BASS FISHING
FUNDAMENTALS

BASS FISHING FUNDAMENTALS

ENLARGED AND REVISED SECOND EDITION

KEN SCHULTZ

THE STEPHEN GREENE PRESS
Lexington, Massachusetts

First published in 1981 by World Angling Services
This revised edition first published in 1986 by
The Stephen Greene Press, Inc.
Published simultaneously in Canada by
Penguin Books Canada Limited
Distributed by Viking Penguin Inc.,
40 West 23rd Street, New York, NY 10010.

All photographs by Ken Schultz unless otherwise indicated.

LIBRARY OF CONGRESS CATALOGING IN PUBLICATION DATA
Schultz, Ken.
Bass fishing fundamentals.
Includes index.
1. Bass fishing.   I. Title.
SH681.S36   1986   799.1'758   85-30238
ISBN 0-8289-0577-0

Printed in the United States of America by
R. R. Donnelley & Sons Company, Harrisonburg, Virginia
Design by Mary A. Wirth
Set in Goudy Old Style

To Virginia Schultz and the late Edward Schultz, my parents, for giving me youthful summers at Kirk Lake and an exposure to the outdoors; and to my wife, Mary Jane, for her patience, encouragement, assistance, and understanding.

FOREWORD

About fifty years ago a friend of mine who worked for Du Pont sent me a batch of nylon monofilament in various thicknesses with a note saying it was a new product and was being suggested as a replacement for the silkworm gut then used as leader material by fly fishermen. Gut leaders were a nuisance because they had to be soaked before using, which meant carrying leaders and tippets in a metal box between pieces of wet felt; otherwise they were brittle and breakable.

I thought this was pretty nifty and would add precious minutes to my fishing time, and tied up a half-dozen leaders with the newfangled material, using the same barrel knots I had used to tie gut leaders. A few weeks later, I was fishing under the covered bridge at a campsite on the upper Beaverkill, and when an enormous brown trout began rising steadily to the green drake mayflies that were on the water, I tied a fanwing Royal Coachman to the nylon tippet. After studying the trout's pattern of rises, I cast to where he was due to show. When he took the fly (which matched the naturals in size if not in color), I set the hook and hoped the monster would go upstream into the fast water instead of downstream into the tangle of brush left by a spring flood, which it obligingly did.

This was by several pounds the largest brown trout I had ever seen, much less hooked, and I remember being pleasantly surprised at my lack of panic during the fifteen or twenty seconds before the line went slack and the fish was gone. I knew I hadn't put undue pressure on the trout as it bored upstream and couldn't understand what had happened until I saw, by the curl left by a knot when the leader parted, that a barrel knot hadn't held. It hadn't broken—it had *slipped.* It wasn't until after talking to other pioneer users of this still experimental material that I learned that nylon required an extra turn or two when barrel-knotted, and that even a Turle or clinch knot needed an extra hitch or twist to be trustworthy; also that nylon, unlike gut, had to be cinched up tight. (It cost me a five-pound smallmouth bass and the hair-frog I left in its lip to learn about clinch knots tied in nylon.)

The point is, ignorance of the characteristics of a new development in tackle had cost me what would have been the biggest North American brown trout of my life, and it was a long time before I finally stopped having bad dreams about it and forgave the Du Pont people.

This book is meant to—and does—fill you in on a lot of the new materials and tackle and techniques of angling for the most popular of American game fish, the black bass. Ken Schultz is a keen and knowledgeable angler with a lot more experience with these species than most of us ever get a chance to acquire, and this updated version of a useful book should be of real help to any bass fisherman, including this one, who is sometimes confused by the variety of new lines, lures, rods, reels, and other piscatorial paraphernalia that clutter up your tackle dealer's shelves. It should help you unclutter your own shelves and perhaps help you cope with that once-in-a-lifetime lunker.

—Ed Zern

ACKNOWLEDGMENTS

My sincere thanks go to the editorial staff of *Field & Stream,* past and present, who always help make my prose and photographs worthy of print; to the anglers who are the subject of these photographs and who graciously took time out from good bass fishing to accommodate me; to my wife, Mary Jane, who shot many of these photos and provided illustrations; and to all the fishermen who have shared their bass angling moments, opinions, and techniques with me.

CONTENTS

PART III   SKILLS, SAVVY, AND TECHNIQUES

APPENDIXES

INTRODUCTION

I was almost finished revising this book when a friend called to ask a question about the effects of weather changes on bass. New to bass fishing, he said he'd been reading and rereading the first edition of this book and had found it most helpful—his experiences and observations were shaping up just as I'd written about them. The evening before, he'd caught twenty bass, the most bass he'd ever caught at one time, including his biggest largemouth to date.

When he asked how my fishing had been, I confessed to having been bass fishing only once in several weeks because I was finishing the revisions for this book. "Revise it?" he asked. He was honestly surprised. "What more could you possibly add to it?"

"A lot," I told him. "I didn't say enough about jigs in the first edition, so I'm adding to that. There are some significant new things about line to talk about. The sections on worm and stick bait fishing are being expanded, and the sonar field has changed so much that I'm adding to that information. I've written a more detailed section on flipping. And the information on rods and reels needed a major updating. When I wrote the first edition, there were no magnetic-spool braking bait-casting reels; now they're the heart of the bass reel market."

"Right," said my friend. "You know I bought three magnetic reels based on your advice last year."

"I'm also adding a whole chapter on spring fishing techniques," I continued, "because it's so important to bass fishermen, and another chapter on catching big bass."

"Ah, that's great. I'd love to see them."

I appreciated that call. For one thing, it's always nice to hear compliments about this book. I've received many, and they are always genuine. I feel good knowing that people are benefitting from this book; some digest it so thoroughly that it's like a fishing bible to them. People who buy and read a book on bass fishing really want to learn, and they seem very willing to express their thoughts and communicate with its author. On a prorated basis, I've gotten more correspondence and comments from the thousands of people who bought the first edition of this book than I get from the millions who read my monthly articles in *Field & Stream* or my weekly syndicated newspaper column.

So I'm delighted to note that this edition is a lot better than the first one. I've learned a few more things and more thoroughly experienced and perfected bass fishing techniques in the intervening years. This edition contains major revisions and additions. It brings the reader up to date on the latest lures and line and electronics, and puts past and current technique information into proper perspective.

Despite the changes, the basic concept of this book remains unchanged. My intention originally—and now—was to produce a book about bass fishing that was basic, functional, thorough, and informative—a book that would help make almost anyone a better bass angler.

I've devoted roughly half of this book to a detailed review of what equipment to use and how to use it. This is not merely a glossy overview. I've done this deliberately because bass fishermen are as much interested in the equipment and paraphernalia of bass fishing— especially lures—as they are in the actual where-to-find and how-to-catch information. Furthermore, the practical aspects of what to use, and where and how to use it effectively, form the foundation for bass angling success.

I've continued to keep this book free of anecdotal accounts of my own experiences. I don't believe you want to be entertained here. You want straightforward information, and you don't need to be convinced that I know what I'm talking about. At the same time, I've tried not to get too technical. The ultra-scientific end of fishing, including the perplexing terminology, can be reserved for those who are searching to know it all or who have to impress others with the vastness of their understanding of all elements of the aquatic world. If you are hoping to find information on the hypolimnion, mesotrophic lakes, color spectrum analysis, and the like, look elsewhere. I have kept the level of bass fishing information in this book fairly simple, using plain language. For all but a relative few, bass fishing is a fun pastime, not a business.

I don't think I'll ever know everything about bass fishing, and it's probably best that no one ever does. This book reflects the best I can offer at the moment, and I unequivocably guarantee that it provides the foundation for becoming a good, knowledgeable bass angler.

—Ken Schultz

PART
I

THE
QUARRY

1

THE HOME OF
THE BASS

Some time ago I helped create a gamefish map of the United States. In selecting the species to be covered and coordinating their locations, I realized that no freshwater fish had a wider range in this country than largemouth bass. This fact didn't surprise me, but at the time I hadn't thought about how black bass, largemouths in particular, ranged so far and how few other freshwater gamefish were so adaptable to such diverse environments.

Classified as a warm-water species of fish, bass thrive in relatively fertile lakes, where water temperatures are warm enough for most of the year to be conducive to their growth and normal feeding activity. This is not to imply that bass are well suited only to temperate climatic conditions.

Largemouth bass are so adaptable that they thrive in all states but Alaska, as well as north and south of our borders, and in Europe, Japan, and Africa. This statement cannot be made for any of our other popular gamefish. Smallmouths, though not quite as extensively distributed, are found from the Mississippi River drainage east, most abundantly concentrated in those areas with generally cool, deep-water lakes and free-flowing rivers. Cleaner waters, colder temperatures, and less turbid conditions characterize the smallmouth's domain.

Although largemouth and smallmouth bass co-exist in many regions and in many individual bodies of water, and although their physiological makeup is essentially the same, they differ in habitat, spawning, and feeding requirements. To be successful, the bass angler must understand both the similarities and discrepancies between these fish.

Their behavior is governed by their temperature requirements and their desire for the protection and security afforded by cover.

When a locale offers cover, comfortable water conditions, and adequate feeding opportunities, it meets the primary considerations in the life of a bass.

Bass, like all fish, are cold-blooded, meaning that their body temperature corresponds to the temperature of the water around them. Largemouth bass are most active when the water temperature is in the 60 to 78 degree bracket. The 65 to 72 range is their optimum temperature, but they function well above and below this. Smallmouths like it a little colder, with 55 to 72 being their active range and 62 to 68 their optimum.

These temperatures are merely ranges and general guidelines. I have found smallmouths feeding actively when the water temperature was in the mid-40s, and largemouths feeding in shallow lakes where the water temperature was a scorching 92 degrees. Both species can tolerate extremely cold temperatures, including life in well-frozen northern lakes and ponds. Largemouths survive in 90-degree-plus water temperatures but smallmouths are not well suited to 80-degree-plus conditions, though they occasionally do briefly habitate such water.

Bass are the most popular sport fish in America. Largemouths, such as these, are found in all states except Alaska and in a wide range of environments.

Black bass are opportunists. They adapt to the circumstances in any given body of water, within reason. Where they have the choice, they will generally seek the temperature of water that is most comfortable for them, provided that they can find forage there. However, they can, and often do, subsist in locales where the water temperature is above or below their preferred range. This may be because environmental conditions mandate this, as in the case of extreme southern lakes and ponds where the summer water temperatures are very high, or because the only available cover for feeding opportunities can be located in this water. Whatever the reason, bass can acclimate to regional conditions. This adaptability adds to the complexity of understanding bass while at the same time contributing to the challenge of finding and catching them.

Every body of water goes through a cyclical transformation through the course of a season. In early spring the surface layers and shallows warm up first. As the surface water surpasses 50 degrees, bass become a little active. When the shallows are warm enough, the bass spawn. Depending on locale, this occurs from mid-spring to early summer. Eventually the upper layers warm past the preferred temperature range, and the fish begin to go deeper, where water temperatures are cooler. In the fall the upper layers and the shallows cool off. Bass react to these changes in accordance with the type of water they live in, the amount and location of food supplies, and the availability of cover.

Black bass can be found in creeks, ditches, sloughs, canals, and many little potholes that have the right cover and forage, but they principally live in reservoirs, lakes, ponds, rivers, and streams.

Reservoirs, which are man-made bodies of water, have been created for water supply, hydroelectric, or flood-control purposes or a combination of these. They usually have some features that many natural lakes do not, such as large coves, lengthy feeder creeks and tributaries, submerged timber and structural objects, and submerged river and creek channel beds. They are also subject to extremes in water level fluctuation and changes in the level of bass populations, and in some cases may be affected by current, either from tributary sources or from water usage connected with water supply and hydroelectric demands. There are lowland reservoirs, which are basically shallow and broad, and highland reservoirs, which are essentially deep, long, and relatively narrow. Some reservoirs are fairly uniform throughout, differing only in the fact that the deepest water is by the

Small, relatively shallow bodies of water, like this Florida phosphate pit, are home to big and small bass alike and can offer excellent fishing.

dam and the shallowest at the head of the lake by the main tributary. Other reservoirs sport many characteristics and feature a wide variety of bass habitats.

Natural lakes tend to have less good bass habitats in the open-water mid-lake sections than do man-made bodies of water. They are usually more consistent in the level of their bass populations, yet they are prone to rapid aging, due partially to natural processes, but primarily to nutrient buildups as a result of changes in water quality and the amount of particulate introductions. Found in all sizes, natural lakes feature many of the same characteristics as reservoirs and ponds.

Ponds are essentially small lakes or small reservoirs and are somewhat scaled-down models of the latter, depending on whether they are natural or man-made. They characteristically possess an abundance of bass cover and are some of the best and most reliable bass fishing holes to be found. It is my suspicion that there is more good bass habitat per acre in most ponds than there is in the average lake or reservoir, and that this primarily contributes to the success of these waters.

Rivers and streams are an altogether different type of home for bass than reservoirs, lakes, or ponds. They vary considerably in size and water classifications. Current is always the foremost factor here, but a bass is a bass, and he will seek the protection of some type of cover in all flowages, just as he does elsewhere.

Home to a bass in any body of water can be a variety of places, dependent upon the water conditions at a given time of the year and other factors. There is some basic survival-related reason in the choice of a residence, though, whether it be temporary or seasonal. A bass may pick a particular site because it offers comforting shade from direct sunlight, an ambush point from which to catch prey, or protection from predators (this is a basic instinct in bass of all sizes, even though the main predator of mature bass is man).

Both largemouth and smallmouth bass are oriented toward cover, usually toward bottom. Most of the preferred food is found in or near cover of some form, so this, plus the need for security and protection from sunlight, is a factor in their specific habitat preferences.

Smallmouth bass have a much narrower habitat preference than do largemouth bass. In their northernmost range, where water temperatures are unlikely to exceed the low 70's throughout the summer, smallmouths may be found in shallow to mid-depth environs throughout the fishing season. But where water temperatures in shallow and near-shore areas exceed the low 70's for a long time, bass move deeper. Smallmouths are regularly found in lakes with at least modest depth, generally of 15 to 25 feet or more. Shallow lakes usually only support these fish if they are spring-fed or are located in northern environments where cool summer evenings temper the effect of daily warmth.

Smallmouths typically inhabit rocky terrain. Their native range is typified by somewhat infertile, natural, rocky-shored northern lakes. Their expanded range now includes southern impoundments with shoreline and deep-water rock structure. Smallmouths don't inhabit lily pad beds or grass fields, though they may be caught along the edges of such vegetation. They aren't found around stumps and timber with sandy bottoms, though they may use such objects as cover in rockier locales.

Smallmouths are located around rocky points, craggy cliff-like shores, rocky islands and reefs, and rip-rap shores. They prefer golf ball- to brick-sized rocks if they have a choice, but larger rocks, including boulders, are also suitable. In the spring, prior to spawning, smallmouths in lakes that are completely rock-laden prefer to be near large rocks, and you may be able to work a shoreline quickly by keying on every big boulder in shallow water.

Smallmouths prefer a rocky domain. A shoal or reef, such as this one on New York's St. Lawrence River, is typical habitat.

Perhaps the primary reason for the smallmouth's fondness for rocks is that they harbor crayfish. Where crayfish are abundant, they are the principal food for smallmouths. Crayfish dominate the stomach contents of smallmouth bass that I keep and clean. I've noted that at least half of these fish have nothing identifiable in their stomachs, while three-fourths of the remainder contain one or more crayfish. Certainly smallmouths eat whatever is most abundant in their environment, and they'll readily consume small fish when they are plentiful or when the proper opportunity presents itself. But crayfish are their staple.

Largemouth bass are found in all imaginable situations. Call these factors cover, objects, structure, or what-have-you, bass seek them out, and we can roughly separate them into visible (that which can be seen in relatively shallow water) and nonvisible (existing entirely below the surface and usually in moderate depth or very deep water). Visible cover includes logs, stumps, lily pads, brush, weed and grass beds, bushes, docks, fence rows, standing timber, bridge pilings, rocky shores, boulders, and points. Submerged cover includes weedline edges, stone walls, timber and stumps, creek beds, house foundations, roadbeds, points, ledge-like dropoffs, humps, shoals, and islands. Submerged cover is generally in deeper water than visible cover.

All of these examples of prime habitats for black bass are true wherever bass are found. In some lakes bass may prefer one type of cover and in another, nearby lake prefer a different type of cover. The selection of habitat is influenced by many conditions. The point is that, under the right circumstances, bass will utilize any of the types of cover previously mentioned, in any region where they are found. A good habitat consistently produces catches of bass. Large bass often inhabit the most desirable locations, but other bass will make this their domicile not long after the former resident has been removed by an angler. Though I hesitate to make this anthropomorphic analogy, it makes a valid point: whenever a well-built house exists in a choice location, it is seldom wanting for a tenant.

Though we have discussed the types of water inhabited by bass and the preferred locations in that water, we have not discussed the

Big bodies of water and those with an abundance of structure offer bass cover and forage, and provide anglers with a wealth of places to fish. The author caught this largemouth bass from a backwater area on Missouri's sprawling Truman Lake.

condition of the water itself. Bass can, and do, thrive in water of marginal purity and quality. Largemouths are most tolerant in this regard. Smallmouths are more apt to thrive in clear, fair-to-good-quality environs. In waters that have become stagnant through the eutrophication (aging) process, the oxygen levels at the deeper, cooler sections may have a marked effect on the well-being of these fish, and such bodies of water may eventually become unsuitable for them.

Polluted waters don't seem to have an adverse effect on the behavior of bass. Chemical pollutants are found at various levels in bass in those waters where chemical contamination is severe. Although this may have a biological effect on the fish, such as influencing the viability of the spawn, it does not seem to alter behavior.

The turbidity of bass water varies markedly from one lake to another across the country and even varies in a particular lake through the course of the fishing season. Many of the larger lakes and reservoirs in northern areas are reasonably clear. Light penetrates deep there, and bass are either well secured in what thick cover might exist or are more likely deep enough to avoid the discomfort of light. In such waters you can see a brightly colored lure 6 or more feet below the surface. Here, bass tend to be spooky, and a refined fishing presentation, utilizing small- to moderate-size lures and light line, is very beneficial. Other waters may be blue-green colored and allow visibility for 3 to 6 feet below the water's surface. Such a condition is considered very clear by many Southern anglers, who never see the ultra-clear waters of mountain-region lakes.

Many bass waters are off-colored, allowing limited visibility. This is the only type of condition some anglers see, and it does not require such a stealthy approach or light line use as the clearer waters do. Muddy, milky, slate-gray, and tea-colored water is common in many reservoirs after heavy rains; farmland runoff, sediment from tributaries, and bank erosion cause this condition. You may only be able to see a light-colored lure a few inches below the surface. In some large lakes the upper ends are only affected like this while the lower ends remain relatively unchanged, or at least unaffected for several days. In still other bass waters, particularly in Florida, the high tannic acid content gives the lake a blackish-brown tint. In all these highly turbid waters, where visibility is limited, bass are likely to be relatively shallow and holding tight to cover, especially in the early part of the season and when water temperatures are not excessively high. Turbid water can be good for fishing success, and certain types of lures, such as big spinnerbaits, crankbaits with good vibration qualities, and noisy surface baits, are well suited to angling under these conditions.

Bass, as you undoubtedly realize by now, can adapt to a variety of conditions within the parameters of their biological capabilities. Unlike that of striped bass, or trout, or muskies, a bass's habitat is basically the same type of condition that is found in every state. Look at the next lake or pond you go by. The odds are good that right in front of you will be some type of suitable bass habitat, another home for the most sought after gamefish in America.

2

FACTS OF LIFE

Bass, like other fish and animals, are controlled by certain biological and physiological traits. Bass have specific reproductive, sensory, and feeding abilities. These and many other elements in the life of a bass are important to the angler, helping him to understand and appreciate his quarry.

GROWTH

One of the most fascinating aspects of the biological history of a bass is its growth rate. Few anglers know the age of a given bass or comprehend how long it has taken for a particular fish to reach its current size. Nor do they realize that growth rates differ between largemouths and smallmouths, as well as between bass of different geographical regions and sometimes between bass in lakes within the same region.

The growth of any bass is dependent upon water temperatures, length of growing season, food supply, and the extent of competition in its particular body of water. The growing season for bass ranges from year-round in the southernmost areas of Florida to barely four months in the northernmost locations, such as Vermont, Maine, and Ontario. This is a function of climate. When water temperatures are cold, the metabolic rate of a bass is very low, and the fish is dormant. When temperatures are hot, the fish's metabolic rate is high, but it does not necessarily get optimum benefit from its food consumption. At extremely high temperatures, bass are usually sluggish. When water temperatures are in the middle of these extremes, bass will feed and grow. Obviously, the longer the water temperature is in this range, the more growth there will be. This is why southern bass generally grow larger (but do not necessarily live longer) than northern bass.

Between the two species, largemouths and smallmouths have a similar growth rate in their first three or four years in areas where both fish coexist. After that, however, the largemouths begin to outdistance their cousins. Overall, smallmouths have a slower growth rate, a fact probably related to their diet. A typical smallmouth bass reaches sexual maturity when it is 3 to 4 years old. At this time, it will be between 9 and 11 inches long. A 16-inch fish, which might weigh about 3 pounds, would probably be 8 years old. In the most northerly reaches of its range, it would be even older. A 5- or 6-pound smallmouth, recognized as a trophy everywhere, is obviously one of the elders of the bass world.

Largemouths, on the other hand, grow slightly faster. In the North, a sexually mature 10-inch bigmouth would be a 3-year-old fish. A 19-inch, 5-pound largemouth in that same area would be 7 to 8 years old. In some areas of the South, a largemouth can reach 10 inches in its first year, primarily due to the difference in its growing season. For this reason, it is difficult to make comparative judgments about trophy-size bass between these geographical regions. The catch of a 7-pound bass in New York, for instance, where that fish is well over 10 years old, is akin to the catch of at least a 10-pounder (possibly a 12-pounder) in a southern area, where such a fish would also be 10 years old.

To further illustrate the disparities in ages and sizes of fish, take the example of the 13-pound 9-ounce largemouth bass that was caught at Truman Lake, Missouri, in April 1985. Just 5 ounces shy of the state record, that fish was aged by fisheries personnel at 12 years. It would be extremely unlikely to find a bass that size of a similar age in Northern waters. This partially explains why bass over 8 pounds are very rare in the North (fishing pressure has something to do with the availability of old and large bass, too). Yet by comparison, that 12-year-old, mid-America bass may be smaller than a 12-year-old bass in the state of Florida.

There is, moreover, a difference in growth rates between the "Northern" and "Florida" subspecies of largemouths. A Northern large-mouth is any fish that is not a "Florida" bass. Floridas grow excep-

These 3- to 4-pound smallmouth bass, taken from a New Hampshire lake, are much older than similar-sized fish from a mid-America locale. Average water temperatures and length of growing season are the primary factors.

tionally fast in areas with a temperate year-round climate. The Florida strain, however, does not acclimatize well to the colder water of northern regions; in fact, it may not adapt at all. However, transplanted Florida strain bass are doing very well in several Texas locales and in Southern California, where many huge bass in the 15- to 20-pound range are caught. Many people think the next world-record largemouth will be taken there. (The present record, 22 pounds 4 ounces, has stood since 1932 and was caught in Montgomery Lake, Georgia.)

Growth rates also differ in geographically close waters. This does not occur frequently, nor is the difference often substantial. Such a situation indicates extraordinary circumstances in the population of one of the two groups, with one possibly having too little forage, resulting in an overpopulation of bass and stunted fish, and the other having abundant forage and little competition, resulting in a slightly faster than usual growth. The latter situation would most likely exist in a newly created lake, where bass grow fast and the population booms for a few years before the lake matures.

LIFESPAN

The age of any fish can be determined by analyzing a scale under a microscope. Fish scales look like a cross section of a tree trunk, with definable annular rings that can be counted to determine age. You can't determine exactly how old bass get, but they have been reported to have lived up to 15 years. The older a bass, the harder it is to reliably determine age by checking its scales.

Although there's no scientific support for the fisherman's assertions that female bass grow larger than males, the large trophy-class bass of both species are females. Males do not live as long, on the average, as females and since a fish's ultimate size is a function of its longevity, perhaps fishermen have rightly explained the female-larger-than-male phenomenon.

SPEED AND STAMINA

Bass have little reason to do any long-distance swimming; instead, their physical abilities allow high-speed movement for short distances. Fisheries biologists have calculated that bass can burst up to 12 miles per hour. That may not sound fast, but it's considerably faster than you can retrieve a swimming or diving plug. There is no question that an angler cannot retrieve a lure faster than a bass can swim. If a bass wants the bait, it is capable of running it down. However, it may be alarmed by such a speedy retrieval, and although capable of capturing the object, it may not be inclined to do so. Moreover, bass are opportunistic fish; they're not accustomed to working extraordinarily hard for their meals.

Bass seldom make long, sustained runs during the course of a fight. They may make several speedy dashes, dive for cover, or leap in an attempt to throw the hook, but they do not fight for a long time. Their stamina varies with water temperature and the strength of your tackle.

Bass are generally sluggish fighters in very cold or very warm water, yet I have caught hard-fighting largemouths in 90-degree water and in 45-degree water. Stamina and fighting characteristics can vary within a particular lake, so I can make only general assertions about this characteristic. Some bass fight sluggishly even in optimum temperature water, when you expect them to be very aggressive, and others fight well when you expect them to be lethargic. Chunky fish have a tendency to be spirited fighters. Shallow largemouths usually fight well and will jump more often than deeper bass. Furthermore, smallmouths are generally known for slightly superior fighting abilities than largemouths.

INTELLIGENCE

Scientists have not pegged the intelligence level of bass, nor have they satisfactorily equated this factor with that of other gamefish. My observations lead me to conclude that bass are capable of learning and generally recognize and avoid situations that they have encountered before, and that threaten their well-being. There are plenty of situations where heavy fishing pressure on a given lake has resulted in poor angling, in part because the easy-to-catch bass have been caught off the banks long ago, but also in part because bass have become wise to the ways of anglers. Whether this is intelligence or not, I can't say, but I do think that bass become accustomed to seeing lures and quickly learn to avoid that which appears unnatural or is deemed to be threatening. For this reason and because fishing pressure is so intense in many areas, anglers will benefit from proper presentation and retrieval techniques.

Laboratory experiments, incidentally, have proven that bass have the ability to differentiate between conditions that portend reward or safety and those that do not. This smidgeon of evidence proves that bass have some learning ability, though how this relates to their natural environment is uncertain. Conversely, bass can be caught repeatedly, even on the same lure that they have fallen to in the past.

In recent years I've conducted a tagging and fishing study of largemouth bass on a small lake. Out of 727 bass tagged, I personally recaptured 39, and other anglers recaptured 88. Several fish had been caught twice more after I tagged them, and one 13-inch largemouth was caught and released four times within a year. The earliest that any bass was recaptured was five days. That fish fell for different lures and had migrated across the lake in that time. The longest recapture period during 4 years was 3 years and 9 months, and that fish had gone from one end of the lake to the other. Most fish were recaptured in the same place or close by. Two-thirds of the fish succumbed to a different lure the second time around, though one that didn't was caught twice in thirteen days on the same lure in the same place.

What this all means is that bass are often savvy enough to avoid capture, but not necessarily smart enough to avoid recapture. I noticed on this lake, however, that bass seem to have become conditioned to the lures I'd been offering them, and that, although the population had not apparently decreased, the fish were not as readily fooled as they were in the past. You always wind up asking yourself if the fish you caught were just dumb, extra-hungry, or protective, or if the presentation of something that resembled food was very good? An answer isn't always apparent. That's why I rely on presentation as being critical to bass angling success.

3

REPRODUCTION

Bass begin spawning approximately when the water temperature reaches and exceeds 60 degrees. Not all the bass in a given lake spawn at the same time. In very small lakes, they do; in others, especially large lakes with different arms where water temperatures vary, spawning continues over several weeks.

Bass generally reach maturity and are capable of reproducing when they reach 10 inches in length. The male selects a nest site in shallow water and fans debris away. The female deposits the eggs, when ready, with the help of the male, and then she will abandon the nest, leaving the male as a sentry.

Guarding males can be effective against individual intruders but not against a school of fish, such as bluegills and perch. The well-being of the overall bass population demands that balanced fisheries populations exist in a given body of water. If a lake is overrun with panfish, they will diminish the bass population through exceedingly heavy predation of eggs and fry. To maintain and restore the total fisheries balance, panfish must be brought under control.

The nest site of bass is generally in shallow water. The depth is usually 1 to 4 feet deep for largemouths, but may be up to 6 or 8 feet if light (and warmth) can penetrate. It can be the same depth for smallmouths, too; however, smallmouth nests are often at the deeper end of this range. The dish-shaped nests are fairly large, usually at least 2 feet in diameter. Some anglers confuse bluegill or sunfish nests with those of bass, but the nests of the former are smaller, close to one another, and sometimes in the open. Moreover, bass spawn before bluegills and sunfish have even constructed their nests. Bass will not make nests too close to other bass nests, and they like to have a large

object, such as a stump, log, or rock, nearby, generally to the back-
side of the nest.

Nest sites are usually found on shorelines and in coves where the
water is warmer than in other areas and where the nests are fairly well
protected from strong winds. The north, northwest, and west banks
of creeks, bays, coves, and the like are often favored by spawning bass
because they warm up first.

Female bass are capable of carrying and depositing thousands of
eggs. Prior to spawning, as much as 10 percent of a female's body
weight may be the egg mass. A large number, but not all, of these
eggs will be deposited on the nest. One nest may contain the eggs of
more than one bass, as a male will attempt to bring other females into
the nest site where they, too, will spawn. Older bass generally have
more eggs than younger bass, and the eggs tend to be slightly larger.
Eggs that are not ripe are not deposited; these form the beginning of

SPAWNING BASS IN COVES

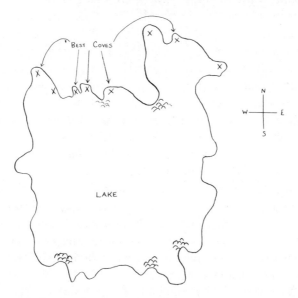

In lakes where the water level and habitat are conducive to spawning, largemouths
usually move into the north coves, or the shallows along north coves or shorelines
in the spring. Sunlight and wind from the south warm up these areas first. This is
especially true if there is a creek coming into the locale. If you have a thermometer, you can check the water temperature at various areas of the lake—you may
find as much as five or six degrees difference.

the next egg mass. Female bass, caught in late summer and fall, carry eggs. This does not mean that they have failed to spawn but that they will be carrying eggs throughout the winter.

Only a fraction of the spawn survives beyond the fry stage, and fewer still, become adults. Predation and environmental factors take their toll. If a particular year-class of fish (young of that year) has been subjected to particularly damaging ecological conditions, in subsequent years that generation of fish will be noticeably absent from the fisherman's take. A premature heat spell, for instance, warms the water early and prompts bass to take to their nests; if that is followed by a cold spell with lowered water temperature, the fish will be driven off their nests, influencing that generation's survival. If the bass have already spawned, the colder temperature will seriously affect the fry. If the bass have not spawned, some will later return to the nests, but others will not.

Keep in mind that just because the water temperature is favorable and the time of the moon is right, there's no guarantee that bass will rush to spawn. A certain biological adaptation is in process, and bass instinctively know when the time is right—when their eggs are ripe and when their urge should be heeded—and they will not spawn until then, regardless of how "right" everything else seems to be.

Another common environmental factor that affects spawning-time bass is a sharp upward or downward change in the water level, as would happen in some hydroelectric or water supply impoundments, and in the case of flooding. With receding water, bass will either be forced to leave nests that have already been made, or they will find a severely decreased amount of suitable spawning habitats. In either case, the reproductive efforts for that year-class-to-be will be severely impaired. Rising water may put the nest too deep and in colder, less sun-warmed water, which can also have a negative effect. Many bass that have made nests and then left them when the water level changed do not make new nests and simply absorb their eggs. This, too, can contribute to a missing age-class of bass.

Anglers, through the removal of bass on the nests, are also a factor in the survival of the fry. Since females are only on the nests for a relatively short period of time to deposit eggs, the male is the one that is usually caught. He builds the nest, fertilizes the eggs, and then stays on the nest site for a long time, guarding the eggs and fanning silt off them. Some studies show that when the male bass is caught and released, he generally returns to the nest. Removal of the male, however, results in mortality of the unhatched eggs and near-total mortality of what newly hatched fry might exist.

Spawning time is the period when big bass are most likely to be caught. Aggressive females loaded with eggs can be enticed into striking a lure before spawning. A male bass guarding the nest can be aggravated, and both sexes can be caught (male first, though) during spawning. Bass don't eat at this time, but they will strike objects that come close to or threaten their nest site. A live baitfish, a plastic worm, a spinnerbait, and a few other lures can catch spawning bass, as long as they appear to be a threat to the nest and the eggs and are placed in the midst of the activity.

Bass will be eager to eat after spawning is completed, though don't look for them to be super-aggressive immediately afterward. They go into a withdrawal stage and may take up to two weeks to get in sync and start striking terror among their prey.

The issue of fishing during the spawning period is a complex and controversial one. Some anglers have misgivings about fishing during that time. Yet, some fisheries biologists maintain that fishing during the spawning season is seldom detrimental to the bass population. This issue is influenced by such variables as the size of a given bass population, number of predators, growth rate and length of growing season, water temperature, and extent of fishing pressure. Ideally, each body of water should be evaluated on its own merits in this regard. In areas of high fishing pressure and in small bodies of water or where growing seasons are short, the removal of spawning bass can detrimentally influence the fish population.

I've never understood why the fisheries departments of neighboring states could not agree on how to treat spawning bass. For instance, in New Jersey and Connecticut, you can fish for and keep bass early in the spring and through the spawning period, but in the state sandwiched between them, New York, the bass season doesn't open until the third Saturday in June, when most of that state's bass have spawned. Nevertheless, it seems to me that where bass are protected during the spawning period, there should be a limited creel (only one or two bass until after a certain date) and an artificial lure requirement to minimize injuries to fish. Some states have this.

I've caught a lot of bass in many states just before and during the spawning period, always with artificial lures and always releasing the fish. These fish have not been unduly harmed by the experience, so I feel confident in saying that where moderation is practiced, fishing for bass during the spawning season can be reasonably non-detrimental.

Unless anglers exercise voluntary restraint and are sporting in their pursuit of bass at spawning time, they will ultimately have regulations imposed on them. We're heading that way now. That is not all bad. Many states that were lax with size and creel limits have moved to lower creel limits and to increase minimum size limits. This has helped improve bass fishing. So, to a large extent, the practicality and future possibility of fishing for bass through the spawning season is up to you.

4

SENSORY ABILITIES

Bass have sensory abilities; their senses function independently or in conjunction with each other and to varying degrees and purposes.

Vision, of course, is one of their senses and thought by some anglers to be dominant in the fish's activity. Though not necessarily dominant, it plays a major role in their behavior. Bass have an extremely wide field of vision. Each eye is capable of 180-degree sight on offset planes, meaning they cross and produce binocular vision in front of the fish. Bass, like all sighted fish, can see objects above the surface. They cannot see through it, but they can see objects mirrored upon it, in what biologists call a circular window. Objects directly overhead appear proportionately largest. When an angler wants to get close to a fish in clear, calm water, he would best keep a subtle profile.

Prominent factors associated with bass' vision include color perception, water depth and clarity, and available light. Bass, like all fish, are sensitive to light, having no natural eye covering as humans do. This partially explains their preeminent activity at dawn, dusk, and on cloud-covered days, as well as their relative need for light-protective cover or depth.

The clarity of the water and its depth also play a role. Regardless of clarity, distance and depth have a similar effect on bass' ability to see, as well as on the relative visibility of the objects they are looking at.

Water clarity is relative, since one man's soup is another man's coffee. I have seen some anglers (typically on a southern Corps of Engineers impoundment) call water clean that another (typically on a natural, clear northern lake) would think is filthy. The majority of bass waters are slightly turbid, and in these waters, where human sight is limited to a few feet, vision is of restricted importance to a bass.

This has a direct bearing on the lures used by fishermen. In waters of marginal to poor visibility, the most important features of a lure are its action and vibration patterns, not appearance. These qualities appeal to another, more important sense, that will be reviewed shortly.

In moderately clear and very clear water, appearance, in addition to action and vibration, assumes an important role. This is where the size, shape, and overall look will visually influence a bass. For this reason, using crankbaits as an example, a natural-finish design has merit.

The ability of a bass to perceive color and its reactions to color stimuli are interesting aspects of its vision. Yes, bass can distinguish colors. No, they do not see them in exactly the same way as humans do.

The retina of a bass's eye contains both rods to receive light and cones to measure color. Because there are more rods than cones, they see well in dim light and poorly in bright light. Some tests show that red is the most visible color to a bass, with violet and red appearing the same. Yellow and orange are also highly visible. These colors have the greatest intensity, compared to blue and green, which have the least visibility and the lowest intensity.

An intriguing phenomenon is at work in underwater color visibility. What the human eye and fish's eye see above water is not the same as what they see underwater. Some colors stand out better than others, and background and light penetration are key factors, so saying what is or is not the most visible color to a bass may be oversimplifying the matter. What is visible is relative to water clarity conditions.

Water also acts as a filter, and colors with long wavelengths are more readily absorbed. Also, fluorescent colors are highly visible underwater (due to the effects of ultraviolet light) at considerably greater distances and depths than their fluorescent-deficient counterparts.

Color, of course, plays a big role in the selection of lures. Lure color has the greatest significance for bass in shallow- and clear-water areas. The deeper you fish and the more turbid the water, the less important the color. In many situations, using a lure color that contrasts with the background is best. Dark colors are generally more useful in clear water and on bright days, while light colors are effective in turbid water and on dark days.

Chartreuse is an example of a very successful bass color. Most

Why did this bass take a black plastic worm in murky water, while another bass nearby might fall to a white spinnerbait? Bass respond to color and to lure action and vibration, though there is no certainty that they are relying on one sense to locate prey all or most of the time, or that they are using all of their senses.

popular with spinnerbaits and used with white, it is effective in moderately dirty blue-green water. The visibility of these colors, combined with lure action and the conditions in which they are fished, account for their success. Incidentally, the company that produces the chartreuse chemiluminescent lightsticks, used so successfully for nighttime swordfishing and now for Great Lakes salmon fishing, found that color to be the most visible color underwater. Though matching the color of lure to the conditions may be important to your success, don't be fooled into thinking that color alone is the basis upon which bass strike your lure. Obviously there are no red or blue baitfish swimming in our bass waters, so remember that for bass, color is rarely more important than lure action and retrieval technique.

One final area where color and vision might play a role in bass behavior is with fishing line. If red, yellow, orange, and fluorescent colors are so visible underwater, then bass should be able to perceive such colors and fluorescence in monofilament line. They can, and the stronger the line, the greater its diameter and the more pronounced its underwater appearance. Researchers determined through laboratory tests that bass can distinguish between different colored lines and between fluorescent lines, and that the most readily recognized line was fluorescent yellow.

Does this indicate a need to fish with the best-camouflaged line? I think not. There are too many good anglers successfully using brightly colored or fluorescent lines to discount their effectiveness. At one time I fished with nothing but fluorescent yellow line and had high regard for it. I have stayed away from that for several years now, because I use the same tackle for other species, including trout and salmon, which I believe are more wary of line color than bass, and because I believe the added visibility of such line to be of most value in trolling situations. To be safe, lines in green, blue-green, clear, and blue hues are least readily visible. And all lines lose visibility as turbidity increases. Remember also, that the higher the strength and diameter of your line, the more visible it will be, regardless of color.

Blindness does occur in fish, and they survive. There have been many recorded instances of blind bass living to a plump old age; these fish were apparently able to use other highly developed senses to avoid capture and to prey on food fish.

The most acute sense a bass has is its hearing. Hearing is activated through two modes: the inner ear and the lateral line. The inner ear, a complex structure of interlocking rings, is sensitive to high frequency sounds. It plays a minimal role in the angler's efforts.

The lateral line, which extends the length of the fish and is sensitive to low frequency sounds, is the most important sense when vision is limited. This applies to the detection and location of prey and predators, as well as the detection of sounds in the environment. Though sound travels differently through water than through air, most of the sounds heard by bass are of low frequency.

Underwater sounds are very pronounced. A jet aircraft takeoff, heard on land at a distance of 230 feet, is only 20 percent greater than the underwater sounds of a 25-horsepower outboard motor heard at 45 feet. And that motor sound is 25 percent greater than that of a loud automobile horn heard at a distance of 3 feet. Pretty noisy, huh?

The sound of a moderate conversation, as held by fishing partners, is not noticeably transmitted through the water and is of little consequence to bass. But sounds made in a boat, which are transmitted directly through vibrations to the fish, are noisy and alarming. Common sounds that bass detect include those made by outboard and electric motors, and shore noises (transmitted through vibrations). These sounds are all picked up via the lateral line.

Some evidence indicates that bass become conditioned to these sounds, but the conscientious angler should minimize his noises. For instance, shutting the outboard engine a considerable distance from the area to be fished is worthwhile. Also, a sustained low-speed electric motor operation is preferable to the more alarming start-up, shut-off operation.

Bass detect lures at night, particularly surface lures, via their sounds and vibrations. This is also true for lures used in limited visibility situations and for plastic worms in any condition where they cannot be seen. This also applies to the detection of other fish and bait. Signals received through the displacement of water by baitfish are relative to the fish's shape and fin movement, so it is possible for bass to not only detect the presence of a fish without seeing it, but also to detect its approximate size and species.

For lures to be successful bass-catchers, they must have properties

Bass have a particularly keen ability to locate prey through their lateral line, which extends the length of the fish and is particularly important in situations where vision is limited.

that resemble bait in the way they appeal to the lateral line of the bass. The action of a constantly moving lure is critically important. A tight, fast wiggle in a crankbait is more desirable than a wide, slow action, because the former more closely mimics the body and tail movement activity of baitfish. This action and vibration, coupled with the introduction of BBs in the cavities of some lures to appeal to a bass's acoustic abilities, are the choice assets of good bass-catching lures. Manufacturers have realized this for some time and have worked to develop products that stimulate bass. There is still a lot to be accomplished as more is learned about the interactions of bass and other fish.

Interestingly, bass that have been deprived of their lateral line function as well as their vision are still able to locate and capture prey in laboratory experiments, albeit with more difficulty than normal. This suggests some reliance on other senses.

These other senses include smell and taste. A bass's sense of smell functions through four small openings on the snout; water is drawn through the two forward openings, passed over smell-sensitive tissues, and ejected from the two rear openings. Bass have only recently been considered to have significant smelling ability, and how important this is to their feeding and general behavior is open to conjecture. Manufacturers of specialty masking or attracting agents claim that bass have a highly developed sense of smell and that they may choose to feed on some prey as a result of association with certain odors. Unconvinced of this, I am extremely suspicious of the supposed merits of this argument. The predominantly turbid and still-water environment of bass does not seem to lend itself to regular association with smell-related stimuli. It is largely speculative whether bass detect human odors or other unsatisfactory odors on lures, such as plastic worms or jigs. In my opinion the ability of a bass to smell and its reliance on this sense is subordinate to visual stimuli and to action and vibration patterns. It should also be noted that bass have tastebuds in their mouth and on the upper lip and tongue, though these are not well developed. Until biologists do more research involving these senses, questions such as whether a bass quickly rejects a lure or worm because it smells or tastes funny cannot be answered except speculatively.

Bass also have the ability to feel. The surface of their body reacts to touch, and surface nerve endings are sensitive to temperature changes as well. Bass have been known to scratch and to chafe against logs in a manner associated with relieving an itch or purging external parasites. Again, this sense is underdeveloped. It is evident that the two most developed senses of a bass are also the two most utilized in the eating, reproducing, and surviving process.

5

FEEDING BEHAVIOR

The most dynamic aspect of black bass is their feeding disposition. Bass have large mouths and large stomachs and an appetite to match. They are not dainty, delicate feeders like stream trout, nor menacing chompers like pickerel and pike. When a bass eats, it goes to town. Under certain conditions it may attempt to stun its prey first, but usually it swallows the prey whole, either chasing and capturing it or simply sucking it in head-first unawares.

Bass, particularly largemouths, have a tremendous vacuum-like suction ability. When they get near their prey, in one swift action they can open their mouths wide, flare their gills and force an immense suction that rushes water into the mouth and out the gills while directing the object of consumption right into the gullet. You may have experienced an occasion, when using a surface lure, where the water around your plug suddenly opened up and the plug disappeared into the mouth of a fish; this is the powerful effect of the bass' feeding mode.

Bass eat all kinds of creatures, but they do have a marked preference for certain organisms. The bass-catcher knows that bass are primarily meat eaters. This is related as much to their biological makeup as it may be to their disposition, since bass lack the enzymes that permit digestion of vegetation. As fry, bass begin to eat zooplankton (small crustaceans), graduating to insects, fingerling fish (including each other), and then larger fish and crayfish as they grow.

On the whole, bass are basically found in relatively shallow water (not much deeper than 30 feet) and near shore or some protective cover. Though some bass do wander, the species is not a deep open-water roamer like trout, salmon, or striped bass. They relate to objects, bottom, and specific water level zones, as do their prey.

The primary forage for adult largemouth bass is baitfish and crayfish. Baitfish may take the form of shiners, bluegills (bream), shad, alewives (also called sawbellies or herring), minnows, and other small creatures, depending upon their abundance and accessibility. Smallmouth show a marked preference for crayfish. Their baitfish preference runs to the fingerling-size shiners and minnows, and to a lesser extent, alewives and small panfish; in streams, insects may make up a large part of the smallmouth's diet as well. Fingerling-size fish, whether of forage or gamefish species, are probably the number one food item for largemouths.

When shad or alewives are abundant, bass will consume them, but I suspect they are not usually the primary food fare. For one thing, gizzard shad grow large and soon reach a size where they are too big to be prey for most bass. Secondly, gizzard and threadfin shad and alewives are open-water cruisers, sometimes found deep, but only occasionally wandering by the usual lairs of bass. At times, bass will corner a school of these fish and tear into them, or will take advantage of the passage of these fish into their domain. As a rule, though, bass are not constantly foraging on these species unless their regular fingerling fish or crayfish quarries are unavailable or conditions bring them into regular and frequent contact. The latter situation occurs on some impoundments where shad follow submerged creek channels and venture near the channels or flats or points that attract bass.

Some of the more exotic food fare for bass include frogs, salamanders, water dogs, snakes, mice, baby ducks, worms, and tadpoles. Much hype has centered on the bass's propensity for eating, including such occasional mouthfuls as these. Such creatures, however, are just an incidental and opportunistic part of the diet. Of these, frogs may be the most regularly consumed animal, though only in those waters that have the habitat preferred by frogs and a correspondingly sizable population.

Bass are regularly caught on live worms by bait fishermen. This is something of a phenomenon since earthworms seldom find themselves in the water naturally. Just as puzzling is why bass are so frequently duped by plastic worms, which perhaps represent earthworms or snakes or leeches, none of which is a significant factor in the daily diet of a bass. This mystery is lessened when we learn that plastic worms are not effective because of what they represent. They are effective because of other factors, which will be covered later in the book.

To maximize your fishing effectiveness, keep in mind the type of bait predominant in the diet of the bass you intend to catch, but don't feel that it is essential to match the forage explicitly. Lures that resemble bait that is not part of a regular diet, can fool fish. Plastic worms and spinnerbaits are prime examples. In clear-water fishing conditions, close representation of the bait may be warranted. In turbid waters where visibility is limited or in tight cover situations, you will often be more successful with a suggestive lure rather than an imitative one, capitalizing on the behavior of the bass.

Bass strike a lure or attack prey for a variety of reasons. They sometimes exhibit specific feeding patterns, but this can vary from lake to lake and even among fish in the same population. Bass feed during the day and at night. They feed year-round as well, though less frequently in colder weather (and barely at all in frigid water). As you might expect, the rate of feeding is correlated to the water temperature. The metabolic and feeding rates peak at the optimum temperature range. Below that it decreases. At 50 degrees and below, feeding and general movement drop off significantly. During the winter, bass may feed as infrequently as every two weeks, at which time they do not grow. At optimum water temperatures, however, a bass may digest its food somewhere in a range of 14 to 24 hours.

Though I haven't kept records regarding the stomach contents of bass I have kept and cleaned, I estimate that 60 percent of the largemouth bass had empty stomachs while 40 percent had one or more organisms in their stomach. For smallmouths, the breakdown is more even, with about half having some form of bait, primarily crayfish, in their stomach. This indicates that bass not only feed when they are hungry, but when they have already consumed some form of prey. Indeed, I have caught bass that have just consumed large shad, that have had the tail of a good-sized catfish sticking out of their gullets, and that have recently filled their crop with other delectables. This indicates that bass strike for various reasons.

All fishermen, and particularly bass anglers, are fascinated by lures. They have a greater interest in learning about a successful lure (its size, shape, or color) than they do about what habitat the fish was caught in, what other tackle was employed, what time of day it was, or what other conditions may have been present. This pre-occupation with lures may be due to the nature of the quarry and to its feeding activities, which at times are indiscriminate and unfath-omable and at other times almost calculative.

Many questions surround the feeding behavior of bass, sparking this interest in lures. For instance, why would a bass strike a lure in situations where it can easily see the lure, its color, and the color of the line extending through the water to the lure? Why does a fish strike something that does not look like its accustomed prey (a spin-nerbait, for example) or smell or feel like the prey? Is it because the skill of the angler, imparting life to a lure, is just as important as the lure's appearance, and sound? Is it because the bass is in a feeding mood and is indiscriminate about its meal? Could it be that it is upset about the intrusion of what it perceives as a subordinate creature into its domain? Or is it, as has been suggested, that a bass is just plain dumb?

Many lures, like this jig and pork chunk, don't particularly resemble nor-mal bass forage, yet they attract fish. Bass strike a lure for many reasons, not the least of which is that they are extremely opportunistic fish that have a reflexive instinct to attack objects that ap-pear vulnerable to them.

Bass strike a lure for all these reasons and then some. Primarily, however, bass strike a lure or attack prey fish because they are hungry or because they possess a reflexive, almost killer, instinct that is vital to their opportunistic nature and to the survival-of-the-fittest aspect that pervades the animal kingdom and all its predatory creatures.

There is nothing difficult to comprehend about the element of hunger. And reflexive attacks are part of the scheme of underwater life. Remember, there is a lot of competition in every body of water, and the motto is either *Eat or Be Eaten* or *Eat Now Before Another Fish Beats You to It*. Bass do strike because an opportunity suddenly presents itself, and capturing and killing this creature is something they are accustomed to doing. Bass are also protective; they take up residence in a particular area they seem to have reserved for themselves and guard this domain against intrusion.

Bass have other attributes that also relate to their feeding and lure striking behavior. They can occasionally be agitated into striking by repeated presentations of a lure or bait. More likely than not, the fish will move off and return in a short while when confronted with this situation but sometimes they strike out, as if in anger. Some fish also seem to be checking a fish or bait out, as it comes by, perhaps even following it, as if curious. We ascribe these attributes to humans, however, and I don't believe that bass actually have these emotions. They can be impulsive, domineering, reflexive bullies, if you will, and their apparent displays of anger or curiosity are more likely protective behavior.

There are dumb bass too, but in these days of intense fishing activity, in all but the most remote, isolated, or private waters, the dumb fish have been caught, leaving the warier progeny behind.

Hunger, reflexive action, protection, and competitiveness are the main reasons for a bass to feed and to strike lures or bait. Its whole existence revolves around this. It is an opportunist. It will lie in ambush, waiting for the right kind of meal to come by, whereupon it will pounce on it and retreat to the protection of its ambush point.

Bass are not high-class jewelry thieves. They are thugs, the street toughs of the underwater world. Their nature is to be compulsively aggressive. They are repeat offenders, unreformable. And it is this aspect about their feeding behavior that so endears them to anglers.

PART
II

THE
EQUIPMENT

6

RODS AND REELS

A visit to the local sport shop nowadays can be an exercise in bewilderment. Racks are full of fishing rods of all sizes, actions, purposes, and prices. Considering that everyone has varied needs and tastes, as well as a limit to how much fishing tackle they want to possess or what they can afford to purchase, the tasks of advising about and selecting bass fishing tackle become increasingly difficult.

Rods and reels suitable for bass fishing have come a long way in recent times due to technological advances; attitudes toward equipment needs have also changed. Except in special circumstances, heavy tackle is no longer considered unequivocally necessary to land big bass; light tackle has merit when conditions permit, and bait-casting equipment has evolved into very functional gear.

Most fishermen not only angle for bass, but panfish, trout, walleyes, stripers, and other sportfish as well. I've observed, however, that many anglers with a limited tackle supply are generally mismatched (undergunned in most instances) for a lot of bass fishing situations, though their tackle might be appropriate for other fishing. Does this mean that bass fishing requires special types of tackle? No. It does mean that a sensible approach to tackle selection for bass fishing—as well as for other types of fishing—is warranted.

The first step in selecting tackle is to assess your needs, likes, and abilities. What types of bass fishing do you do? What kind and size of lures do you use, and does a special type of retrieve mandate a particular style of tackle? What is the nature of the cover you fish? Is it thick and tough on tackle or sparse, offering lots of open-water angling? How much of your time is devoted to bass, and how much to other species with the same tackle? What is your level of skill at

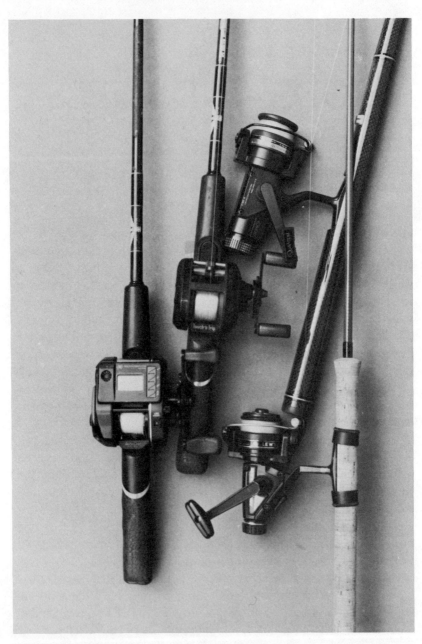

No one outfit will do the job for all of the varied conditions in which bass are found. Today's crop of rods and reels are very sophisticated and eminently suitable for bass fishing.

fishing various lures and in playing fish? What is your personal attitude toward the tenuous question of what constitutes "sport" in sport fishing? Are you interested mainly in catching big bass or fish of all sizes? All of these subjects, and more, play a part in the determination of the right bass tackle for you.

The idea of one outfit for bass fishing is dead today for all but the one-lure, one-technique fisherman. Serious bass angling involves a range of fishing conditions, lure styles and sizes, and fishing methods. Adaptability, versatility, and preparedness are keys to success, and your fishing tackle must be able to meet the respective tasks.

The equipment options open to bass fishermen run the gamut from ultralight spinning to heavy bait-casting and fly fishing. Fly fishing is probably the least practiced method of bass fishing, although it is very challenging and a lot of fun. In my opinion, fishermen would be best off if they mastered bass fishing techniques with other forms of tackle and fully understood the habits of their quarry and varied fishing conditions, before taking up the fly rod. For this reason, I am not going to discuss fly fishing in this book, but, rather, deal in detail with other techniques and equipment (much of which is applicable to bass angling regardless of tackle used).

At one end of the bait-casting and spinning tackle spectrum there is heavy and medium-heavy equipment. This tackle borders on the unsporting side at times, considering that the majority of bass caught by all anglers weigh less than 2 pounds. In locales where brush, timber, and grass are exceedingly thick, and big bass are reasonably numerous, strong equipment has merit, but within reason. Super-heavy tackle does help anglers free lures from impenetrable tangles and it does help manipulate lunker bass in tight quarters. But when you honestly evaluate the situation, how fair is it to catch bass with a broomstick-type of rod and 25- or 30-pound-test line? There is good medium-action equipment available that will handle big bass and bad conditions and still be sporting. With it, you can use medium strength line, switching to heavy line when the worst conditions are prevalent.

Light- and medium-duty tackle, packed with 4- to 14-pound-test line, can handle the majority of bass fishing circumstances (with a few notable exceptions, such as flipping and vegetation fishing, which will be discussed in later chapters) and still retain an element of fun and good sport in the bass-catching process. The best advice I can give, then, is to use equipment that best does the job under existing circumstances without sacrificing the element of sport. For bass that usually isn't ultralight gear but it often is light. On a line pound-test basis, and assuming you have a balanced fishing outfit, I would classify the categories as follows: Ultralight: 2- and 4-pound-test line; light: 6- and 8-pound-test line; medium: 10- and 12-pound-test line; medium-heavy: 14- to 17-pound-test line; heavy: 20-pounds and over.

As I've classified it, ultralight tackle is impractical for standard largemouth fishing. And in many situations light tackle borders on the impractical as well. Both are acceptable and even desirable for smallmouths, however. The principal reason for this lies with the nature of these fish. For the most part, the smallmouth resides in open water and when hooked does not have to be powered away from obstacles other than the bottom. Bronzebacks aren't caught in grass or lily pad clusters or around stumps and logs. In many regions they inhabit relatively clear, deep lakes. Because they are an especially wary fish, delicate presentations involving light, thin-diameter line, small jigs, and other diminutive lures, and corresponding rod and reel combinations make light and ultralight tackle a fundamental part of smallmouth fishing success.

A largemouth, by contrast, is a close-quarters, object-oriented scrapper. Largemouths found in or near weeds, stumps, bushes, fallen trees, rocky ledges, boulders, lily pads, and such—in effect, most of the areas where they live—have to be forced away from these objects after being hooked, or they may be lost. Since this covers most of the places where largemouths are found, the importance of this element is significant. With light and ultralight tackle it is difficult, if not impossible at times, to properly work weeds and lily pads and to finesse a weedless spoon, plastic worm, surface lure, or even a spinnerbait through them.

Ultralight gear is incapable of properly handling crankbaits except for the small, shallow-running variety. Diving plugs put a hefty bow in a supple rod and cannot adequately be fished at the depths (and bottom terrain) where they are meant to be used. For certain types of surface plugging, ultralight rods are a hindrance to activating the lure properly, and they lack the muscle to set the hook adequately in plastic worm fishing.

Setting the hook is the least common denominator of all the troubles that afflict light-tackle bass anglers. Many fish that are played momentarily and lost on light or ultralight gear are sacrificed because

Most bass fishermen prefer medium-duty tackle because of the nature of the cover that the fish inhabit. Though big fish can be caught, the average bass is small, and anglers should use equipment that best does the job under existing circumstances without sacrificing the element of sport.

of inadequate hook setting. That's not to say it can't be done. It can, but it's difficult. And that is true for most aspects of light-tackle bass fishing. It can be done. It can be fun. But it requires some finesse.

A would-be light-tackle bass angler must have a good ability to handle the equipment and a sensible attitude toward using it. It is not sport to use willowy rods and hair-thin line, let a fish run until it's exhausted, and then release it to an uncertain fate. And it is not sport to toss a light-lined plug into a batch of timber where a big bass will wrap you up and break off, toting your terminal tackle in its dentures.

There are many fishing rods available that will provide good service as bass fishing tackle. But there are many rods being used by bass fishermen that actually hinder their efforts. These rods are too stiff or too soft or too heavy to allow adequate, comfortable fishing.

Bass fishing with artificial baits principally involves these different angling devices: spinnerbaits, crankbaits, worms and jigs, floating/diving plugs, and surface lures. With a good rod, one that has guts and sensitivity, you can effectively fish the first three categories. For the others you still need a rod with guts but with a softer tip action to impart effective lure motion.

For crankbait fishing and worm and jig fishing, the soft-tipped or limber action rod is a severe handicap. It takes a rod with backbone to set the hook as well as to feel the action of the lure. One of the biggest problems beginning worm fishermen have is that their learning is hampered by the use of a rod that is too light and too whippy for the subtleties of the task. The same is true of crankbait fishing. With a limber, soft-tipped rod you can miss—not even detect—many strikes. If you switch to a stiffer-action rod, you'll notice the difference and begin to detect those soft strikes you were missing before. The rod needn't be as stiff as a baseball bat, either. A stiff-tipped rod is difficult to cast and not sensitive enough to lure action. A strong, sightly flexible butt section does provide needed strength for hook setting and for playing a fish, particularly a big one or a good fish in thick cover.

These attributes apply equally to spinning and bait-casting rods. There is not much justification for advocating one system over another for bass fishing, as long as you understand the conditions that you will be fishing under, realize the demands you will have to make on your fishing tackle, and can utilize that tackle to its fullest capability. Spinning tackle is more functional on windy days than bait-casting, particularly if it is necessary to use small baits or to be casting into the wind. Spinning reels are easy to use and not as prone to line fouling or backlashing, though the latest bait-casting reels are also remarkably good in this regard. On the flip side, a good bait-caster can usually be more accurate than a good spinning rod user, and bait-casting reel drags are generally of better quality.

Which gear to use is largely a matter of personal preference. I'm partial to bait-casting rods for most bass fishing, particularly for crankbait and worm fishing and working in heavy cover. A bait-casting rod offers slightly better casting control and is much more conducive to the use of big lures (I call a spinnerbait a big lure by virtue of its overall size) and baits weighing over ¼ ounce.

My preference runs to 6-foot bait-casting rods, which are advantageous for casting (as opposed to short, 5-foot models), though admittedly a little harder to use in close quarters, and I prefer straight, rather than pistol-grip, handles. The long rod helps you achieve distance, if that is necessary, makes fish playing and control better, and

Bait-casting gear is preferred by most avid bass anglers, especially those after largemouth bass. Casting accuracy, level line winding, smooth drag performance, and an ability to handle big bass are among its attributes.

helps get crankbaits deeper. I'm 6-feet tall, however, and a shorter fisherman might find the same advantages in a slightly shorter rod or might find my 6-foot rod too long for his fishing comfort.

Spinning-tackle fishermen looking for medium-duty equipment will find $5^1/_2$- to $6^1/_2$-foot rods to their liking. Since I primarily use bait-casting tackle for bass, my own spinning tackle for these fish consists of light-action rods equipped with 6- or 8-pound-test line, which is primarily used for fishing floater/divers, some surface lures, small jigs, and light spoons and spinners. My choice is for long spinning rods, in the $6^1/_2$- and 7-foot category, because the open-water fishing that I do with this tackle (for largemouth bass, but especially for smallmouths) complements this nicely. These same rods are used for lake and stream trout fishing as well as in fishing for other open-water light-tackle fish, so they fill more than one equipment need. Many spinning rod anglers, however, prefer shorter sticks for bass, usually having a slow taper so they are not limber (and use them for jigging). For ultralights and smallmouth fishing, I still prefer a long rod, but most ultralight models are in the 5- to $5^1/_2$-foot range.

With spinning tackle you may find, as I do, that a top-and-bottom sliding-ring reel seat, rather than a fixed reel seat, provides best feel and best rod comfort. The majority of spinning reels available, particularly the medium- and heavy-duty models, feature fixed reel seats. The adjustable seats allow you to position the reel foot where the combination of rod and reel feels most comfortable to you. These also enhance the sensitivity of a rod and help transmit feel from the tip portion down through the butt into the seat.

For cold-weather fishing, I suggest wrapping the reel seat with electrical tape. This somewhat insulates the handle and keeps your hand from touching cold metal; some anglers with adjustable seats take the sliding rings off the rod and keep their reel permanently affixed to the rod with tape.

Trying to determine the action of a rod is tough to do by mere feel, yet it is even tougher to do when buying, sight unseen, from a catalog. Although it may cost you more to go to a fishing tackle dealer, he may be knowledgeable enough to assist in the selection of tackle (mass merchandisers and discount store sporting goods section clerks are woefully deficient in this regard). There, you can not only handle and flex the prospective purchase, but you can actually put your own reel on the rod and maybe tie on a few lures or cast a dummy plug. This is the best way to determine if a rod suits your needs and anticipated fishing applications.

An alternative is to find other anglers who are satisfied with the rods they use for various bass fishing conditions and try their equipment yourself. This way you can judge the performance of a rod that you may then wish to buy through a mail-order supplier or from a tackle dealer or sporting goods store.

The best combination of characteristics in any good bass fishing rod is one that has strength with sensitivity and is light in weight. If you will be doing a lot of fishing, for many hours at a time, the weight factor will become significant. The trend in reels in recent years has gone to down-sized, streamlined products that are light, have minimal

Spinning has merit in open water fishing circumstances, as in fishing for small-mouth bass where fish don't have much chance of finding an obstruction to cut your line off.

line capacity, and essentially fit in the palm of your hand. New materials and manufacturing processes have made rods lighter yet stronger, too. This is where graphite and boron rods shine.

The best graphites are light, strong, and sensitive. They are also fragile, in the sense that they will not stand up to continued abuse. Knocking them against the boat, dropping other rods and reels on them, and doing other seemingly innocuous actions can do more harm to them than it would to fiberglass rods. I have broken a lot of graphite and boron rods over the years, but not one has been broken in playing a fish. Some have broken during casting, some during retrieving a lure, and some in shaking a snagged lure free. These instances were incidental to fishing and probably resulted from a crack or fissure in the sidewall of the rod. What this means is that you can confidently apply maximum pressure to a fish while using a graphite or boron rod, but you can't repeatedly bang it against the gunwale of your boat or jab it in a corner.

Deciding whether to buy a graphite or boron rod is difficult for the budget-conscious angler and for the beginner unsure of his needs. The decision is further complicated by the fact that many rods labeled graphite are really composites of graphite and fiberglass, and the manufacturers seldom indicate the percentages of composition. Rods that are all or mostly graphite are lighter than those that are mostly fiberglass. Though lighter than fiberglass, graphite rods tend to be stiffer. And they are more expensive. For sensitivity in detecting a strike or feeling what your lure is doing, graphite and boron rods are a definite asset for worm and jig fishing; of marginal value in surface fishing; and of some value in crankbait or spinnerbait fishing. In all areas, they are beneficial for hook setting.

I use graphite and boron rods for all types of bass fishing, and they excel in all areas. Experienced anglers and fishermen who do a lot of fishing will appreciate the lightness, strength, and sensitivity of this equipment. A beginning angler should consider starting with a top-quality fiberglass rod, however, or a graphite-fiberglass composite. He can learn with this, hone his angling abilities, make the mistakes that everyone does, and work up to the next level as he becomes more familiar with his needs and skills and can appreciate the difference that this equipment affords. To some extent, this is like having the best and latest camera. If you have never worked a camera before and go buy the best available, you can't possibly appreciate its abilities or get the most out of it. Just as the possession of a good camera cannot make you a good photographer, having the best tackle cannot make you a better or more successful angler; it's how you use it and what you do with it that counts.

Fishing rods are only part of the equipment picture. Reels, too, have come to have a significant place in bass fishing since the early 70's. Technological innovations and advances in recent years have made bass fishing reels, particularly bait-casters, extremely sophisticated, functional, and high quality. Many manufacturers currently have spinning, spin-casting, and bait-casting reels that are well-suited to bass fishing applications.

In the purest sense, a reel is nothing more than a device to hold your fishing line. In practicality, a reel aids casting, lure retrieval, fish playing, hook setting, and more, and thus, it should be evaluated on many fronts. The quality of construction and materials is one factor by which to judge a reel, but also important are weight, drag, retrieve ratio, cast control, freespool, and line capacity features.

Light weight is desirable in a reel, particularly if you expect to use it continuously for long hours of fishing. Many of the latest reels feature all or partial graphite construction or graphite and titanium components that help decrease overall weight. This makes reels easier for anyone, especially youths and women, to use, and easier for all-day casting. With the larger, older reels of the past you usually experienced wrist fatigue at the end of the day. Petite bait-casting reels, which hold no more than 100 yards of 12-pound line, are popular, and if the line capacity of these is suitable to you, then small reels are a good choice.

Line capacity is not much of a factor in bass fishing; if you just use the reel for bass fishing, you rarely need more than 100 feet of line, and then only because you have made an extremely long cast, as when sending a lure to a distant school of feeding fish. The common casting range in largemouth fishing is 30 to 60 feet. Furthermore, when hooked, bass don't run away. They bulldog it, look for cover, and try to throw the hook or break off on an object. If you'll be using a bait-casting outfit for other forms of fishing as well as bass fishing, and where greater line capacity is needed (such as striped bass fishing), go for a wider spool model that will hold 200 yards of 12-pound line or approximately 150 yards of 17-pound line. If not, a narrow-spool reel is just right.

With spinning reels, consider the size of line you'll be using. Light- to medium-action spinning and spin-cast reels are more than adequate for bass angling. Check the manufacturer's chart for line capacity, and note that smaller reels are not meant for use with heavier, large-diameter lines and that big reels shouldn't be used with light, small-diameter lines.

The cast control is an important feature on bait-casting reels that serves to prevent backlashes caused by spool overruns. It is basically a spool-braking device. Most of the latest and best bait-casters now augment or override their standard cast control operation with magnetic spool braking. Magnets on the sideplate of the reel are adjustable and allow you to place a precise range of pressure on a reel. Gradients from zero (no magnetism) to 10 (the most) allow you to adjust spool braking pressure according to the situation and your skills.

Under general fishing conditions, most good casters keep the magnetic cast control knob set at 3. Casting light lures or casting into the wind are conditions in which you might increase spool-braking

Magnetic-spool breaking devices have made bait-casting reels easy for almost anyone to cast. They are featured on the sideplate of the Ryobi (*center*) and Daiwa (*right*) reels here. In contrast, the older Childre reel (*left*) features a conventional centrifugal cast control mechanism.

tension. Casting heavy lures and aiming for long distances are situations in which you can decrease tension.

In theory you can take your thumb off the revolving spool and cast without applying thumb pressure and not have a backlash. That's why these modern reels are said to be backlash-free. However, it is possible to have spool overruns with these reels, so the smart angler will still use an educated thumb while he casts with the magnetic spool-breaking device at the preferred setting. Using these reels, a good caster can go all day without having a significant backlash (unless, of course, he hooks the line of the guy casting behind him; there is no reel that will help prevent a snafu in that situation).

Magnetic spool-braking reels are excellent for fishermen who are new to bait-casting. A beginning bait-caster can set the magnetic control high (say 7 or 8) and make short- to medium-length casts until he is satisfied that he is reasonably comfortable with the equipment. In doing so, he will avoid the problem that his predecessors faced, of having to untangle horrendous spool-overrun bird's nests that inevitably resulted from learning to thumb conventional bait-casting reels. As he develops confidence, he can relax the magnetic tension until he is casting at all distances with accuracy and without backlashes.

For years, fishing with bait-casting reels was such a chore that few people wanted to have anything to do with them. And when spinning reels, with their ease of castability, became available after World War II, bait-casting tackle took a back seat as functional angling gear. Today, the situation is markedly changed. Not only is bait-casting tackle functional, it is probably more functional for many largemouth bass fishing situations than other types of gear and is unquestionably preferred by avid bass anglers. This shift has occurred only in the last ten to fifteen years, as such functions as level-wind, cast control, and drag systems evolved from technological manufacturing advances.

Drag systems enter the picture in all kinds of reels, of course, but don't come into play for many bass anglers. In my thinking, a smooth drag system is essential for any high-quality reel, whether you expect to use that feature or not. Light line and light tackle users, particularly spinning rod fishermen, will call upon their drag more often than other bass anglers, due to the nature of the fish and the equipment, but if the drag is inadequate it overshadows the other features of the reel. How to use and set your drag is discussed later in the book.

Fast retrieve ratios are another aspect of modern reels that are important to bass anglers. Spinning reels have had high-speed retrieves for a long time. In the past few years some bait-casting reels have sported retrieve ratios as high as 5.2 to 1 and even an extremely fast 5.36 to 1.

High-speed retrieves are not needed in most bass fishing circumstances, especially in lure retrieval. At top speed you are often reeling a lure in much too fast for the likes of the fish. However, they are beneficial when you need to retrieve a lure quickly to make another cast, such as in reaching a moving school of bass busting shad on the surface. High-speed retrieves especially shine when you are playing fish, especially big bass and fish in heavy cover, or when fish must be hauled out of or steered around bad objects, or when a bass rushes the boat. Often a bass will rush the boat after it strikes your lure. To set the hook or control the fish, you need to catch up with it quickly.

Occasionally a fast retrieval ratio can be an aid in working a lure, such as in speeding up a crankbait or spinnerbait or in recovering slack line. It does require less handle-cranking effort on the part of the angler. However, a fast retrieve reel can lull anglers into retrieving their lures faster than the fish like, because of the high speed. Many an angler who uses a high-speed retrieve reel has found that his mind slipped while he was fishing crankbaits for bass in cold water, and was inadvertently bringing his bait through the water faster than the somewhat lethargic fish were willing to take it. If you use a high-speed retrieve reel and keep in mind that you need to turn the handle slowly at certain times, then you shouldn't have any problems, and the advantages will far outweigh the disadvantages.

The wave of the future in bass fishing reels may well be with electronics. In time we may see reels, especially bait-casters, with electronic influence over such basic functions as cast control. Presently, electronics are only used for display purposes in providing information. Daiwa has an electronic display spinning reel that tells time and sports an alarm that sounds when the drag tension is reaching a near-critical point. They also have a microprocessor-equipped bait-caster that monitors relative retrieval speed via an LCD readout screen on the front of the reel. Called the Daiwa Microcomputer Procaster, it uses an LCD readout to tell you how far you cast, the speed of your retrieve, the amount of line on your reel, the strength of line, the depth of your lure, and more via audible signals and programmable visual displays. If more manufacturers come out with similar products in the future, these may be a big part of the bass fishing game in time, especially when the price (they are currently selling at about $140, which is a lot to spend for a bass fishing reel) comes down.

After using this particular reel for the better part of a year, I can say that I like it, but that I'm not sure it's what every bass angler needs. The reel features a magnetic cast control, and casting with it is excellent. Knowing how far you've cast is nice, but not a necessary element of bass fishing. It really doesn't matter whether that stump by the bank is 40 feet away or 55 feet away; if you're able to cast to it and are in the right position for the best presentation, you will. Length of line out is of paramount importance to trollers, so I expect that, in time, these reels will be of supreme value to striped bass, trout, and salmon fishermen, who aim to set their lines out a certain distance and to get their lures down to a particular depth.

This reel is a little heavier than most other bait-casters, and some anglers will find this uncomfortable, though I have not. The lure retrieval speed can be of value, provided you train yourself to get into the habit of looking at the reel. Most anglers look at the water in front of them, following their lure in and looking for fish, places to cast, and so forth. Retrieving is an automatic act. The Daiwa LCD reel has a bar graph that ticks off retrieval speed. I found that the graph jumps easily from low to high positions, but that you can determine a relative retrieval speed. In crankbait fishing this can be of some value, though I haven't encountered a situation where I needed to use the same rate of retrieve over and over in order to catch fish. Being able to determine how deep your lure is, however, is valuable to bass anglers who are jigging in deep water and fishing for suspended fish. It can also be valuable in setting bait out at a certain depth or in getting a slab spoon down to a certain level (as when fishing for white bass or stripers).

This type of reel will become a part of the avid bass angler's inventory, but I feel confident in saying that most bass fishermen can survive without it. Trollers, on the other hand, should be grabbing the advanced versions of these reels and getting them into use as quickly as they can.

Another thing that has happened in the past few years to bait-casting reels is the emergence of high-quality left-hand retrieve reels. For decades, Garcia was the only manufacturer to have a bait-caster that had a handle on the left side of the reel. Bait-casting reels seem to have been invented by a left-handed person, because the handle traditionally has been on the right side of the reel. This is a problem that is only appreciated by the beginning bait-caster.

The majority of bait-casting reels sport a right-handed retrieve, meaning that if you cast right-handed, you must switch the rod from your dominant hand to your left hand after casting, holding the rod and reel (and retrieving lures and playing fish) with your left hand while reeling with your right. This is contrary to how right-handed anglers use spinning and spin-casting tackle and requires some adjustment. A few years ago, Shimano came out with a Bantam left-hand-crank bait-casting reel, then followed it up with a similar reel in their magnetic spool-breaking series. These were the first top-quality reels that had a left-hand retrieve and were truly made for right-handed anglers. Now Garcia and Daiwa have produced top-quality reels with this feature as well. Now, Shakespeare and Ryobi bait-casters permit either right- or left-hand retrieve, as is done with spinning reels. We'll probably see more of these reels in the future.

I have recommended the left-hand cranking bait-casters to many anglers who are just beginning to use bait-casting tackle and who are already familiar with spinning gear. Most of these people, who have no preconceived notions or developed habits with or about such tackle, adapt to it well. The standard right-retrieve bait-casters, of course, are fine for left-handed fishermen. Anglers who are right-handed and who have been using a right-crank bait-caster for years will find it difficult to make the switch. They are too used to doing it the traditional way. Also, to make the switch you need to replace all of your current right-retrieve bait-casters with left-retrieve models, as having both in your boat makes your fishing confusing when you change from one type of reel to another.

Still another new development in reels for bass fishermen is the "flipping" reel, or a reel designed specifically for flipping. One of these, which I've been using for over a year, is the ABU-Garcia Ultra Mag XL Plus, which has all the standard high-quality features of most bait-casting reels plus a knob that allows you to strip off line instantly by depressing the Thumb Bar line release without having to turn the handle to engage gears. It makes it very easy to strip line off as conditions warrant without having to stop and engage gears. When this feature isn't used, the reel functions as a normal bait-casting reel and can be used for any bass fishing application. Another flipping reel, the Shimano Brush Buster, also sports a no-backlash line-stripping feature, but is useful only for flipping.

Still other developments in reels of late have been lever drags, direct drive, and one-hand-casting spool releases.

Lever drags have dual drag settings: locked-down strong for hook setting and normal for fish playing. I haven't had much experience with these as yet, but it seems to me that an angler who uses his drag properly needn't have a stronger hook-setting mode and often doesn't have time to fumble for the control to back off on the drag if necessary. This system originated with big-game ocean reels, and is fine in that application, but a little too much for freshwater bass fishing.

Direct drive is useful for anglers who don't want to use their drag at all but who wind in reverse, or backpedal, the handle. If you do this while fighting a good fish, however, and you lose your grip on the handle (maybe it's wet), you'll have a wildly careening spool, an inevitable overrun, and bruised knuckles. Again, a high-quality drag, set properly, should suffice for most anglers.

The one-handed casting releases come in the form of a bar between sideplates or a pushbutton on the sideplate, and they allow you to release the spool for casting by using the thumb on the hand that holds the reel. With other reels you have to use a finger on your non-casting hand to reach over and depress the spool-release button before casting. This one-handed operation does simplify casting and saves you a fraction of a second of time. For some people, however, the position of the spool release, especially between sideplates, is a little low on the reel or a little hard to depress, and therefore uncomfortable on the thumb.

These features are becoming standard on the more expensive and top-of-the-line bait-casting reels, and some, including the lever drags and one-hand casting (plus stern-mounted drag control), are being featured on spinning reels as well. One-handed casting with spinning reels is accomplished via a lever that allows you to lift up the line and open the bail with one finger. Previously, you had to open the bail with the hand that wasn't holding the rod.

Of the other significant changes in spinning reels in recent years, spool design is the most obvious. Spinning reel spools used to fit inside the bail housing; that often led to line tangling around the shaft under the spool. Today it's hard to find new reels so designed. The skirted spool, which shrouds the shaft and slips over the bail housing, has swept through the industry and successfully curbed tangling.

The drag systems on spinning reels have improved dramatically, too. The popularity of light monofilament line made it necessary to have a forgiving reel, one that would yield line when strong fish applied extreme pressure. Multiple-disc, spring-loaded systems that could be set at various adjustments evolved. Rear, or stern-mounted, drag-adjustment knobs have also become popular, though there are many fishermen who still prefer the older style of top-mounted adjustment.

In the past few years, spinning reels have gotten lighter, too. Some models now feature all or partial construction from graphite composite materials. Previously, they were made from zinc alloys or die-cast aluminum. In addition to convenience, such reels are more resistant to corrosion, and you can expect to see more of this trend in the future.

Featured clockwise from upper left are Zebco Cardinal, Childre Speed Spin, Zebco Quantum, and Garcia-ABU Cardinal spinning reels. The Zebco Cardinal is an older reel, with a spool that sat inside the upper part of the reel, though it was the forerunner of stern drag controls. The other reels, which are new products, sport some of the features, including skirted spools, line capacity charts, partial graphite construction, and rear drag, that have become standard on top-quality modern spinning reels.

As you can see, reels have come a long way in recent times. I expect they will continue to become lighter and generally more functional fishing tools that do far more than simply store line.

Among bait-casting reels I've had good use out of Diawa Procasters, in the standard and Magforce versions as well as in the microcomputerized PT10 version mentioned earlier; Ryobi's V-Mag Lite bait-caster; Lew Childre's reels; and the ABU-Garcia reels. Among spinning reels I can recommend the old Zebco Cardinal reels, especially the 3 and 4, if you can still find them (a few people have squirreled some of these away); Lew Childre's Speed Spin models; Shakespeare's Sigma Pro (formerly the Sigma Supra); and ABU-Garcia's Cardinal 700 Series.

As for rods, I'm partial to Fenwick graphite and boron 6-footers, in the HMG 605 bait-casting designation. I've used these rods successfully for not only bass fishing, but also for catching stripers, lake trout, salmon, char, and other species. They are a little long for tight casting situations and for underhanded casting from low boats, but that's the only area in which they don't compromise. Among other bait-casters I use and like are some top Daiwa, Skyline, and Childre models. Among spinning rods, a host of fiberglass, graphite, and boron models fill the bill.

These recommendations are based on my personal experience. Other rods and reels that I haven't used or used enough to form a personal opinion may be as good. You'll notice that I haven't discussed spin-casting tackle here, not because it isn't functional in its own right, but because I don't think it can compare with bait-casting or spinning tackle in many critical areas of bass fishing, including drag performance, casting accuracy, fish-fighting, and control.

When you do select a rod or reel for bass fishing, be mindful of the equipment you expect to use with it. The concept that most anglers use for matching rod and reel is one of balanced tackle, which basically means that the two products should complement each other. You can't use a medium-duty spinning reel with an ultralight action rod, nor a miniature reel with a heavy-duty rod. The combined outfit should be neither too heavy in the tip section nor too heavy in the handle.

Most of the rods and reels that are considered appropriate for general bass fishing fall into the top-of-the-line tackle series of the respective manufacturers. This means that they cost more than the bottom- and mid-series equipment, but they're made of better material and with better components.

Price is not always an indicator of quality. For example, some graphite-fiberglass composite rods have a small percentage of graphite, are heavy, and are not as good as comparable all-fiberglass products; yet these rods are much more costly, presumably due to what the consumer thinks is "high" graphite content. The fishing tackle market, however, is very competitive, and price is usually one guideline for quality.

Buy the best equipment that you can afford from the start, and take good care of it; the tackle market is volatile and subject to changes annually based on trends, fads, and technological developments. Those who bought top-quality reels five years ago and who have fully mastered their attributes are sacrificing little to the 1986 angler with the latest rod and reel. Possession of quality tackle is no replacement for angling savvy, but it will help your fishing by fortifying your attitude and confidence.

CARE OF RODS AND REELS

Fishing rods need and consequently receive very little attention. After years of use or if they are subjected to substantial abuse, the ferrules may come loose or a guide may break off, but throughout the season there isn't much you need to do to them, particularly if all your usage is in freshwater.

Fixed reel seats can occasionally use a mild dose of WD-40 to keep them operating smoothly. A broken tip-top can be made temporarily serviceable by cutting the rod down to just above the next guide or by putting a new tip-top guide on the place where it broke, but the action and feel of this modified rod will be inferior to its original design. You can usually get a broken tip guide off by melting the finish and glue with a match, then twisting. For short-term use, you may be able to fit the guide foot over the broken rod top and use a fast-drying glue or epoxy to keep it in place. Write the manufacturer and buy a new tip section for that model rod if it's a two-piece rod.

Always keep the brochure or warranty slip that accompanies a new rod. Mark on it the model number, size, weight, and any other pertinent descriptive data, and save this so you can positively identify the product years later, if necessary, for repair or replacement. This can also be done for reels.

New or replacement guides can be put on a rod by you or by a fishing tackle dealer who services equipment. Though it is best to replace a guide with one of similar style and certainly with an identical inside ring diameter, something different can do in a pinch. To replace a guide yourself, place the guide into position, apply a light coat of glue over the guide foot, wrap the foot from the interior out as neatly as possible with strong thread, tie it off, and cover with a coat of lacquer.

Many anglers are concerned about their rods taking a "set" as a result of being in a poor position for a long time. My fiberglass rods seemed to get a slight bend to them after years of use, but they function fine. You may want to hang your rods by the tips from a hook in the wall or ceiling or use some retaining holder that keeps them in an upright position. Probably the worst offense is to lean a rod up against a wall. This forces the rod to be bent unnaturally in that position for a long time.

It is also not a bad idea to check your rod guides occasionally, verifying the smoothness of the inside ring where line passes. A nicked guide will abrade your line, thus weakening it. Running a Q-tip or piece of nylon hosiery through the guides will detect such a problem. Replace guides that are so damaged.

Also check the sidewalls of your rods once in a while. Most rods that break from fishing use do so because of a nick or fracture in the material, probably incurred from hard contact with some object. This structural failure may not be so serious as to hamper the rod's performance, or it may take one very demanding experience to put more strain on the bad spot than it will bear. You can't do much about this other than recognize that it can happen and take precautions to be careful with your equipment.

The one modification that I make to my fishing rods is to whittle the bulbous end off all my bait-casting rod handles, making them into straight handles. Use a belt sander, if available, to smooth the material off and give the handle a more polished appearance. Though you will be hard-put to find a modern bait-casting rod with a no-pistol grip, straight handle, I prefer them this way because they're easier to cast with two hands and fit into a rod holder better for other types of fishing.

Reels are more likely than rods to need attention during the course of a fishing season. The key features of a reel that need occasional inspection and that malfunction the most are; the drag, anti-reverse, bail-catch, bail arm, level wind, and cast control.

A little lubrication goes a long way for preventive maintenance, as does a periodic cleaning. Manufacturers find that the reason most reels are returned for service is that they have become fouled with dirt and grime and need to be cleaned.

It also pays to occasionally check all nuts and screws, tightening them as necessary. Sometimes sideplate screws become loose after taking a pounding while you're running a boat in rough water, and you don't realize it until you later make a cast. Loose items seem to pop off at the worst time and, if lost, can hamper the service of the reel until replaced. I speak from sour experience in this respect, though I admit to not checking for loose parts frequently enough. Even new reels, I have found, should be scrutinized.

Every time that a reel has been used in saltwater or brackish water, hose it down with freshwater. Do this with a moderate spray of water, rather than a heavy one. If a hose is not available, cleanse the reels under a faucet or in a shower.

If there are major problems with a reel, my advice is to send it back to the manufacturer or a qualified repair center. Some folks like to tinker with their equipment and repair or modify it. That's fine for them. Not me. If it's not working right, I send it back to the manufacturer or the repair center. I have a lot of tackle so I can spare a reel if it needs repair work, but the average angler wants his reel fixed immediately. My suggestion is to send the reel by United Parcel Service. UPS delivers coast to coast in four working days, less if the distance is closer. I have sent reels recently to Daiwa, ABU-Garcia, and Shakespeare and gotten them back within ten days, which in my opinion is a reasonable time.

One of the most important elements of a reel that warrants watching is the drag. It's a good idea to release drag pressure at the end of the day's fishing. This relieves tension on the drag washers. Few people do this. Many of those who do, forget to readjust the drag the next time they go fishing.

No matter how frequently I use my tackle, I have made it a habit to check the drag on each reel before a day's fishing. I adjust the drag tension as necessary and check the start-up operation. A familiar problem is the failure of the drag to release line smoothly when it is initially demanded. Because the drag is stuck or tight, it takes more start-up pressure than normal to allow the drag to function. Often this start-up pressure exceeds the breaking strength of the line, and the result is a broken line and a lost fish. Check this before making that first cast—you won't be sorry later.

Most of the modern bait-casting reels are equipped with two-grip handles, but older models were only supplied with single grips. My preference is for double grips, and I replaced the single-grip handle on my older reels with these. These two-grip handles are referred to as "power" handles by some, but this is a misnomer. Their real advantage is singular and simple: the grips are easier to latch onto and you don't need to see them to locate them readily. Not everyone appreciates these handles; fishermen with very large hands and big fingers find it awkward to use two-grip handles, but they can replace them.

Fortunately, modern rods and reels can withstand reasonable wear and tear without too much consideration from the angler. Don't overlook your tackle completely, however. A little preventive maintenance and common sense will keep quality tackle in top shape for a long time.

7

LINE

Line is to fishing tackle as sewing thread is to a dress shirt. Remove all the sewing thread from a dress shirt and what happens? The collar detaches. The cuffs come off. The sleeves come off. The buttons drop off. What remains is the makings of a shirt without the vital ingredient. What's lost is the essential connection that brings it all together and allows it to function as a shirt.

Now think about your fishing tackle. Remove the line and what happens? There is nothing to run through the guides. The spool of the reel is empty. The hook or lure is unattached. You have the makings of a fishing outfit without the vital connection that makes it function.

When most people look at a shirt, do they visualize the sewing thread? No. They see fabric, color, design, and buttons. When most fishermen contemplate fishing tackle, what comes to mind? The first thing is the lure or bait. Then the type of rod and reel. Often over-looked and usually unappreciated is the most necessary—and impor-tant—element. The difference between the two is that you don't have to be aware of the importance of your thread in order to wear a shirt. You *must* recognize the role of your fishing line in order to be a successful angler.

Line not only makes all of your other tackle function, it plays *the* prominent role in the three most important factors of catching fish: presenting the lure or bait, hooking the fish, and landing it. When all aspects of fishing technique and fishing tackle use are taken into consideration, line becomes the single most important piece of equipment.

Because of the prominent role that monofilament line plays in

Whether you are trying to force a bass out of heavy cover, setting the hook, or simply casting a lure, your fishing line plays a vital role. The more you know about the capabilities and performance of line, the more effective you can be.

fishing today, it is essential that anglers understand how to use their line to its utmost capability. The more you know about the funda- mental aspects of line use and performance—for bass as well as for other fish—the better angler you will be.

Fishing line is one of the least expensive, least understood, and yet most important factors in angling. A reel filler spool of line costs less than any rod or reel, less than some lures, and less than two or three of the more popularly used plugs, spoons, or spinners. You can catch fish without a rod or without a reel, but you can't catch them without some form of line.

Nevertheless, most fishermen know little more about line than what they have read in advertisements and the meager and insufficient information contained on product packaging and labeling. Worse yet, they do not exercise sufficient care in the handling and treatment of the one piece of equipment that is the most vital link between them and the fish.

Modern monofilament line is so much superior to what was avail- able to fishermen earlier in this century that many people have been lulled into thinking that their line needs no more attention than a simple fishing rod. Then, too, the average bass fisherman seldom catches fish large enough to really test even the poorest line and his own abilities, which again leads him to overlook that line. This is a mistake. Proper care, use, and attention to your line does more than mark you as a knowledgeable, fastidious bass angler; it pays dividends over and over again in ordinary day-to-day fishing situations.

UNDERSTANDING FISHING LINE

It is not necessary to understand the many technical aspects of manufacturing fishing line. It is helpful, however, to have a basic, non-technical familiarization with line, because all of the properties of interest to your fishing applications are related to that manufacturing technology.

In today's marketplace we have monofilament, cofilament, and braided Dacron line. Braided Dacron, which is technically a multi-filament line (the Dacron filaments are weaved together), accounts for less than 2 percent of all line sold in the U.S. For all practical purposes, it is ancient history as a fishing line and is used by very few bass fishermen.

Through 1985, monofilament—which means a single strand of line but which has become synonymous with nylon—line sales accounted for 94 percent of all line sold in the United States. Nylon monofilament has become extraordinarily popular with anglers since its refinement and premium introductions in the 1950s and with the introduction and refinements in top-quality spinning and bait-casting tackle. Nylon monofilament line, as the name suggests, is a single-component product formed through an extrusion (molten plastic formed through a die) process.

Cofilament line is a new category of fishing line that first became available to anglers at the end of 1985 in a product called Prime, introduced by Du Pont. A cofilament is a multicomponent coextruded fishline. That means the product is comprised of two or more filaments, merged in the manufacturing process into one unit. Prime, which was the only cofilament line on the market when this book was written, has two filaments that exist in a sheath-core relationship. The sheath, the outer portion, is Du Pont Stren nylon monofilament. The core, the inner portion, is a polyester monofilament. Polyester is not a nylon. Polyester and Stren nylon are vastly different polymers.

When you cut a piece of sufficiently high diameter Prime cofilament and look at the end of it with the naked eye, you can see that this line has a sheath and a core. It is these materials and their relationship to each other that give Prime cofilament a marriage of the best features of nylon monofilament and braided Dacron. I'll discuss these attributes later in this chapter.

Cofilament line looms as the premium line of the future. It will appeal to anglers who want to fine-tune their fishing, who are among the more serious and studious anglers, and who are willing to pay its approximately 40 percent higher cost.

Both nylon monofilament and nylon-polyester cofilament lines are polymeric byproducts of crude oil processing. Nylon alloys, a mixture of various types of nylon, are used to form fishing line also. None of these materials exist in nature. Although the lines possess the same derivatives, the way they are processed and extruded and the way their molecules are compounded determine the different characteristics of the line and its properties. This accounts for the differences in properties among brands of nylon monofilaments and between monofilaments and cofilaments. Additionally, premium-grade lines receive more quality control attention, more introduction of additive ingredients, and more attention in the finishing processes than non-premium line. As a result, they cost more.

THE PROPERTIES OF LINE

The characteristics of any fishing line include some degree of breaking strength, stretch, knot strength, memory, uniformity, and resistance to abrasion. Color is an additional feature, though not one that affects the basic performance aspects of the line.

BREAKING STRENGTH

The most prominent feature of any line is its strength, that is, how many pounds of pressure must be applied before the molecules in the line part and the line is broken. (Perhaps the foremost desired feature is durability, but this is a function of all the properties of line.) All spools of line are labeled to indicate their breaking strength. This in itself is misleading, since the actual breaking strength of line indubitably varies from the labeling.

The primary reason for this confusion is the fact—unknown to 99 percent of the fishermen—that there is a significant difference in how a line breaks when it is dry versus when it is wet. Monofilament line absorbs water, which alters its performance from a dry to wet state. The wet breaking strength is always less than the dry breaking strength. My tests in this regard have shown a range from 9 to 23 percent less, but 15 percent is about average.

It is meaningless to take a piece of line, wrap it around your hand, tug on it, and proclaim it has great strength. This is dry strength, and since your line is wet when you fish, dry strength is meaningless. For many lines, including some of the supposedly better and so-called "premium" lines, the wet breaking strength is greater than the labeled strength of the line. The point about all this information regarding breaking strength is that unless you buy a "class" line, you don't know what you've got because the manufacturers are not explicit enough with their product information. A line that is labeled as 12-pound-test, for example, is actually so designated to assure that it will break *at or above* 12 pounds in a *wet* condition. Most break above their labeled rating, though a few regularly break below it, which, of course, is a serious deficiency. One frequently run advertisement by a line manufacturer compares its 10-pound line with those of others and says theirs is stronger, but when you look at the figures they give, you can see that what they really have is a 17-pound-strength line. That's deliberate mislabeling, not greater strength.

You should realize that there are two classifications of line: "test" and "class." Class lines are predominantly used by saltwater big-game tournament fishermen and by any anglers specifically interested in establishing line-class world records (world records are kept for all species based on strength of line used as well as in all-tackle designations). Class lines are guaranteed to break *under* the labeled strength in a wet condition, in order to conform to the world record specifications of the International Game Fish Association (IGFA), which is the repository for world record fish. Class line is more expensive than test line and is only differentiated from test line in the wet breaking strength feature; its other properties should be similar to those of test lines. To illustrate the breaking strength difference, anglers fishing with a class 12-pound line are fishing with a line that will break at slightly less than 12 pounds in a wet state, while those fishing with a good-quality test 12-pound line are using a product that will probably break between 13 and 14 pounds in a wet state. That may not sound like much but there are situations when this is a considerable difference. Anglers who are seeking to establish records or who want to be absolutely sure of the wet breaking strength of their line will find class lines to be worthwhile, although they only account for a small part of the fishing line market and an even smaller percent of the bass fishing line market.

The basic strength of a line directly relates to its diameter. The greater the breaking strength, the larger the diameter. The primary reason for switching from a "heavy" line to "light" line is that lighter line has a fine diameter and is less obtrusive to fish. Here, too, manufacturers differ, and the line with the highest breaking strength may not be the one with the largest diameter (within the same category of line).

Among lighter lines there is only a minute difference in diameter between different brands. Heavy lines, from 20-pound-test and up, however, can have a significant difference. Line diameter is more of an influence on abrasion resistance.

ABRASION RESISTANCE

Abrasion resistance is one of the most difficult qualities of line to measure, because no laboratory test has yet been devised that accurately reflects the abrasive contact that line is subjected to during fishing conditions, in a dry state. Some lines are more abrasion resistant than others, either due to greater diameter or to the molecular composition of the line itself. Determining the differences among brands is subjective, although some lines do seem to be considerably more resistant to abrasion than others. However, you can only make this judgment through use. Lack of abrasion resistance is Dacron's biggest drawback; Dacron doesn't compare favorably in this respect to even the poorest nylon monofilaments, and the poorest of these don't compare favorably to premium nylon monofilaments or to cofilament.

Bass fishermen do have to contend with abrasion. There are circumstances when you have to cut off nicked line every half hour or so while fishing, because the terrain that you are working is so tough on your line. The lighter the line you use, the more damaging abrasion can be. Contact with rocks, trees, stumps, and emergent grasses can wear heavily on your line, so selecting a line with satisfactory abrasion resistance is important. No nylon monofilament or cofilament line completely withstands abrasion, however.

STRETCH

All lines stretch. The issue is how much they stretch and how this impacts your fishing.

Stretch is both good and bad. It allows for mistakes in fighting a fish, inadequate drag setting, or countering sudden close-to-the-angler surges by strong fish; yet it hampers the inattentive angler who forgets to keep all of the slack out of the line when setting the hook.

Some lines have more stretch than others. Dacron has no stretch, but braided Dacron stretches a little because the braids have some give and pull tighter when extreme tension is applied. The average percent of stretch in nylon monofilaments, according to tests I've conducted in the past, is around 30 percent in a wet state. Line has more stretch in a wet state than in a dry one. Lines that have high stretch (I've seen over 45 percent) are great for casting, but terrible for hook setting and playing fish because they have the elasticity of a rubberband. Lines with too little stretch are inelastic and may break easily under sudden impact. The cushioning effect that has been provided by lines with a controlled stretch feature has been vitally important to many anglers.

The few anglers who fish with braided Dacron do so because its extremely low stretch gives them much greater hook-setting power. Some offshore big-game trollers use a braided Dacron line because of its hook-setting effectiveness when striking a huge fish that is usually a long way behind the boat.

Stretch is one of the areas where cofilament line differs markedly from nylon monofilament. Prime has a much lower stretch factor, and it behaves much more like Dacron line. The polyester core of this product does not absorb water; it is stiff, and it controls stretch and contributes to sensitivity.

The low stretch-high sensitivity aspects of Prime cofilament give the fisherman improved hook-setting ability, more control in playing a fish, increased sensitivity to feel what a lure or bait is doing, and an increased ability to detect strikes. Having used Prime extensively this past season, I can attest to its virtues in these respects. After a

Line stretch is a factor in many areas of bass fishing, particularly when setting the hook and when fighting strong fish near the boat. Some lines stretch less than others, offering greater control in playing a fish and more sensitivity for detecting strikes and feeling the movements of your lure.

lot of fishing and particularly when jig or worm fishing for bass, you'll recognize differences in stretch and sensitivity.

A simple way to detect the decreased elasticity of Prime cofilament as it relates to a typical angling situation is to take a 40-foot length of wet Prime cofilament and a similar length of wet nylon monofilament and connect one end to a firm object and the other to identical fishing rods. Set the hook on each. The lack of stretch and the greater hook-setting ability of Prime cofilament will be immediately apparent.

A similar way to test this, using the same length of wet line, is to measure the lengths of these lines when you apply an equal amount of pulling tension on them. For instance, if you take a 40-foot length of wet 8-pound-test Prime cofilament, connect it to a good scale and pull on it until only 1 pound of pressure is exerted, you'll see that the line stretches 14 inches. Take a wet 40-foot length of a good-quality nylon monofilament, do the same thing, and it will stretch 30 or more inches—more than twice as much.

In addition to having low stretch, Prime cofilament is a far more sensitive product than other fishing lines. This is a feature unique to cofilament, and one that is easier to appreciate while using the product rather than reading about it.

This example helps to illustrate the point: Take a 40-foot length of wet line. Apply enough tension on the line (pull it with the line connected to a force gauge or a reliable scale) to stretch it just 1 percent, or 4.8 inches. This is similar to what might happen when a fish takes your lure. When you compare the force necessary to achieve this 1 percent stretch between Prime cofilament and other lines, you'll find that it takes three to four times less pressure to stretch Prime than it does to stretch other lines. This directly relates to sensitivity. In other words, with Prime cofilament you have between a 300 and 400 percent better chance of feeling that strike. You may have seen the movies of fish sucking in a lure a short distance and then spitting it out, without the fisherman ever knowing that he'd had a strike. Those scenes illustrate the difference that stretch and sensitivity make.

I have singled out Prime because it is the only product of its type available as of this writing. With this first generation of cofilament line, anglers have a product that minimizes the negative aspects of stretch in fishing line and maximizes the benefits. This is particularly relevant to bass angling, and I expect that other companies will produce a cofilament line to serve anglers who are looking for the best of all worlds.

Although Prime cofilament and nylon monofilament lines are vastly different, they are similar in terms of ultimate elongation. Ultimate elongation is the amount of stretch that a line will take before breaking. Good quality lines have an ability to return to their normal state after severe pressure and stretching and to maintain basic strength. Stretch is not a permanent condition, then, under average fishing conditions. However, lines that have seen the severest stress warrant close examination. If in doubt about the continued serviceability of your line, replace it.

LIMPNESS

The molecular structure of nylon is such that nylon monofilament or cofilament lines form a memory when placed in a certain position (such as being spooled) for an extended period of time. Lines with less memory are said to be limp and are more castable than stiff lines. This factor is important in light-line angling. Some lesser quality fishing lines tend to be stiff, contributing to spooling and twist problems and making casting difficult. Castability is related to limpness (which engineers refer to as bending modulus). The most castable line would be one that was as limp as a noodle, but it couldn't possess the other qualities necessary for a good fishing line.

Castability is not only affected by limpness but also by water absorption (wet lines cast better than dry lines) and line diameter. The greater the diameter and the stronger the line, the harder it is to cast. With nylon monofilaments, the stiffer the line, the less stretch it has but the more difficult it is to cast. Thus, there is a dramatic tradeoff between castability and stretch in nylon monofilaments.

Cofilament is different in this respect. It has low stretch but castability similar to premium nylon monofilaments. To put this into angling perspective: to engineer the low stretch of Prime cofilament into a nylon monofilament, you would have to increase the stiffness of that nylon monofilament $4^1/_2$ times, but you'd get a line that you couldn't cast. It would be extremely stiff, and it would be $4^1/_2$ times more difficult to cast. The bottom line here is that Prime cofilament is limp and castable without being stretchy. That is one reason why fishermen will be buying this product in the future.

KNOT STRENGTH

Nylon monofilament and cofilament lines become weaker when you put them in water. And once you tie a knot in the line, it becomes weaker yet. Furthermore, knots that are tested in a wet condition (as they would be when fished) are weaker than when in a dry condition. Manufacturers claim that their technological processes produce molecular formations that result in specific knot strength abilities for their line. Since the same knots are tied with various levels of expertise by different individuals, this is hard to verify when comparing knots tied by one angler to those tied by another. Nonetheless, if you are tying knots carefully and uniformly, and they're not holding, it could be because the knot strength of the line is deficient.

UNIFORMITY

It is reasonable to expect that what you get at one end of a line spool you should get at every point along that spool to the end. With premium lines you generally do. Sometimes, however, the manufacturing processes may alter the diameter of the line in certain spots or in some way alter the characteristics in unidentified areas. You may find a spot that is thicker than the rest of the line. Here, the molecules have not been well oriented, and this part of the line will be weaker than the rest. Conversely, a thin spot will be stronger. With the premium lines on the market today, you should encounter none of this. With the bargain-basement specials—those lines selling for $1.99 for a 2,000-yard spool—you get what you pay for: junk.

LINE USE

LINE TWIST

Probably the greatest problem that most fishermen experience in relation to line is twisting. Many anglers incorrectly blame their line for twisting problems. If your line twists and you think it's because the line is no good, take a brand-new consumer spool of that line, lay out how many feet of it you want, and wait for it to twist. You'll be waiting forever. The point is that you have to do something to make line twist; it doesn't twist by itself. Line twist can occur as a result of improper spooling, improperly playing a fish, having too loose a drag, using certain lures without a swivel, fishing in swift current, and using a lure that is not running properly.

If the problem is a faulty lure, you'll need to adjust the lure so it runs without spinning or else try using a split-ring, snap, or swivel-snap, all of which aid in preventing spinning and twisting. Certain lures, such as most spinners used in flowing water, require the use of a swivel-snap to prevent twisting.

If your drag is too loose, it will slip while you are reeling in, in the course of fighting a fish. This results in line twist. Similarly, if you crank a fish by forcefully reeling it in with spinning gear, instead of pumping, retrieving line, etc., you will put a bad twist in monofilament line.

You'll know that your line is twisted when you retrieve a lure by watching how it dangles from the tip of your rod. If it begins to rotate, the line is twisted. Another way to tell is if coils develop in the line when you give it slack. Often an angler will be retrieving a lure, let it momentarily rest, and not notice that a coil develops near the reel. He continues retrieving, only to pile line up on the reel arbor on top of the loose coil. During a subsequent cast he is likely to get a bird's nest of monofilament, the severity of which will depend on how twisted his line became.

Twisted line is not difficult to cure if you are in a boat or near running water. Nylon monofilament and cofilament line will untwist itself if you let a long length of it out behind your boat, with nothing attached to the end of it (no snap, swivel, split-shot, hook, or lure, etc.), and drag it along for a few minutes. The faster your boat travels the quicker the line unravels. Reel the line back in and you're ready to attach terminal gear and fish. You can achieve the same effect on moderate- to fast-flowing water by letting the unweighted line float downstream and then hold it in the current for several minutes. This has the same effect as dragging it behind the boat.

Line twist can be impossible to cure if the problem has not been recognized until the line is a mass of twists and curls. When line twist is this serious, cut off the problem section and start anew, being careful to remedy the cause of the twist before fishing again.

FILLING YOUR REELS

Many problems experienced by anglers using nylon monofilament or cofilament line actually begin at the first step of line use, in putting new line on a reel spool. How you put line on and how much of it you put on are keys to minimizing difficulty.

The best performance of your line and reel is achieved when the reel has been spooled properly. This means filling it to within $^1/_8$ to $^3/_{16}$ inch of the edge. This allows you to achieve good casting distance and accuracy and permits better drag functioning. A full spool also provides more line for playing a large fish, though this is not relevant to bass fishing.

If you overfill a spinning reel, line will fall off loosely when slack is given, causing snafus to develop; several loops of line will pile up and jam in the spool or in a rod guide. Also, line can become pinched in the side flanges of the spool of an overfilled bait-casting reel.

A properly filled reel allows you to achieve good distance in your casts, particularly with light lures. An underfilled reel hampers your casting range, since more coils of line (causing more friction) must come off the spool. After a period of time, through cutting frayed line, tying knots, and experiencing breakoffs, your line will become too low on the reel. In addition to hampering casting in some fishing situations, you could be in danger of hooking a big fish that will take all of the remaining line off the reel (depending on the capacity of the reel and whatever other species of fish you encounter besides bass; as mentioned in the previous chapter, bass are not likely to run all the line off your reel unless you have hardly any on to begin with). Additionally, drag pressure increases as line on the reel arbor decreases, creating a sometimes difficult situation for the angler when fighting a strong, surging fish.

You can put twist in the line by improperly spooling it, which happens often to unknowing or inexperienced anglers. Monofilament line has a memory factor, and it returns to its "memoried" state after being used. Line thus develops a set in that position in which it has been placed for a long time, such as the plastic spool on which it is wound for packaging.

Line on a consumer spool not only has taken a set, it actually is slightly coiled already, which is an inherent part of the manufacturer's spooling process. Though you have no way of knowing this, the manufacturer has huge bulk spools of line in its plant from which it fills the smaller retail spools. Line that comes off the extreme periphery of a full bulk spool has less coiling than that which comes off the core of the bulk spool.

Fill your reels properly for the best performance—bait-casting and spinning reels should be filled to within $1/8$ to $3/16$ inch of the edge. Spinning reels, in particular, are prone to twisting if not filled correctly.

You and a friend could conceivably possess the same brand of line in the same pound-test, and one would be noticeably more coiled than the other. The reason is probaby that they came from different locations on the bulk spool, or that they were produced at different times (in which one batch of line was more coiled than the other). In any event, the longer that line stays on the retail spool, the more its coils conform to the diameter of the spool.

Many anglers have told me that they were dissatisfied with a certain brand of line because it was "too coily" or twisted "too easily." This complaint has been applied to all the major brands of line. You'll find that coiling is less pronounced in the top-grade lines.

Now that you understand the inherent characteristics of your packaged line, you need to know how best to put it on the reel. Line on bait-casting reels, which are aptly called level-wind reels, is fairly free of twisting problems as a result of spooling. This is because the line is wound straight onto the reel arbor in a direct, level, overlapping manner. The spooling suggestions that follow can also be applied to bait-casting reels.

Open-faced spinning reels and spin-casting (closed face) reels pose many problems in line spooling for beginning fishermen. This is because these systems actually put a slight twist in the line as it rotates off the bail arm and onto the arbor. If the line is of poor quality or if it already has a fair degree of manufacturer-instilled coiling and the angler improperly spools it onto his spinning reel, the result can be twisting, curling, coiling line—endless trouble unless it is run out behind the boat and rewound.

The first secret to successful spooling is watching how the line comes off both sides of the manufacturer's spool. Take line off the side with the least apparent coiling. Then apply moderate pressure on the line before it reaches the reel.

Here's a good technique for proper spooling: Place the supply spool on the floor or any flat surface. The line should balloon or spiral off the spool as you pull it up. After you've threaded line through your rod guides and attached it to your reel, hold the rod tip 3 to 4 feet above the supply spool. Make 15 to 20 turns on the reel handle and stop. Now check for line twist by reducing tension on the line.

Lower the rod tip to one foot from the supply spool and check to see if the slack line twists or coils. If it does, just turn the supply spool upside down. This will eliminate most of the twist as you wind the rest of the line onto the reel. If the other side has more of a coiled or twisted nature to it, go back to the first side and take line off while it is face-up. The trick here is to take line from the side that has the least amount of coiling. In effect, this method counter-spools the line on your spinning reel and cancels the curling tendencies that would otherwise exist.

I do not recommend using a pencil or other object inside a spool to let that spool run freely while you put line on your reel. This seems to compound the spooling problem.

Keeping moderate tension on the line with one hand as you reel with the other is also important. Do this by holding the line between your thumb and forefinger with your free hand. A loosely wound reel results from not applying spooling tension and causes loops of line to develop on the reel spool. Excessive tension, however, can bind the line up and allow more line to be spooled than necessary, as you will later find when the line bunches up after being used and spooled naturally by reeling.

CHANGING LINE

In a sense, new fishing line is like a new automobile. When you purchase a new car and drive it off the dealer's lot, it becomes a "used" or old car. When you put new line on your reel and fish with it, it becomes used. A new automobile that is driven frequently, but is garaged and only taken on the best roads, is likely to stay in top condition longer than one that is used daily, constantly exposed to the elements, and driven on every type of road condition. Line is very much the same. The age of the line is much less important than how much and under what conditions it has been used.

The primary reasons for changing line are that it is too low on the spool, it's very old, or it has had such extensive, stressful use that a cautionary replacement seems warranted.

When line becomes too low it hampers casting and reduces effective drag settings, so it needs to be refilled. Many reels have large line capacities and yet, when a reel has too little left on it for good casting, it still has usually half of its capacity left. If the line has not been on the reel very long, it is still worth using. You should consider taking this off by tying the end to a tree or post in an open area (or on the water) and backing away so the line does not bunch up or become tangled. Take this off, put on a suitable amount of backing of stronger line, then take the end of the monofilament that you hitched to the post and tie this to the backing. When your spool is full, you have the fresh, unused back section of old line for fishing.

If you have a large-capacity reel, but will only need a third or half of it for bass fishing, and will not need it for other kinds of fishing, attach a backing to the spool before putting new line on.

If you wish to replace the full capacity of line on a reel, simply strip it all off and discard it in the garbage. You can do this fairly quickly by giving it the old clothesline palm-to-elbow wrap. Another method is to use an electric drill. Affix an old consumer spool or some large-capacity object in the drill bit head, set the reel on free spool or reduce the drag setting to the least amount of tension (this is also a way to break in a drag), and run the drill until the line is off. A third method is to use the new Berkley Outdoorsman line stripper. I haven't used it, but several people who have tell me it does a fast job of peeling line off a reel.

Old line needs to be replaced completely, as does line that has been used often in punishing fishing conditions. Some anglers have had line on their reels for years—so long that they have no idea how old the line may be. They'll be sorry when a big fish comes along or when there is a lot of action, and the line won't hold up.

How long line may be used before being replaced is a question with no set answer. This depends on how much fishing you do, the strength of the line, how large and hard-fighting the bass that you regularly catch are, how much care or abuse your tackle receives, and the original quality of the line. An angler who fishes only a few times a year would be well advised to change his line at least once a year, preferably before the start of each season. A slightly more frequent angler should change it at least twice a year. And anglers who fish regularly should change their line every few weeks. I use a lot of reels in a wide range of fishing conditions and for many species of fish in the course of a season. Some of my reels may go all year without being changed (but will be changed before next season), while others—the most heavily used—may be changed half a dozen times or more.

The type of fishing circumstance can also serve as a guide. Fishing in unobstructed water puts less demands on a line than does fishing around rocks, logs, timber, docks, and the like. In a week of fishing in heavy cover, I have changed line (actually stripped off the top layer and replaced it with fresh line) two or three times. Light line, because of its thin diameter, requires more frequent changing than heavy line.

INSPECTING YOUR LINE

You can't tell much about the thickness of line by feeling it, since variations are generally in thousandths of an inch. You could use a micrometer to measure the diameter, but very few anglers have reason to own or regularly use this costly piece of equipment.

You can detect abrasion by feel, and this is quite important. A nick, cut, or fray in line can weaken it, sometimes by as much as 50 percent or more. A 10-pound-test line, which would ordinarily need 10 or more pounds of pressure to break it, may only need 5 or 7 or 8 pounds if it is abraded. Line breakage as a result of undetected abrasion leads many an angler to question the quality of his line, when in fact he is to blame for not checking the line. Therefore, periodically running your fingers over the first few feet (more if necessary) of line to detect nicks or frayed areas is a good idea. When you do find such spots, cut off the damaged section of line. If, for some reason, you find it hard to detect abrasion by feeling the line, try running it through your lips.

Abrasion usually results from underwater contact with objects and fish, though it can happen after a portion of your line contacts tree limbs or stumps when you get a lure hung up. Occasionally, however, imperfections in your rod or reel cause abrasion. A nick or burr on a rod guide, reel pickup arm or level-wind guide, or spool edge can be the culprit. If line abrasion occurs regularly throughout the line or when you're fishing in unobstructed water, you should check the tackle and correct the problem.

Another sign of old line, and possibly well-worn line, is the visibly faded look, which may be the result of age or extensive exposure to sun. This is a result of the fluorescence evaporating from exposure to ultraviolet light. Sometimes anglers find that line on their reel suddenly seems to have lost its strength. The reason usually remains a mystery. Old line does, however, become stiff as the result of the seepage of its plasticizing agent (monomer, which is the white chalky buildup that you sometimes get when spooling line on a reel) and thus, is brittle and weaker. This condition is evidenced in lighter lines

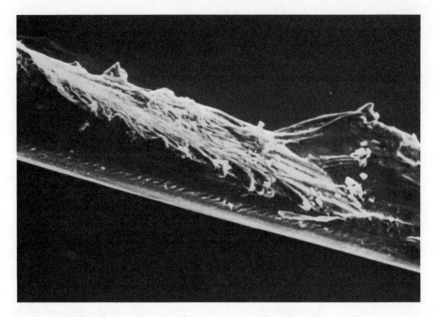

Inspect your line frequently. A nick or cut can weaken line dramatically. Here, 20-pound-test line has been magnified 60 times with an electron scanning microscope to illustrate how prominent line abrasion (which you can barely detect) can be. (*Photo courtesy of Du Pont*)

by failure to hold knots well or by the easy breaking of unknotted sections.

In some cases, this old line is still serviceable once it is soaked in water, but it's good to view fading as a wear indicator and plan to replace the line.

CARE OF LINE

Monofilament is not ageless. Its effective life depends on how it is treated and to what it is subjected. Long exposure to sunlight can affect monofilament, so don't store line, either on a consumer spool or a fishing reel, in a position where sunlight falls on it daily. The ultraviolet elements of the sun's rays are very strong, and to diminish their effect, premium lines feature an ultraviolet retardation element, which prolongs the effective life of the line. The fluorescent characteristic of some line is especially vulnerable to ultraviolet light and will fade in time. The best storage for line is in a cool, dry environment, away from extremes in temperatures and from water saturation, and sheltered from sunlight. This might be in a garage, closet, or basement. Examples of how not to treat line include leaving a spool on the dashboard of your automobile or a reel by a window where sunlight regularly reaches it.

Many anglers lose track of the strength of line on a particular reel or can't recall when they put it on. In some cases they are mistaken as to which brand they are using. This can all be solved by marking the reel. Some line manufacturers supply gummed labels with each spool of their product, so anglers can jot pertinent information on it and affix it to their reel. I use these or some other form of gummed labels to put this data on all my reels, using a number-letter system to code it all. For example, the markings 12/3/86 ST would signify 12-pound-test Stren line put on the reel in March 1986. The marking 12-17/3/86 XL would signify 12-pound-test Trilene XL over a 17-pound-test backing, spooled in March 1986.

You should also be careful about what substances come into contact with your line. Some of these can alter the characteristics of your line in unsuspected ways. WD-40, for instance, which is commonly used on reels to inhibit rust, may leach out some of the plasticizers of nylon monofilament, resulting in somewhat stiffer line. If the line was in contact with water soon after contact with WD-40, there would be no effect. More effect would be incurred if the reel full of line was sprayed with this substance (and some got on the line) after fishing and then stored.

Suntan oil can pose a problem, too. A spokesman for one line manufacturer informed me that suntan oils "generally contain certain active ingredients which can serve to plasticize the nylon monofilament and actually make it softer. There are some constituents in suntan oil that can have a beneficial effect and for a short time, at least, raise the knot strength of the product. Ironically, most of the ingredients in suntan oil tend to have a negative effect when it comes to actual fishing qualities because their plasticizing action causes an increase in elongation and the lines become excessively stretchy." The spokesman also said that there is an active ingredient in some insect repellents that, for a short time, creates dramatic improvements in knot strength. As a precaution, it's a good idea to clean the palms of your hands before touching your line (and lures).

Gas and motor oil can also be detrimental to line if there is contact for an extended period of time. In extreme cases of contact (or soaking) with gasoline, a 50 percent reduction in line strength can occur. Motor oil is not as potent as gasoline.

The most harmful substance to line, even for short contact, is battery acid. This sulfuric acid attacks nylon line properties almost immediately and advances oxidization. Light lines in particular are very vulnerable.

Perhaps more serious is the possibility that these substances may imprint an odor on the line that is not noticeable to humans but detectable to fish. What effect this may have on fish behavior is unclear. It surely cannot be positive.

This information is not meant to alarm you or to complicate your angling. It is not farfetched to imagine that you might spray yourself liberally with bug repellent and then touch your line while tying a knot; or that coils of line might fall on an uncovered battery when you lay your rod down; or that gasoline or oil might be inadvertently spilled on your reel. Just take care to keep such substances off your line for extended periods.

BUYING SUGGESTIONS

Buy quality. Premium-grade nylon monofilament line and cofilament cost more but they are worth the expense. Skip the cheap stuff, even if the local discount store offers enough line to stretch across the United States. Cheap line and poor care make for false economy.

Value-wise, it makes good sense to buy bulk spools if you do even just a moderate amount of bass fishing and line changing. The 1200- and 2400-yard bulk spools are much cheaper per yard than the reel-filler-type packs, plus you know it all came from the same manufacturing batch. When you do purchase new spools, mark the date of purchase on them, so you will have an age reference later on.

Sometimes, reel-filling bargains are found at tackle stores, and if you can get your reel filled with *premium* line at a penny or two a yard, it's a deal you can't beat. Just be sure the retailer doesn't put too much on your reel (particularly spinning or spin-casting models)— the line will pile up on one side when you fish normally with it, causing you to waste the excess.

KNOTS

The strongest your line will normally be is when it is in an unknotted dry condition. But your line is fished wet, and so it is weaker then than when dry but—if it is a premium line—still as strong or stronger than what the label says it is.

Your line must be attached to your terminal tackle—that is the main function of a knot. There are knots and then there are fishing knots. The most basic point to know about knots in relation to nylon monofilament or cofilament line is that they weaken it. Thus, your objective is to tie the strongest, most reliable fishing knots that you can, to achieve the maximum strength possible from your fishing line. If you use a knot that regularly only achieves 75 percent of the strength of your line in maximum stress situations, the knot will break before the line. If, however, you tie a knot that achieves 100 percent of the breaking strength of the line, the line will usually break before the knot. Of course, you want neither to break, but the important point here is that under those extreme circumstances your monofilament line did as much as it was capable of doing. Perhaps the line was too light for the conditions; the fish was too big; the drag was set too loose; or the rod was too soft—but the line did what it was supposed to do.

As a youth, I had no knowledge of fishing knots whatsoever, and no one showed me what to do. The only knot I used was the overhand, which I now know results in 30 to 50 percent loss in breaking strength. I operated under the theory that if one such knot was good, two were better, and three or four were best of all. I do not recall having any particular problems, but I undoubtedly was not taxing the strength of my line to its fullest, since I was primarily bait fishing for panfish, bullheads, small bass, and perch.

Fish alone, of course, do not apply pressure to your line. When you get hung up, which, for some anglers occurs more frequently than tying into tackle-testing fish, you might apply a lot of force to free yourself. In short, there are no substitutes for good fishing knots.

Before I give detailed instruction on knot tying, I must first preface it by saying that knot performance, even with the most detailed instruction, varies from one angler to the next. People vary in the way they form their knots, how many wraps they make, how fastidious they are in tying, and so forth. A good knot is only as good as the

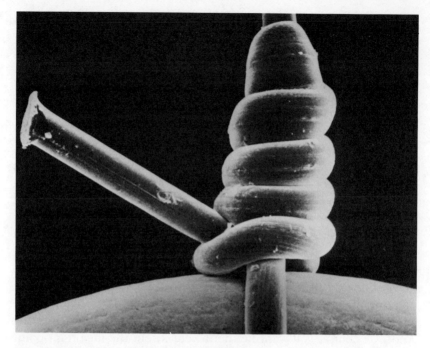

This magnified photograph of an Improved Clinch Knot demonstrates the perfection necessary for full strength. Good knot tying is the result of precise, even-handed procedures. (*Photo courtesy of Du Pont*)

angler tying it. Much is to be said for practice and for achieving uniform knot tying, so that once you have mastered a given knot and have come to use it for bass fishing, you can expect it to perform reliably time after time.

Here are some fundamental pointers for effective knot tying:

1. Be neat. Keep your twists, spirals, and other steps uniform so that when you draw your knot closed, it is neat and precise.
2. Snug all knots up tightly with even, steady pressure. Knot slippage under pressure can cut the line, so watch the knot for evidence of slippage and redo it if necessary. Don't pop the knot to tighten it.
3. Wet the line as an aid to drawing it up smoothly. If your hands are wet and will wet the line, fine; if not, place the knot and line in your mouth momentarily.
4. Be careful not to nick the knot with your clippers when you cut off the protruding tag end. This can form a potentially serious and weakening defect.

5. If your knot breaks repeatedly when you tighten it, check your hook eye or lure connection for rough spots that are cutting the line.
6. Use plenty of line to allow you to complete your tying steps without difficulty.
7. When using double lines keep them as parallel as possible and avoid twisting them as the knot is being tied.
8. Test your knots occasionally with a scale to see if you are getting the performance you need. You can do this by tying the line to the hook of a reliable spring scale. Have someone wrap the unknotted line around his hand several times, using a towel or cloth to keep from getting cut. While your accomplice pulls on the line, you hold and watch the scale, noting at what amount of pressure the line or knot breaks. If the line broke, your knot held; if not, check your knot tying.

Using this scale is also a good way to monitor the basic strength of your unknotted line as well, though this test should be conducted when the line and knot are wet. Don't be too alarmed if your knot breaks before the line, but that the breaking point reached is still quite high. A typical top-quality 12-pound-test line will break in a wet, unknotted condition when roughly 12.8 pounds of pressure is applied. A wet knot delivering 95 percent strength will break when 12.2 pounds of pressure is applied, while one delivering just 90 percent will break at 11.5 pounds. If you have a knot that delivers consistent breakage at or near the labeled strength of your line (which in this example is 12 pounds), then you should be satisfied with it unless you can do better or can find a better knot.

Certain lines seem to accommodate particular knots better than others. This may be due to differences in molecular structural formations. According to the manufacturers, knot strength is a characteristic that is built into fishing line and massaged in the finishing process, so it would seem that this quality may be stronger in some brands than in others. Most of the time, though, knot failures are due to improper tying rather than to the properties of the line itself.

IMPROVED CLINCH KNOT

My favorite knot, the Improved Clinch, is the one I use in most of my fishing (bass and otherwise) for making terminal tackle connections. It is best used for lines under 20-pound-test. Tied properly, this knot can give 90- to 100-percent strength; poorly tied, it may yield only 75 to 85 percent, which is insufficient, especially for a light line.

To tie the Improved Clinch (not cinch) Knot, pass the line through the eye of the hook, then make five turns around the standing part of the line. Thread the end through the loop ahead of the eye and then bring it back through the newly created large loop. Moisten the knot with saliva and note that the coils are spiraled properly and not overlapping one another. Pull firmly to tighten up. Test knot with moderate tension and clip off the loose end.

Personal testing of this knot has shown me that six spirals are best for line through 12-pound-test and five spirals for 14- to 17-pound-test. For 20-pound-test and over, I make four spirals and often use a pair of pliers to pull on the loose end and snug up the knot.

If you experience slippage with this knot, you may try running the line through the hook eye twice before completing the other steps. This is called a Double Improved Clinch Knot. A variation on this is the Trilene Knot, which also features two turns around the hook eye but in which the tag end comes back through both turns and then is snipped off.

PALOMAR KNOT

Line manufacturers say this knot is easier to tie than the Improved Clinch and more consistent. Because it is easier to tie, fewer anglers experience difficulty with its use. Tied properly, it yields 90- to 100-percent strength and is meant for terminal connections. I use it mainly for tying leader tippets to flies, since it is a smaller profile knot than the Improved Clinch.

To tie the Palomar Knot, double about 6 inches of line and pass the loop through the eye of the hook. Tie an overhand knot in the doubled line and pass the loop over the entire hook. Moisten the knot, pull on both ends, tighten, and clip the tag end.

The only problem encountered with this knot is using it for large, multihooked plugs, where a longer loop must be created to allow the big lure to pass through it. You should also take care not to twist the doubled sections of line.

THE UNI KNOT

This knot is a very versatile creation with applicability to most bass fishing situations. It can give 90- to 100-percent strength as a terminal tackle connector. I use it primarily to tie two lines to one another or to tie leader to fly line.

To join two lines of fairly similar diameter, overlap each about 6 inches. Hold these in the middle of the overlap with your left hand and make a circle with the line extended to the right. Bring the tag end around the double length six times, pulling snugly after the last turn. Repeat the process in reverse direction on the other side. Pull the two sections away from each other to draw the knot up; moisten it, then pull it firmly and clip both loose ends. Quicker and easier to tie than the time-honored Blood Knot, this is equally reliable.

LOOP KNOTS

There are several good specialty loop knots; these include the Surgeon's End Loop and the King Sling. Perhaps because I am lazy, I have not bothered to tie these, but instead use a Uni Knot or an Improved Clinch to form an end loop. With the Improved Clinch, I merely placed my finger between the hook eye and the first spiral to form a large loop. I then tied the knot as usual, pulling it snugly to my finger at the end. I then pull firmly on the tag end to cinch the knot down. This holds fairly well for most fish, but under severe stress the knot will slide toward the eye and hold fast, now being a complete Improved Clinch again. Afterward, I cut off this section and retie the knot. A loop knot is valuable in fishing crankbaits, some surface lures, and some shallow-running plugs.

LINE TO REEL KNOTS

Again, there are several routine methods of attaching line to reel arbor, but I have never bothered with these. I use an Improved Clinch Knot for this, too, and have never experienced difficulty.

OTHER KNOTS

There are other knots that may prove useful in specialized circumstances. These include the Albright Special, a hook snell, and the Bimini Twist. The last knot, which creates a double length of line, is usually thought of in only saltwater big-game trolling situations, but it also has merit in light-tackle freshwater use, where you might want to have a strong 10- or 12-foot leader section on light 6- to 12-pound-test line.

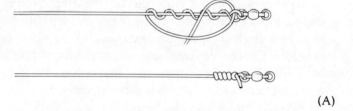

(A)

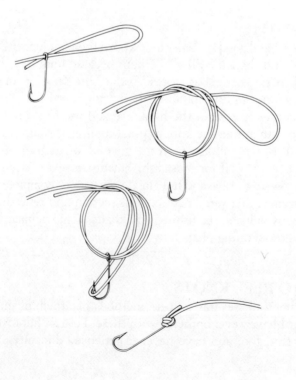

(B)

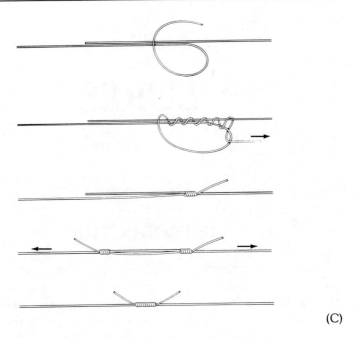

(C)

Shown are the steps for tying: (A) an Improved Clinch Knot; (B) a Palomar Knot; and (C) a Uni Knot to connect two lines. (*Illustrations courtesy of Du Pont*)

8

LURES

INTRODUCTION

So, you're just putting together your bass fishing equipment; you've got that new tackle box, and you want to fill it up with a bunch of the best bass-catching baits you can find. Trouble is, where do you start, and with what? This chapter will help you with those choices, but first some general comments about bass lures and their attributes and applications are in order.

All lures are designed to perform a specific function. In most cases, their success or failure is primarily due to the way the angler uses them. The fisherman who knows his quarry and matches his lure selection to the habits of the bass and the prevailing conditions is the one who is the most consistently productive. The angler who is completely familiar with the characteristics of each lure and can make the lure work to its maximum designed ability is the angler who will score when the chips are down. Therefore, the more you know about your lures and the fish you seek and the better you understand the conditions in which you seek them, the better prepared you will be to make a knowledgeable lure selection.

There is a host of lure types available to fishermen. Many of these overlap in application and technique, but others are suitable only to particular conditions and require specialized usage. In general terms, lure choices shape up for bass fishing as follows.

For shallow-water fishing, where everybody most likes to chase bass, floating/diving plugs and spinnerbaits get the call. In the plug category, minnow-imitating balsa or plastic lures that float at rest and dive only a foot or two on retrieve are traditional, proven baits.

Spinnerbaits are excellent lures, particularly in the spring when fish are shallow and also when fishing vegetation. They can also be used quite effectively in deeper water, crawled slowly across the bottom, or jigged.

For medium-depth angling (4 to 12 feet) you'll generally want to fish with a straight-running, dive-to-the-bottom-on-retrieve lure. Bottom-hugging bass plugs such as these have come to be called crank-baits, and they are manufactured in shallow, medium, and deep-diving versions, all of which are determined by the size and shape of the lip protruding from each one. Medium and deep divers are usually the most useful to bass fishermen, and these come into play in spring, parts of summer, and fall, in many locales. Worms and jigs are also highly effective bass baits in this depth range.

For deep-water fishing (from 10 feet on, though often in shallower water as well), the bass angler without a plastic worm or who doesn't know how to use it, is in for a rough time. Bass seek the comfort of

Though there are many types of lures for bass fishing, you must match the lure to the conditions and be able to retrieve it skillfully.

cooler, deep water in late spring, summer, and early fall, and plastic worms are probably more effective than all other lures combined, at these times. Another bottom scrounger, particularly effective on small-mouths, is the jig. This can be fished extremely effectively in very deep water (and at any depth) as well as along rocky, sharp-sloping bluffs and shorelines, and on underwater mounds.

Surface fishing, a favorite technique of bass anglers, is generally less productive than below-surface methods at most times. Because of the habits and habitat of the quarry, there are generally fewer times when surface techniques have merit. Surface lures run the gamut from soft plastic floating baits to wood or plastic plugs that twitch, wobble, chug, and sputter.

There is a *time* and a *place* for all lures. Remember above all else that *each lure is designed to do a certain function and that such function must be coordinated with the current fishing conditions.* A lure won't catch fish merely because it is supposed to. There are good lures and bad lures, good times to use them and poor ones, good usage of the lures and bad usage. A lure also won't catch bass merely because it "looks good." The bottom line in the lure business is that the product must catch *fishermen.* Most anglers, in turn, expect the lure to catch fish. But these expectations are misguided. Cars don't drive; they are driven. Guns don't shoot; they are shot. And lures don't catch fish; fishermen do. Lures are just a means by which an angler can accomplish his goal.

Not that the lure isn't important to this success. Obviously it is. But there's a lot more to productive bass fishing than possessing a well-stocked tackle box. Recognizing the abilities of a lure, using it to its full potential, and injecting a dose of angling savvy are all vital factors in the game. With this in mind, let's analyze each category of bass lure in depth.

CRANKBAITS

In bass fishing, no lure comes with a no-cut contract. Nothing is certain to catch fish anywhere or at any time, but a crankbait rates highly on my priority list of bass lures.

"Crankbait," a term that has reached popular usage in modern times, has come to be associated with various treble-hooked diving and sinking plugs that have a built-in vibrating, wiggling, swimming action. The term orginated from the fact that the simplest and most practiced way to fish such a lure is to chuck it out and crank the reel handle steadily to bring it in on a nonstop retrieve. This is not the only way to use this lure, nor is it necessarily the best, but the mere throw-it-and-reel-it-back nature of this plug has resulted in the name.

For any bass fisherman, even one with the most meager selection of lures, several crankbaits ought to be mandatory tackle box fare. Although crankbaits only have a fair degree of versatility in their usage, they have several notable characteristics. The first is that they are easy to cast. A novice fisherman who has mastered the very basic casting motions will have no difficulty tossing out a crankbait, even under windy conditions, provided that the lure is not too light or too heavy for the rod, reel, and line he is using. Nor will he find his line fouling around the hooks or the hooks becoming entangled. Because of their streamlined shape, crankbaits do not meet the air resistance

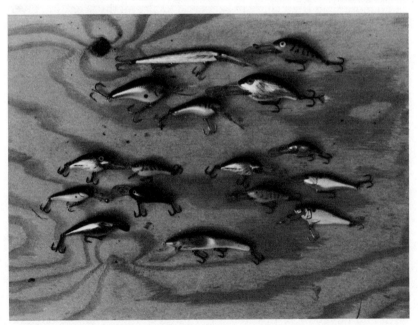

Crankbaits come in a wide range of body styles, sizes, colors, and patterns, and run to various depths depending on the size and position of their lip and the speed of retrieve.

that some other types of lures do, so they do not have a tendency to tumble in the air and will fly well even if the cast is poorly executed. The set of hooks are usually well spaced to avoid reaching one another, and I have not seen crankbaits with hooks that were too large for the body of the plug.

Crankbaits are also relatively easy to fish with. While it seems that bass blast these lures with profound determination most of the time, it is a fact that the combination of a basically quick retrieve, the swift attack of a bass on what it thinks is a rapidly departing prey, and the usual two sets of treble hooks, all lead to slam-bang action at the moment of impact. A bass will often hook itself on the lure (nonetheless it is important for the angler to set the hook). I believe these factors add up to an excellent hooking potential and consequently more fish caught per strike than with many other lures.

Crankbaits also have a good capacity for catching legal-size or filleting-size fish (12 inches or better). Although I have caught very small bass on very large crankbaits, it is the nature of these plugs to catch more than their share of keepers. Despite all the attention given to lunker bass, I think most fishermen are satisfied with an abundant number of keepers.

Crankbaits also fit well into the most-used bass fishing method: plugging the shorelines. There are advantages and disadvantages to constant shoreline cruising, but it is popular with fishermen. If you spend the whole time plunking the shore, you'll probably catch stray bass, and the crankbait is a good lure on stray bass.

The crankbait, then, is a generally effective bass lure and a good plug for beginning or semi-experienced bass fishermen. I've had many such anglers with me, and some experienced fishermen who were not familiar with crankbaits for bass, and all were impressed with the action of these lures and the fish-catching success they brought. Many promptly purchased several crankbaits of different makes, types, and colors afterward.

The design of crankbaits has gradually changed in the last decade. The older, bulbous "alphabet" type plugs have given way to slimmer, deeper-diving models. These new models are smaller in length and girth and have longer lips that allow for deep diving on the retrieve, and more built-in action through a tighter, better-controlled wiggling pattern.

Most crankbaits have clear plastic lips, which are presumably less

It's especially important to get your lure on or near the bottom; choose a crankbait according to the depth you need to fish.

visible to fish than metal or colored plastic ones. I have found little difference in fish-catching ability among these different lipped baits, although there is an action difference between rectangularly fronted lures and ovally fronted lures.

It is the lip, of course, that generally controls the standard running depth of the lure and contributes greatly to its action. The larger the lip, the greater the running depth. The exception to this are lures that are not designed to float and that sink immediately to the bottom. These, too, may have smallish lips but it is their weight, the amount of lip you have out, and your method and speed of retrieve that determine their working depth.

Depending upon lip size, crankbaits can be classified as shallow, medium, or deep diving, covering a range of depths from 2 to 12 feet. (There are, incidentally, large crankbaits suitable for pike, muskie, and striped bass angling. These reach much greater depth and are generally trolled, rather than cast, but can occasionally be used for catching big largemouth bass.) Ideally they should run on or close to the bottom. It is clear that certain baits have applications for working specific bottom depths. As a whole, bass-fishing crankbaits have most application in waters to 12 feet deep. Greater depths are better scoured with other types of lures, such as jigs and plastic worms.

The standard fishing technique with crankbaits is the cast-and-crank method. It is probably used most of the time by crankbait fishermen, and it works. But it is not enough to plop down on the lake and whiz this lure along any old place. Keeping in mind the depth of water you want to work, it is generally a good idea to retrieve fast in warm water and slow in cold water, and fast in clear water and slow in muddy water. Regardless of water color, however, I have found it a good technique to work sharp shoreline dropoffs by casting in close to shore and retrieving a deep-diving crankbait as fast as I can. Rocky shorelines are particularly good for this. Largemouth and small-mouth bass alike respond to this tactic, and often the strike will come after a few feet of retrieve. If you fish like this for most of the day, you'll have a noodle arm that night, but that may be what it takes to catch fish. If the bass aren't responding to this technique, try other lures or other crankbait-fishing methods.

If you are working the shoreline without results, you may be only scratching a short section of the bottom. Depending upon how sharp the dropoff is and if you're casting into shore from your boat, the lure may not be reaching all of the bottom that it should and therefore isn't getting to the depth of water where the fish are holding. Instead, then, cast parallel instead of perpendicular to the shore and make sure that your plug is working the right depths.

Bottom scratching is critical in most bass fishing situations with crankbaits. Try to keep your plug rooting along the bottom, over objects, and along impediments. This is no problem with the right floating/diving crankbait. For the sinking version, let it settle to the bottom (or count it down to a particular level) and make your retrieve at a rate slow enough to keep the plug on or as close to the bottom as possible.

Floating/diving crankbaits are exceedingly buoyant, a feature that adds a different dimension to their fishability. If you stop your retrieve, these plugs will bob toward the surface like a cork. You can take advantage of this feature in your fishing techniques. A pull-pause action is easily accomplished by retrieving in the standard fashion and

stopping momentarily, then repeating the procedure. In its most ex-
aggerated form, this can be extended to stopping the retrieve long
enough for the lure to float to the surface, and then resuming the
retrieve. Try making the lure hesitate by stumps, brush, and other
objects. This technique can be used repeatedly throughout the entire
retrieve and might be the tactic to stir up otherwise unexcited bass.

The buoyancy of crankbaits varies from lure to lure. Obviously,
sinking models sink and floaters rise. How fast they rise or fall depends
on their density in relation to the density of the water. Some crankbaits
that rise quickly are not as beneficial to anglers as those that rise more
slowly. I have seen times when bass would strike a crankbait only
when its steady retrieve was interrupted by the angler momentarily
stopping the lure so it lifted up slightly.

A few lures have little buoyancy or are neutral in buoyancy. This
genre of lure got its start with the Rebel Suspend-R a few years ago.
Arbogast's Arby Hanger is a popular current suspension bait. These
lures remain stationary in the water when stopped. Suspension has a
lot of validity in fishing crankbaits, which essentially represent small
baitfish. I've observed baitfish and have noticed that they rarely rise
or sink to a significant extent in their natural environment. When
they stop they stay at the same level, using their fins as stabilizers and
relying on their internal organs to maintain their level. Making a lure
stop and suspend at its running level has the most usefulness when
you are fishing over some type of cover that is likely to hold bass. A
good example would be the case of working a crankbait over a submerged grass bed, which likely holds bass buried in the holes in the
vegetation. These bass might hit a crankbait swimming briskly by.
They probably won't be induced to strike a bait that is stopped but
floats back up to the surface. But a bait that is stopped and that hovers
over the grass could be the most attractive offering of all. The same
can be true when fishing over treetops or dropoffs.

Certain places that bass lie are particularly well worked with a
crankbait. This includes rock walls and roadways, underwater islands,
and other irregular features that the lures can reach. Sunken or exposed
bridge abutments are worth working and so is flooded timber; in all
cases fish to, from, over, and around these objects, and don't be
concerned about bumping the lures against them.

The best way to fish a particular object with a crankbait, like a
stump, for example, is to cast beyond it so that when you retrieve,

A rocky or rip-rap shoreline and bridge pilings are excellent places in which to work a medium- to deep-diving crankbait.

the lure will be able to get down to its running depth before it reaches the object. This is only possible, of course, when there is enough area behind the object to permit this. When casting to a long fallen-down log, for instance, also cast beyond the target but position yourself to be able to retrieve your crankbait down the length of the log as closely as possible.

Although floating/diving lures could be used as surface lures in a pinch, I don't think much of using them in this manner. A crankbait is designed for underwater use, and I have yet to find it attractive as a surface lure, although a bass will occasionally strike a crankbait when it is lying still on the surface. When I want to fish the surface, I use a lure that is designed for it. I bring several fishing rods with me, and one is usually rigged with a surface lure in case there is some sudden surface action that I want to capitalize on without having to change lures.

Another possibility with crankbaits is to fish heavy cover with them, a tactic that can be successful on occasion if you can keep from getting hung up or enmeshed in weeds. Six wiggling, vibrating, exposed hooks is not my idea of a weedless bait, though; again, for fallen trees, heavy weed growth, thick lily pads, etc., a specifically weedless lure can be used with more effect and less chance of alarming the natives. (A modification that will make crankbaits a little more weedless is to cut off the front hook of the treble or replace both trebles with double hooks.) Occasionally a crankbait that gets hung up can be freed by giving slack to the line, allowing the lure to float free. If near-shore weed growth is not too great, crankbaits will work well for the shore-based fisherman, too.

One critically important aspect of crankbait fishing that is overlooked by many anglers, particularly beginners, is the diving ability of the lure. If bass are holding at 12 feet on a rocky bank and you are using a plug that you think dives that deep but in reality only reaches 8 feet, you can cast till your arms fall off and be unsuccessful. You must know how deep any diving plug runs to be effective with it. Diving abilities depend on the lure, the size of your line, and the speed of retrieve. Use the information supplied by the manufacturer with his product as a guideline, but don't rely on it. Find out for yourself how deep your lures run.

When retrieving it is not necessary to crank the handles as fast as possible to achieve maximum depth. In fact, some lures lose depth when worked too fast. Crank the lure fast for a moment to get the bait down, then effect a moderate pace of retrieve; this will keep the lure as deep as it will go depending on your line. The heavier the line you use, the greater its diameter, which means it offers more resistance to the water and inhibits lure diving. The lighter your line, the deeper a diving plug will go. If you are flinging long casts, this will make a difference. If you are trolling, with relatively long lines out, this is especially significant. Also, remember that current, if it is present, will affect diving ability. Lures retrieved with the current, or sideways to it, do not run as deep as those worked into it.

Determining the diving depth of a plug can be simple if you fish it over known bottom terrain or around objects of a known depth. For example, find a flat that is 7 feet deep. Try a medium- or deep-diving plug; if it touches bottom you know it will go that deep. Move out a little deeper until you lose contact with the bottom to determine running depth at its maximum. If you're not hitting bottom, go shallower until you make contact.

One trick to crankbait fishing is to keep your rod down at all times. This not only assists in hook-setting and reacting to a strike, but it also allows your plug to run deeper. If your rod tip is close to the water, you'll gain an extra foot or two of depth over someone in the same boat with the same lure, whose rod is angled toward the sky. Those extra few feet could make the difference in getting down where the bass are holding, which is especially relevant in dingy water. To attain the most depth possible, you can kneel or sit down in the boat and lean over and stick the rod tip into the water. The longer your rod is and the further you stick the tip into the water, the deeper the lure will go. Some anglers refer to this as a kneel-and-reel technique. It makes no sense to do this, however, if you can achieve the same thing by using a similar crankbait that dives deeper. On the other hand, you may find a situation where one particular size and color of crankbait is working and you have just one of these; then you may need to do whatever you can to get the lure down to the proper level.

Another key pointer for successful crankbait usage is how to present your lure and position your boat when working the shoreline or a weedline. The best way to cast a crankbait to such areas is by working parallel, rather than perpendicular, to it. When two anglers are in the boat, it is a good tactic for both of them to fish from the front (as when casting from a bass boat), with each one's cast overlapping the other as the boat is maneuvered close and parallel to the area.

The vibration and noise of some crankbaits is another aspect worth mentioning. The best crankbaits have an enticing side-to-side action that does more than look good. It produces vibrations that are detectable to bass and that may signal not only the presence of potential forage, but that of a wounded, erratic-swimming prey. Bass

Keep your rod tip down when crankbait fishing to aid hook-setting and allow your plug to run deeper. To attain the most depth possible, you can kneel or sit down in the boat and lean over and stick the rod tip into the water.

strike some crankbaits they cannot see, such as in murky water or at night, because they have been able to detect that lure due to the water it displaced and the vibrations thereby produced. The better the lure, the better its action and vibration qualities.

Some crankbaits also possess rattle chambers within their bodies. These plastic lures feature one or more BB-like spheres of varying size, which are free to move back and forth in the chamber, thereby creating a rattling noise. I discovered just how pronounced this sound is while testing a plug in an above-ground pool with a vinyl liner supported by a circular aluminum wall and aluminum framing. While testing this particular lure to see how it ran, I heard a distinct clicking sound. At first I thought it was my reel. When I stopped turning the reel handle the noise stopped. I moved away from the pool and didn't hear the noise. I returned and stood next to it and could plainly hear the noise. It was produced by the rattling lure and was resonating off the aluminum walls of the pool. When you put this example into an angling situation, like a rip rap bank or rocky cliff shore, you can see how a rattling crankbait can be very detectable to a bass.

I realize that the food eaten by bass doesn't rattle; however, fish do produce vibrations, and some prey, such as crayfish, may very well produce audible noise as they crawl over rocks. Most important is that the rattle can draw the attention of a bass and make the lure more detectable under low light and turbid water conditions. Sometimes rattling crankbaits are more effective than non-rattlers, but many times

PARALLELING A BANK WITH CRANKBAITS

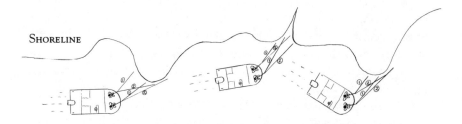

SHORELINE

When working a shoreline that drops off well, it is sometimes best to position your boat close to shore and fish parallel, rather than perpendicular, to the bank. Two anglers should fish from the bow, overlapping their casts. If this is not possible, position the boat perpendicular to the bank, drift with the wind, and use your electric motor to maintain proper position.

there is no difference. However, it pays to realize what the advantages of rattling plugs are and when they can be useful.

The last major criterion for good crankbait usage is color. The color choice of a crankbait should relate to the major forage of the bass where you are fishing as well as to the color of the water and its visibility. Although many colors are available, the best sellers for most manufacturers year-in and year-out are the silver, shad, and crayfish versions. These best resemble the predominant natural forage of bass. As long as you can determine what the primary forage of the fish you seek is, you have a headstart on color determination.

Water coloration is an influential factor, and here there are no guidelines. In blue-green-colored water, chartreuse seems to stand out especially well, and crankbaits in this color, or with some chartreuse undercoating, are quite effective. In sand-colored or muddy water I like light baits that have flash. In tannic acid-influenced dark water, a gold or chrome color in a plug has merit. In very clear water darker colors seem to be less alarming to bass than light, flashy ones. Depending on water color, a more subtle tone to a plug may be all that is needed, using, for instance, a lightly colored crayfish pattern rather than a dark one. I'll discuss color selection in lures further in Chapter 10.

The "natural finish" trend in crankbaits is typical of the fads that spurt through the bass lure manufacturing business. The natural finishes—paint jobs that looked like some form of bait right down to the scale patterns and gill structure—became popular when manufacturers utilized the same devices that had been applied to printing on irregularly shaped surfaces, such as cylinders and containers. This fad was the result of an interest in closely matching the appearance of bass forage items. Exceedingly popular for a few years in the late 70s and early 80s, they are still present and represented in many of the lures available today, but are not a great deal different from their predecessors, only prettier.

As I mentioned earlier, lures must first catch fishermen. The natural finish lures are certainly eye-appealing, but there are two major points to be stressed about them. First, because they look good to you, the angler, you may have more confidence in them and fish them more often and more intensively. This can result in greater productivity; if so, terrific. Second, the best application for a natural-finish plug is in water of high clarity. There, light line use, fine presentation, precise lure action, and lure color and detail can make the difference between catching bass or being frustrated. In water of limited visibility, however, how well your lure looks is less important than its action and vibration qualities.

At times, a touch of red or orange on the belly of a lure makes a difference, and at other times, a green-and-white crankbait, which resembles nothing, is more successful than conventional colors. There aren't always explanations for fish behavior, which is the way it should be and one of the reasons that people like to fish. It pays to have a varied selection of crankbaits in your tackle box, both in terms of colors and diving abilities, so you can handle whatever conditions you may encounter.

There are two remaining aspects of crankbaits that should be mentioned in this section. The first is that crankbaits must run true to be effective. They must run straight on the retrieve, not lie on their side or run off at an angle. Some lures will do this fresh out of the box and some will not. There are ways to "tune" your crankbaits and ways to make them run true. The fine-tuning of these and other lures is reviewed later in the book.

A sometimes overlooked aspect of crankbaits is their ability to do double-duty as trolling lures. I have, at times, caught big bass while trolling deep-diving crankbaits and feel confident in using them in this manner, either on a flat line or aided by a bottom-hugging sinker. Crankbaits are the best lures for trolling, and though many anglers pass up this technique for bass, there's something to be said for it.

In closing, I feel obligated to comment on crankbaits that I would recommend, since I have used and am familiar with just about all of the current ones on the market and because I think a beginning fisherman would like to receive some direction in this regard. At seminars I am always asked to make such comment. I rate very highly the crankbait lines made by a number of manufacturers, including Rebel, Normark (Rapala), Bagley, Sisson, Storm, Bomber, Norman, Cordell, and Arbogast. Regardless of what I write and what you use, remember the words that one prominent lure manufacturer said, "Even the best lure is only as good as the angler fishing it."

SPINNERBAITS

A spinnerbait is one of my favorite lures and my principal spring-time bass-catcher. I have introduced many friends to spinnerbaits, and I recommend them highly for fishermen of all levels of skill, but most especially to newcomers to bass angling. Spinnerbaits are more than able fish-catchers. They are relatively easy to fish and are remarkably weed- and tangle-free to use. More importantly, they are exciting lures to fish.

Surprisingly, some people still look blank when you mention a spinnerbait. This is particularly true in the far northern part of the country. Some folks think you mean a plain spinner, such as a Mepps or Panther Martin, that has a single blade that revolves around an in-line shaft.

But a spinnerbait is a different beast. Looking at it sideways, you see a V-type configuration. The bottom of the V features a lead-headed

Spinnerbaits can sport long or short arms, single or tandem blades, trailer hooks, various blade styles, and plastic curl-tail bodies.

hook with a skirt or soft-plastic grub attached to it. The upper part
of the V features one or two spinner blades, which revolve around
the shaft. The entire ensemble resembles an open safety pin, which
prompted some early users to dub it a safety-pin spinner. When the
lure is retrieved steadily, the blades and upper arm should run vertically
above the bottom part of the lure.

What a spinnerbait is supposed to look like is uncertain. It is not
meant to look exactly like some particular food of a bass, yet it possesses
certain qualities that attract bass, especially in the spring and fall.
Through blade color and movement, a spinnerbait offers visual flash
and auditory vibration. Fish can both see and hear it well. With a
good skirt on the lower half, a spinnerbait also offers pulsating movement and the impression of having enough substance to be worthwhile
chow. Add to this the fact that it can be effectively fished in all but
the thickest cover, and you have the elements of a lure that really
catches bass.

A spinnerbait may also appeal to the predatory, reflexive instincts
of a bass. As I mentioned, a spinnerbait per se looks like nothing a
bass would normally consume. Therefore, a bass must strike it because
he is hungry or because it grabs his eye and looks like something
vulnerable that some other fish will snatch if he doesn't. A spinnerbait
is a good lure for fishing in and around cover, and because bass are
often concealed when this flashy, dicey morsel comes by, the appearance of this lure must trigger a reflexive strike.

Cover is the key word for anyone wondering what places are best
to fish a spinnerbait. Lily pads, grass, stumps, brush, treetops, boat
docks, rock piles, logs, and similar fish-holding places can all be effectively worked with a spinnerbait. Though any level of water may
be fished with these lures, shallow water is where they are most productive.

Formerly, a popular technique for surface fishing with a spinnerbait was "buzzing." With this method, the spinner blades were run
just enough under the surface to create a visible wake through the
water. However, with the popular emergence of buzz baits (which
we'll discuss later), this technique has been more or less dropped from
the lure's repertoire.

The most common technique of fishing a spinnerbait is to retrieve
it close enough to the surface so that you can see the lure through
the water on the retrieve. The depth of water fished below the surface

This largemouth bass took a white spinnerbait with a big willowleaf blade shortly after the lure was cast to the shallow stickups in the background. Shallow-water cover is especially suitable for spinnerbait use.

ranges from a few inches to several feet, depending on the clarity of the water and the structure.

It is not only beneficial, but highly enjoyable, to watch a spinnerbait when it is being retrieved this shallow. Nearly every time, if you can see the lure, you will see the fish strike it. Sometimes a bass seems to dart out of nowhere. Other times it comes from right where expected. This is very much like surface fishing; the excitement of anticipating and seeing the strike is always present. Spinnerbaits are usually struck from the side, suddenly forcing the lure sideways as if it were hit by a gust of wind. When this happens, jam the hook home fast. Another distinct advantage of this technique is that you can see the fish that attempt to strike the bait, too. You can often see if a bass misses the lure, hits short, or is merely taking a close look. Sometimes these fish can be caught with another cast in the same area.

It is also beneficial to watch the lure as it is retrieved right to the boat. Sometimes, particularly on shallow, stumpy flats, a fish may come from almost under the boat after the lure, yet turn away at the last second as the lure nears the boat. Chain pickerel and northern pike are two species of fish that especially love spinnerbaits, and they are also fish that characteristically follow this lure right up to the boat.

It is important to begin retrieving a spinnerbait the moment it hits the water for maximum effectiveness when working the shallows. With spinning tackle, this is no problem, but right-handed bait-casters will have to switch the rod to their left hand during the cast so they can engage the reel as the lure hits the water, or their lure may get fouled initially or fall too deep to fish the nearby cover.

Sometimes bass are holding by objects at a level deeper than your lure is being retrieved, and they will not come up for it. If you are fishing a spinnerbait shallow with no results, let the lure sink out of sight to a depth of between 4 and 8 feet, and retrieve it steadily at that depth. Occasionally, you will have to fish a spinnerbait out of sight along the bottom like this. Some anglers are even more versatile with a spinnerbait and fish it very deep by fluttering it down sharply sloping shorelines, dropoffs, rocky ledges, and the like, using a short-armed spinnerbait (make sure the blade turns freely and regularly when the lure is dropping) and working it in a series of short hops or in a jigging-like motion.

The places where I have most successfully used a spinnerbait are grass, lily pads, stumps and logs, stickups, and bushes. In all cases, get as close to the particular object as possible. Do this by casting the lure beyond the target and bringing it back into contact with it, then continuing on. I usually make several casts to each object, from every angle, paying particular attention to the deep and shady sides of it as well.

An effective method for working weed beds and weedlines is to crawl a spinnerbait slowly over the tops of the grass, when it is submerged a few feet. For grass beds with definable weedlines, however, I may cast parallel to the edge or bring the lure over the top and let it flutter down the edge. For lily pads, it is best to work the channel-like openings, but don't be afraid to throw into thick clusters, work the bait in pockets, ease it over the pads, and drop it in another pocket.

Perhaps the most reliable pattern for spinnerbait fishing, especially in the spring, is working the wood. This includes stumps, logs, and stickups. Make sure your spinnerbait is close to these objects; in fact, bump them with the lure at times—the momentary fluttering of the bait's blades and the object contact seem to produce strikes. Stickup trees, bushes, and floating logjams (as often found in coves) also are productive for spinnerbait users. In these locales, you should get your bait as far back in them as possible before commencing the retrieve. Boat docks and houses, too, fit in this category.

The most popular spinnerbaits are single- and tandem-blade versions. Tandem blades on the overhead arm of the spinnerbait usually feature a small spinner followed by a larger one. These are predominantly for shallow fishing and are best in the spring. Single-blade spinnerbaits, also effective when fished shallow as the season progresses, are a better bait for deeper retrieves.

Most spinnerbaits feature Colorado- or Indiana-style spinner blades. The Colorado is pear-shaped and produces more vibration than the Indiana. The common size is No. 4, which is roughly the size of a quarter. Colorado blades are often found on single-blade spinnerbaits. Indiana blades are teardrop-shaped and produce good vibration, too, though they spin faster, and work well on tandem-blade lures.

A third style of blade, the willowleaf, was less commonly used until the past few years. Spinnerbaits with these long blades have been the trend lately, used on a tandem rig with a big No. 4 or 5 willowleaf in silver or copper behind a smaller Indiana blade. The willowleaf

Stickups, bushes, stumps, blowdowns, and similar woody cover are good early-season spinnerbait terrain.

doesn't offer as much vibration as the other blades, but it revolves freely and produces a lot of flash. Baits with big blades are generally reserved for waters with distinct big-fish potential. This is not to say you won't catch big bass on smaller lures—I've caught big bass on small and large spinnerbaits—but the probability is that you'll catch fewer smaller size bass with an oversized bait.

At least one spinnerbait being made sports a revolving blade in the middle of the lure as well as a blade on the overhead shaft. Although this is a nifty innovation, it doesn't appear to add to the effectiveness of the lure. Another innovation is a spinnerbait with a hook for an overhead shaft, with a revolving blade attached to the hook. This bait is supposed to increase your fish-hooking effectiveness, but in using it, I didn't see this happen. Also, the lack of tandem blades was, at times, a disadvantage.

Something to note on all spinnerbaits is the thickness of the wire in the shaft arms. Thin wire gives you good feel and good lure action but can snap under the strain of a big fish, and, in general, will not withstand as much use as thicker arms. I have had some spinnerbait arms of light wire snap after a lot of use and fish-catching. However, wire arms that are too thick detract substantially from lure action and feel, and are thus undesirable, too.

Formerly, many spinnerbaits featured overhead blade arms that extended well beyond the hook on the bottom arm. This was some help in preventing hangups, but it hampered hook setting. Now many spinnerbaits have a shorter shaft, in which the blade assembly is directly above the hook, which is thus unobstructed. This is a two-edged sword, however. Short-arm spinnerbaits hang up frequently in thick brush and stumps and timber. If you need to roll such a lure over a log it often won't make it, because the overhead shaft is too short to afford any protection. If you take a short-armed spinnerbait that is attached to fishing line and gently try to pull it over your arm, you'll see what I mean; if the hook pricks your arm, it will stick in a log. For such times, a long-armed spinnerbait is best.

Spinnerbaits have to be periodically tuned to be kept running properly. A good spinnerbait runs straight, without twisting 360 degrees or leaning off to the side. You can adjust a spinnerbait so that the blades and hook run vertically in the water by bending the entire overhead shaft arm in the opposite direction from which it is running astray. For example, if the bait is leaning to the right side as you look at it during the retrieve, bend the overhead shaft to the left until you achieve a vertical running position.

The spinner blades on these arms come in different colors and impressions. Silver and copper are most popular, followed by gold, and painted white, chartreuse, and orange. Most are hammered or otherwise indented to reflect light rays and create flash. Copper, generally the favorite of most anglers, is good for slightly turbid and off-color water. Silver works well for me most of the year, especially in the spring and in clear water. Painted blades, most notably chartreuse, have worked well when murky-green water conditions were present.

As for spinnerbait bodies, color is sometimes unimportant and sometimes crucial. White is good for the early season and in murky water. Then all-chartreuse and chartreuse-and-blue (or black) combinations take over. On many occasions, the color of skirt makes no difference in the number or size of fish caught.

The material of the skirt and how it is applied is important, however. Most spinnerbaits today are supplied with rubber-tentacled or "living-rubber" skirts, but they used to be primarily dressed with vinyl skirts. Vinyl skirts should be replaced by rubber skirts. Rubber holds up better in cold water and offers much better body-swimming action. The disadvantage in rubber is that the tentacle arms have a tendency to stick together in the tackle box; you can avoid this by sprinkling some talcum powder in the compartments that house your spinnerbaits and by using trays that allow you to store spinnerbaits with the skirts hanging loosely rather than bunched up. If the legs get molded together, pull the skirt off and replace it with a fresh one.

The best way to apply a rubber skirt is as follows: hold it up so that the tentacles hang straight down, then turn it upside down so that the tentacles come out and over the stem of the skirt, resembling small streams of water being shot out of a fountain. Now thread the stem over the hook point and the shank until it fits snugly on the base of the lead head. This backwards skirt produces far more pulsating action than a straight-back skirt would.

It's a good idea to dress up spinnerbaits, especially large ones, still further, by adding a curl-tailed worm, grub, or pork chunk to the main hook. I'm partial to 3-inch twin-tailed soft plastic trailers, which swim feverishly just behind the skirt, and give a valuable extra dimension to the look of the lure.

An important modification on a spinnerbait is a trailer hook.

This is how a well-applied rubber skirt and trailer hook should look.

Trailer hooks account for many bass that would otherwise be lost. It is not necessary to use them all the time, but it doesn't hurt, especially if the fish are visibly striking short or hitting merely to stun. The trailer hook should ride in the same direction as the spinnerbait hook. To keep the trailer hook from sliding off, use a blocking method. A small piece of rubber tubing (which can be had from the body of a discarded rubber skirt) works best. Place a small ring of this material over the eye of the trailer hook, then bring the point of the spinnerbait hook through the eye and tubing, and secure it.

Most spinnerbait fishing, and, thus, much of this information, is directed at largemouth bass. But in the spring, smallmouths can be caught on spinnerbaits. Spinnerbaits are very effective lures at that time, particularly when the fish are shallow and are in shoreline areas completing spawning.

My experience has been that spring and early summer are the best times for spinnerbait use. In spring and early summer, spinnerbaits allow you to cover a lot of ground effectively and quickly, while you watch your lure work and see strikes. Midsummer is generally not a very good spinnerbait time, although in some well-timbered lakes where bass remain relatively shallow, spinnerbaits are effective. As the water cools in early fall, spinnerbaits again become reasonably productive lures.

There are a lot of good spinnerbaits on the market, including many that are made and sold within a certain region, so you shouldn't look far to find something suitable. If you keep a supply of extra blades, barrel swivels, trailer hooks, and skirts to be able to modify your spinnerbaits as necessary, you'll be able to enhance the lure's effectiveness and increase your angling successes.

SURFACE LURES

Surface fishing for bass is exciting no matter what time of year you choose to do it. Summertime is probably when bass fishermen give the surface the most pounding—early in the morning and late in the day. Bass, however, are bottom- and cover-oriented fish, and you usually have to get down to the level at which they are holding if you expect to catch them regularly. Nonetheless, surface fishing not only can be exciting, but at certain times it does have much merit, if you understand when and where to be working the top.

Surface fishing is generally restricted to relatively shallow water areas—12 or 14 feet—and to areas with cover. It is important to work a surface lure in locales that provide cover for bass; unless you are casting to bass feeding on schools of baitfish in open water or trying to call bass out of the tops of submerged trees, it is usually unproductive to fish most surface lures in open, deep-water areas. Also, being an accurate caster and having full mastery over the workings of your lures is important in surface fishing.

These, then, are the keys to successful surface fishing for bass: knowing when, and when not, to use them; knowing what type to

Surface fishing is the most exciting way to catch bass, though it is not always productive. Overcast conditions, early and late in the day, when a light ripple is on the water, and fishing around shallow cover are some of the keys to having surface fishing success.

use and how; knowing where to use them; knowing when to quit fishing on the surface (a common mistake is to stick with surface fishing long after the surface activity has petered out); and being able to put those lures in the position where they will be most productive. We'll cover the what, where, when, and how subjects shortly.

Basically, any lure that is worked as a topwater plug or as one used within the first 1 to 3 feet of the surface, falls into my categorization of surface lures. Essentially, there are four types of surface lures: popping and wobbling plugs, floating/diving plugs and darters, propellered lures, and stick baits. We'll cover each category separately.

POPPERS AND WOBBLERS

There are two distinct lures in this category: those that pop or chug and those that wobble. The former would be represented by such plugs as the Arbogast Hula Popper, Cordell Near Nuthin', Burke Flex-Plug Popper, and the Pico Pop. The latter is characterized principally by lures like the Heddon Crazy Crawler and Arbogast's Jitterbug. All these plugs are strictly for use on top of the water.

A popper, to my way of thinking, doesn't resemble the actions of any popular form of bass bait. Nothing that I've seen in the water deliberately calls attention to itself or makes pop-pop-popping or chug-chug-chugging sounds. A remote possibility is that this noise is construed by bass as the surface-feeding activity of other fish. More likely, this sound simply attracts feeding fish or calls some out of hiding for curiosity's sake.

All poppers (also called chuggers) have a concave, soup-bowl-type mouth. They function mainly as a noisemaker and attractor. They should not be worked in a continuous-retrieve manner, but should be utilized with pauses of varying duration during the retrieve. Generally, the slower a popper is worked, the better. The actual popping or forward chugging motion is made by jerking your rod up or back, not by reeling line in, to achieve the proper movement. It is best to keep your rod low and pointed toward the lure; this helps you keep slack out to work the lure well and to be in the best possible position to react to a strike.

When you pop this plug, you can do so with varying degrees of emphasis. Seldom is it worthwhile to jerk the rod hard to create a loud commotion. This can be an effective technique for schooling striped bass, but only occasionally is it warranted for black bass, and this, too, would likely be when they are schooling and chasing baitfish pods near the surface. When the surface is calm, you need only to effect a mild popping noise; a loud noise under this condition would probably be alarming to bass. When the surface is disturbed by a mild chop, you'll have to make a slightly noisier retrieve, and this condition warrants making your plug make louder pops.

If it appears that bass are feeding fairly actively, you can shorten the time between pops, but it is usually best to maintain long pauses, several seconds in duration, between them. Poppers are obviously time-consuming lures to use, and do not cover a lot of area very well. On the other hand, when worked slowly and enticingly in places with good concentrations of bass, they can be dynamically effective. A good tactic with poppers is to let them lie motionless a while after splashdown, then take up all your slack line and gently jiggle the rod just enough to impart the slightest sign of life to the lure. This tactic works well for just about all surface lures and sometimes makes a striker out of a bass that has been attracted to the landing of the plug in the water but might be spooked by the first quick pop.

Poppers work best near cover and in water that is not too deep, roughly to 12 feet. Early and late in the day (particularly in the summer), night, and cloudy days are the best fishing times for this

Wobbling (*left*) and popping (*right*) plugs.

lure. I've seldom had success with poppers until late spring or after mid-fall, and the combination of bright light and noisy lures does not seem to be one that bass favor. I don't recommend continuously using poppers when fishing unless you have exceptionally good success with them and fishing conditions warrant it. Poppers are good for spot-fishing, that is, making a few casts in selected areas and then switching to another, different type of lure. They are also, in my experience at least, better favored by largemouth than smallmouth bass, which you might expect owing to the habitat differences of these fish. Also, poppers (and wobblers) generally are not as productive in waters that are heavily fished as they are in moderately or sparsely fished bass lakes.

Wobbling plugs are used much in the manner of poppers. Wobblers, too, are more effective for largemouths, but I confess to having caught some dandy smallmouths on them at night. Wobblers, in fact, are probably more effective in the dark than at dusk, daylight, or dawn.

Wobblers are characterized by their to-and-fro undulating action. The Jitterbug has a wide, double spoon-filled metal lip that causes this motion, while the Crazy Crawler has two metal "wings" that rock the bait from side to side. The common retrieval method is a straight, continuous motion. At times, though, a worthwhile technique is to make the lure stop and go, or to give it a pull-pause motion, particularly as it swims next to an object like a stump or dock support. As long as there is some cover present or the water is not excessively deep under the boat, it is wise to work this lure all the way back to the boat. These plugs may be hit at any point along the retrieve, especially at night.

Keep your rod tip low and resist the urge to reel too fast. These lures don't have as good an action when retrieved quickly as they do when worked slowly. Moreover, a fast retrieve is more conducive to missed strikes. Many bass strike and miss wobbling surface lures. This may be because they have difficulty in pinpointing the lure's location or more often because they are intending to stun this surface-swimming creature. You may find it advantageous when experiencing a lot of short strikes to fashion a trailer hook behind the lure (if this doesn't hamper the action) or to resort to a more frequent stop-and-go retrieval cadence. For some reason, many fish that strike and miss fail to hit the lure when you toss it out a second time. Try to resist the urge to set the hook the instant a fish slashes at the bait and momentarily wait to feel the fish take your plug before setting the hook sharply. This hard-to-master delay is very effective in fishing weedless spoons in the grass and works well on wobbling surface plugs as well. If the fish misses altogether, try stopping the lure in its tracks and twitching it a little, then moving it a few inches and stopping it. Repeat this procedure again before resuming the retrieve.

My recommendation for color choices in these lures is very light or very dark. My best overall success has been with black wobblers and poppers, but chrome, clear, and frog-patterned models are also effective. The size of lure can vary with the conditions and expected catch. In waters with large bass, or when specifically looking for big fish, I'll use ³/₈- or ¹/₂-ounce plugs. In Northern waters, where bass usually run smaller, I seldom use the largest ones, preferring a ¹/₄-ounce popper most of the time and a ¹/₄-ounce wobbler in the day, going to ³/₈-ounce at dusk and at night.

FLOATING/DIVING LURES
Probably the most universally applied method of surface or near-surface fishing involves the use of floating/diving type plugs. These lures are made either of plastic or balsa wood, are generally minnow-shaped, and sport a small lip that serves to bring the lure beneath the surface at a maximum of about 3 feet on a conventional cast-and-retrieve. (These same minnow plugs, incidentally, will get down to a depth of 6 or 7 feet when trolled slowly and when using at least 150 feet of light line.) Though this type of lure is manufactured in sizes from 2 inches on up to 8 inches, the most practical size for bass fishing is the 4- to 6-inch model, since this is usually large enough to be of interest to a bass and yet still representative of baitfish. Occasionally the larger models will be effective, as will the smaller ones, though generally you'll catch more small bass on the latter (and panfish, too), and they are more difficult to cast.

Floating/diving minnow plugs are highly effective for both large-mouth and smallmouth bass. They will catch largemouths all season long in the right locations, but are more of an early- and late-season bait for smallmouths except in the most northerly waters, where some smallmouths can be found shallow even in the summer.

These lures are most effectively worked in a deliberately erratic fashion to imitate a crippled baitfish. If you have ever seen a dying shad, alewife, sunfish, perch, shiner, or other small fish, you may have noticed how it lies on its side, wiggles its tail fin occasionally, goes around in circles, and sometimes gets up enough energy to swim a few inches underwater before bobbing to the surface. This is essentially the type of activity you want to mimic in the retrieval of a floating/ diving lure. Being an opportunist, a hungry bass is likely to charge such a defenseless morsel (whether it is the real thing or your fake) with gusto, creating an electrifying strike.

To get the most out of this lure you have to fish it convincingly. This is one type of lure in which the action you put into it is directly proportional to the results you get. The first thing I do when fishing this type of lure, as I do with just about all lures, is to reel up the slack line to the point where none is left. I also make sure that my rod is not pointed skyward. The reason for both of these actions is that a bass often strikes a well-cast surface lure shortly after it hits the water or has been retrieved a few feet. If a fish hits that lure while it is first sitting still in the water and you have either slack line or a sky-busting rod, it's very hard to set the hook. You probably won't get another chance at that fish, so no opportunity should be squandered.

How you fish most topwater lures in the first few feet of retrieve is critical to your fishing success. This is especially true of this type of lure. In my experience, though I have not statistically verified this, 90 percent of the bass caught in the daytime on surface lures are taken within half of the total retrieving distance. Using buzz baits and fishing surface lures at night are exceptions to this.

Thus, your objective with a floater/diver is to make it gyrate as enticingly as possible in a stationary position. Keep the rod tip pointed low toward the water and use your wrist to move the rod. Jiggle the rod tip in a controlled, not frantic, fashion. Then jerk the lure back toward you a few inches. Then gyrate it some more, all the time reeling in an appropriate amount of line to keep the slack to a minimum. This is not very difficult to accomplish, particularly if you have a rod with a fairly limber tip. Stiff-tipped rods don't allow for soft lure movement, and I have found that long, light-action spinning rods generally work very well with these lures. The 4-inch size lures, being light, are easiest to cast with spinning tackle and 6- to 12-pound-test line anyway, especially under windy conditions.

Another way to use this lure type is on a straight retrieve, allowing it to run a foot or two beneath the surface. This is more like using it as a crankbait, and sometimes bass strike it this way. But a better technique, especially when bass won't hit this bait on top of the water, is to make it run just below the surface in a series of short jerk-pause movements, running it forward half a foot with each motion. This retrieve is more in the style of darters, those plugs that float but have no significant surface action and are used, solely, just below the surface. L&S MirroLures and Creek Chub Darters are characteristic of this lure type, as was the Bagley B-Flat Shiner (no longer produced), all of which are subjected to the same jerk-pause retrieval technique employed for floating/diving plugs.

The best floating/diving plugs for bass that I have used and could recommend include the floating Rapala, Rebel minnow, Bagley Bang-O-Lure, Smithwick Rogue, and Cordell Redfin. The Rapala and Bagley lures are made of balsa wood, and the Rapala is my favorite in this type of lure; the balsa lure does not seem to rise as quickly to the surface after being pulled under as do the plastic products. Thus, it best represents the behavior of small fish. For colors, the silver version probably out-catches all the others combined. Gold is good under certain water-color conditions, and sometimes, in clear lakes, perch, smelt, and bass patterns may be productive.

Floating/diving plugs.

A new floating/diving plug from Cordell, the Ripplin Redfin, has superb swimming action and holds a lot of promise for bass fishermen. The distinguishing characteristic of this 5-inch-long plastic plug is its thumbprint-like contoured sides. These give this bait an exceptional wobbling swim. An early prototype that I recently used had much merit when fished on a slow steady retrieve, in a jerk-and-pause fashion, and as a topwater bait. Another new lure of this type, which is destined to be a winner, is the Minnow Mate from Sisson Lures. Made by Lee Sisson, who crafted extremely popular lures for several well-known manufacturers until 1985, this has a "ticking" sound chamber and is made of a very bouyant yet durable hardwood. There are jointed and unjointed versions, and the action and sound they produce is outstanding.

Perhaps the best location for the use of floating/diving plugs is over submerged grass that comes to within a few feet of the surface. This lure is not only good for catching bass in such a locale, but also for locating possible concentrations of fish, which may then be tapped by the use of a plastic worm. Any type of relatively shallow cover can be a target for this lure. In less-covered locations, these lures can be quite effective as well, including spots such as long, shallow points; the backs of bays; and rocky shorelines. Smallmouth bass are particularly receptive to these lures in late spring and early summer when they are in shallow water. Look for every sizable rock or boulder and toss a floating/diving minnow plug to it.

In the early part of the season and again in the fall, there is no preferred time of the day to use this lure. In shallow lakes in the early spring, I've had more success from mid-morning to mid-afternoon, after the sun has had an opportunity to have a warming effect on the water; however, this lure is good for spring morning fishing when bass are shaking off the effects of a cool night. Later in the spring you may be able to catch fish on these lures throughout the day. In the summer, early in the morning is the best time, and just before dark can be fairly good. These lures don't produce as well as others, however, at night.

PROPELLERED LURES

Two separate and distinctly different types of lure qualify under this heading: propellered plugs and buzz baits. Both are noisemakers and both are attractors, but beyond that the similarities end.

PROPELLERED PLUGS Propellered surface plugs have provided me with exceptionally good fishing at times for both largemouth and small-mouth bass in all areas of the country. These lures are basically shaped like small cigars or torpedoes; they may feature propeller-like blades both fore and aft, or they may only possess one blade at the rear. They are manufactured in roughly 2- to 6-inch sizes. The 3½-inch-size bait seems best for smallmouths. More wary than their brethren, these fish are less likely to hit very large plugs; the big propellered surface plugs would not be very effective on them. Small and large sizes are productive for largemouth bass, and it is likely that the larger plugs account for the larger fish, too.

The basic technique for retrieving this lure is similar to the surface retrieve of floating/diving minnow plugs, which was outlined previously. The retrieve constitutes a jiggling-jerking-pausing motion that is erratic and representative of a struggling or crippled baitfish. As in fishing with the floating/diving lures, you need to keep the rod down, utilize the rod tip to effectively impart action, and make your wrists do the work.

You can retrieve a propellered plug either quickly or slowly. I lean to the slow retrieve when prospecting for unseen fish and to the fast side when casting to a school of bass that are tearing up baitfish. When working for non-schooling bass, slashing this bait forward, too hard and too far, seems excessive. At this time it takes a slower, more deliberate, convincing action to catch bass. The propellers will make a loud churning noise with some bubbly effect, and this may aid in attracting the attention of bass in the vicinity. A rapid, ripping retrieve is warranted for schooling largemouths, and the noise thereby created seems to imitate the slashing surface-breaking feeding activity common to this situation. At this time, if you can keep with the school and if they stay near the surface, it is possible to have a lot of action on a propellered plug. Northern anglers may not witness this type of fish behavior, as it generally occurs (with varying degrees of frequency) in southern impoundments with abundant concentrations of threadfin shad, where bass have gathered to chase and feed on these baitfish. Even in northern reservoirs with a good population of alewives (shad can't tolerate the cold winters in this region), bass rarely exhibit this surface schooling behavior.

Propellered surface plugs can be fished in the spring, summer, and fall, though summer appears to be the most productive period.

A plug with a propeller on the rear took this bass over submerged grass. Lures with rear blades are sometimes more effective than those with fore and aft propellers, creating a detectable but more subtle attraction.

At that time it is best to fish them for the first few hours of daylight and occasionally in the evening. I have caught most largemouths and smallmouths on these baits between 3 and 10 feet of water. Areas with heavy cover seem to be prime fishing locations; in northern waters especially, shore-hugging weedlines before a gradual dropoff are quite productive. These lures do not work well in deeper water, other than for school situations. I have occasionally had a stray strike from a largemouth or spotted bass in the open, in water 15 to 18 feet deep, but don't count on these lures to call bass up from unobstructed depths.

You won't find an abundance of these propellered surface plugs in most stores, particularly in northern locales, but that's not because they don't catch bass in those areas. They do—as well as pickerel, pike, inland stripers, and saltwater fish. In fact, one of the two times that I have caught two bass, at the same time on the same lure, was on one of these baits. The fish weighed respectively 5 and 2 pounds, and I saw several others come up with those! The top lures in this category that I have used with excellent results are the Smithwick Devil's Horse, Gudebrod's Sinner Spinner (no longer available to my knowledge), Heddon's Dying Flutter, and the propellered Bagley Bang-O-Lure.

BUZZ BAITS   One type of lure that excites the bass's aggressive nature is the buzz bait. This type of lure is thought to be a recent phenomenon, but it's not. Some form of buzz bait has been around for a long time. The Harrison-Hoge Weedwing has been a popular lure with some fishermen and is foremost among old-time buzzers. But a new variation of this evolved with the popularity of the spinnerbait and has resulted in the present-day form of buzz bait.

Two types of buzzers are available: those with in-line configuration and those with overhead configuration. The overhead model resembles a spinnerbait in its construction while the in-line version features a weedless spoon or bucktail behind the blade. The revolving buzz blade itself is of unique design, vaguely resembling an airplane propeller, and having cupped ends that give the lure a clicking, chop-chop-chop sound that accounts for the name of the lure.

The noise of a buzz bait is not only attractive to feeding bass, but also to shallow non-feeding bass. Its effectiveness is not limited to one time of the day, to one season, or to a specific geographic locale. Moreover, in my experience, this lure is an excellent producer of big fish, and certainly of larger-than-average bass. The bait works well in spring, summer, and fall, under most weather conditions, and during the day as well as at night. It is generally not very productive in bright sunlight, but good for warm water and hot weather conditions. I have not yet caught a bronzeback on a buzzer, incidentally, and since its habitat preferences differ markedly from a largemouth,

I don't expect that I will catch many in the future; however, fishermen in various areas have told me of their success with these baits on smallmouths, so apparently they can be of limited effectiveness for these fish, too.

A buzz bait is at its very best in areas with thick cover. It is deadly in emergent vegetation that is not too thick to prevent free lure passage and over submerged vegetation that comes fairly close to the surface. It is also highly effective around brush, in timber, and around any fallen wood that might conceal a bass. The closer you can work a buzz bait to such cover, the better.

A well-designed buzz bait is reasonably weed-free and can be fished effectively in all but dense concentrations of matted vegetation. Even in fairly thick areas, with accurate casting and a little side-to-side rod manipulation, you can pick your spots and work a buzzer. I have little trouble fishing some models of buzz baits with attached trailer hooks in light vegetation. Mid- to late-spring, of course, when lily pads and grass have not fully grown up, is an excellent buzz bait season, provided the water is warm enough.

Bass don't seem to mind how warm the water is in order to hit

Propellered plugs (*top*) and buzz baits (*bottom*).

a buzzer, but they won't come up for it if the water is too cold. The upper 60's is the lower water temperature range for buzz bait action. The summer and early fall are consistently productive buzz bait times, usually in the first few hours of the morning, in late evening, and at night. I often fish a buzz bait in the evening and at night, and it is twice as exciting then as in daytime.

A particularly good feature of buzz baits is that they are basically shallow-water products, as are all surface lures in general. I rarely catch bass on buzz baits in water over 12 feet deep, even if the vegetation comes to the surface. Furthermore, if you want to cover a lot of water for feeding fish and all other factors are right, a fast-working buzz bait will allow you to do just that.

When bass strike a buzzer, they usually crash the bejeebers out of it. There are times, however, when they either miss (this happens a lot at night) or strike short. I think this occurs when the bass are not necessarily feeding, but looking to worry or stun the intruding creature. A lot of short strikers can be caught if you use a trailer hook. This is rigged the same as a spinnerbait trailer. I generally use a trailer hook with a buzz bait, except in thick grass.

There are many buzz baits now on the market. In selecting, I look for these qualities: the ability to be worked effectively at a slow retrieval speed; a bullet-shaped lead head that can cut through the water and ride over the vegetation neatly; heavy-duty-gauge shaft arms; an overall slim profile for lightweight lures to permit easy casting with bait-casting tackle; and large hooks, generally in the 4/0 or 5/0 sizes. I haven't fished with all of the buzz baits on the market, but I can recommend a few of my favorites. These include Norman's Triple Wing Buzzer, an overhead lure that features a three-cupped buzz blade; Floyd's Buzzer, an in-line lure produced by Blue Fox Tackle; the Okie-Bug Buzzer, a good overhead model; and the Strike King Timber Buzz, an in-line lure particularly good for heavy cover and featuring two counter-rotating blades followed by a weedless spoon.

For buzz bait colors, I basically use black, white, and chartreuse, depending on the color and clarity of the water, and the relative lightness of the day. Sometimes, color makes no difference. Whatever a buzz bait represents and for whatever reason bass strike it, it certainly brings out the fighting side of the fish. When that chopping retrieval cadence is interrupted by an authoritative crash of a striking fish, it sparks your adrenaline and makes the spirit want to come back for more. I dare say that the strike in this situation is the climax of the excitement, after which you can't wait to bring in the fish and throw the lure back out, with the expectation that yet another bass will bust it.

STICK BAITS

Excitement and anticipation are the norms for stick-bait fishing, a form of surface angling that I prefer above all else. Unlike my attitude when using other baits, I don't merely think or hope a fish will hit my stick bait, I fully expect it.

That expectation isn't based on a stick bait's appearance. Resembling a cigar or tapered broom handle, this lure is the antithesis of the natural shape and imitation design in vogue with many lures. An artsy paint job may dress up this lure, but essentially it's still a torpedo in costume. Most of the baits that fit into this category are similar in size and conformation to propellered plugs, except that they don't have propellers. They are retrieved much like, and are fished in the same areas as, propellered plugs and to a lesser extent floating/diving lures. Stick baits do not have a lip or concave popping mouth, and

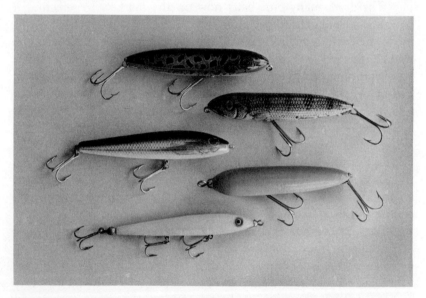

Stick baits don't have a particularly impressive appearance, yet they can be extremely effective at catching bass, particularly large fish. They are lures that require a skillful retrieve.

they are weighted in the tail so the head sits off the water and the tail rests slightly under the surface. Stick baits are also known as "splash" baits or "jumpers" because of their darting activity on the surface and the way they splash and seem to be lurching in and out of the water.

Although appearance has little to do with a stick bait's fish-catching appeal, its activity when retrieved has everything to do with it. A stick bait can't be tossed out with abandon and then cranked back in. The secret of its effectiveness lies in a masterful retrieval technique. All of the action must be supplied by the angler, making the stick bait foremost among lures for which retrieval skill is of paramount importance.

Many anglers find stick bait retrieval difficult to master. Perhaps this difficulty has been a factor in the relatively low popularity of these lures. Stick baits are effective for largemouth, smallmouth, and spotted bass, and also productive at times in angling for stripers, muskies, pike, pickerel, snook, tarpon, and an assortment of other saltwater fish. Stick baits enjoyed limited popularity in years past via the original Zara Spook and then fell into near anonymity except among a coterie of Ozarks anglers until recent years. Lately, fishermen have been finding that these lures can catch fish nearly everywhere. Nonetheless, it's not uncommon to walk into a tackle shop that doesn't stock some kind of stick bait, or to find anglers who are not familiar with them.

The most widely used stick baits today are Heddon's Zara Spook, Cordell's Boy Howdy, Jim Rogers' Walker (formerly known as the Jim Dandy, and made by R&W Lures), and the Rebel Jumpin' Minnow. The Jumpin' Minnow is essentially used by inland striper anglers for surface-busting schoolies, and though it's a functional bait, it doesn't have quite the dynamic action of the Spook and the Walker. The Boy Howdy is fairly popular in Southern bass circles, and though it, too, doesn't swim or walk as well as the others, it is a good splash or jumping bait in the hands of an artistic retriever. The Walker is the least known of the four. It's larger than the other stick baits, being 5 inches long and weighing 1 ounce, and is used mainly on stripers, though it is an excellent bait for big largemouth bass and has muskie potential. It also has a rattling BB inside it. The Zara Spook, the grandfather of the stick bait family, is widely known and even revered in some circles. The largest and most productive of the Spooks are the $3/4$- and $7/8$-ounce versions, which are $4\frac{1}{2}$ inches long.

A stick bait, such as this Zara Spook, sits with the nose out of the water and the butt below the surface. Note the loop knot attached to this plug.

Learning to retrieve these lures came fairly easy to me, as it may to others who are familiar with techniques for fishing floating minnow plugs. The principal stick bait retrieve causes the lure to step from side to side. This side-stepping technique for stick baits is called "walking the dog," a term that originated with the Zara Spook.

To retrieve a stick bait, you must begin with the rod tip at a low angle, preferably pointing toward the water. This permits a desirable angle of pull and allows the head of the lure to lurch in and out of the water most effectively. The all-important lure action is achieved through an adroit combination of rod-tip twitching and reel-handle turning. You make a continuous series of short jerks—never long sweeps—that cover roughly a 6- to 10-inch distance, while at the same time advancing your reel handle perhaps half a turn with each rod-tip twitch to take up slack. By slowing the pace, you widen the lure's path of travel; by speeding it up, you narrow it. ("Slow-walking" and "fast-walking" are the terms occasionally applied to these respective speeds of retrieval.) A skilled stick bait angler can just about keep the lure in the same place, making it nod from side to side while barely moving forward.

If you have a long length of line out, you can effectively walk the dog while keeping your rod tip high. But eventually, as you reel in line, the angle of pull will become too great, and if you keep the rod tip up, you'll jump the bait out of the water and reduce its designed action. So as the length of line decreases, lower the rod tip, a move that also puts you in a better position to respond to a strike.

An advanced technique of retrieving stick baits is one known as "half-stepping." The peak of stick bait retrieval skill, this technique can drive a fish wild. In the half-step, a stick bait moves repeatedly to one side instead of from side to side. Imagine that you're in a position to work your lure past the entire length of a log. If you walk the plug it will dart in toward the log, out away from it, back toward it, out again, and so forth. When you half-step it, however, the plug darts away from the log at first, then comes in, then comes in again, then in again, and so forth, repeatedly butting its nose up against the object as if it meant to climb it or hide by it.

To half-step a stick bait, first jerk the rod tip to bring the lure in the desired direction. Then barely nudge the rod tip, a maneuver that doesn't advance the bait, but causes it to turn its head just slightly outward. Now jerk the rod tip as before, and the lure will dart back in the same direction it last headed. Nudge the rod once again, then jerk it. Again the plug will head inward. If you use the half-step to work the lure around a bush, along a log, or into a big stump, it can be nearly irresistible to a big bass.

A propensity to attract big fish, incidentally, is one of the prime virtues of stick baits. On the average these lures produce bigger fish than most other types, and it seems that the larger the plug, the larger the fish.

One difficulty with these lures is that they are hard to fish from a sitting position, especially from a low seat. Sitting on a pedestal seat or, preferably standing, improves retrieval ability. Also, a relatively limber-tipped rod is preferable to a stiff-tipped one. I use a 6-foot, fast-taper graphite bait-caster for fishing a Zara Spook or Walker, and this is just barely limber enough to work the lure.

Using a snap or a loop knot with the Spook or Walker is especially important. A No. 3 snap (not snap-swivel) works well for many anglers, though I prefer a loop knot to allow the line to go back and forth quickly and unimpeded. Tying a conventional knot snug to the eye of the lure definitely hinders the action. I've found that my baits work best on medium-strength line; stick baits don't seem to perform as well on 8- or 20-pound line as they do on 12.

Stick baits can be productive in all cover situations where you'd expect to find bass. Working specific objects is usually the best bet, but I've had good success fishing blindly over thick, submerged grassbeds and on weedy points. They may be most effective, however, around wood, particularly stumps, logs, and fallen trees, and for calling up bass from submerged timber. They should be worked along the full length of logs and as close to stumps and bushes as possible. When casting to a specific object, land the lure well past your target. Slow-walk the lure up to the object, then fast-walk it past. Vary your retrieval speeds. A moderate retrieve is often best, though there are times and lakes in which bass will not respond to these lures unless you work them slowly and seductively. A very quick, constant retrieval speed is generally least effective.

At times, stick baits will catch fish throughout the day. Wind is sometimes a prohibiting agent. When it's windy, you'd be well advised to abandon stick bait fishing or at least fish with the wind if you must. A light wind that ripples the surface is sometimes desirable, and cloudy, overcast, drizzly conditions are good. Bright sun can also be an inhibiting factor. When the angle of the sun is low, retrieve the bait toward the sun, rather than away from it.

As for colors, my best success is with clear (transparent) Walkers and frog-, perch-, and shad-colored Zara Spooks. I've been experimenting with all-black stick baits but have had little success with them, though I think black should be a good color. Charlie Campbell of Forsyth, Missouri, a friend of mine and probably the dean of stick bait practitioners, once offered me this wisdom regarding color selection: "The darker it is, the darker the color of Zara Spook I go to. The biggest fish seem to come on frog or black, and on cloudy days I go to these colors. In clear water I go to a light color. In the early morning I'll use a dark color until the sun comes up, and go dark again in the evening. For suspended bass and in midday use, I prefer a light color, and the chrome version has proven to be a good daytime color."

As you may suspect, a lot of fish strike or boil after a stick bait and miss it. Many of these fish can be enticed to strike again if you control your reflexes. When fish strike a stick bait, the over-anxious angler often rears back to set the hook and jerks the lure away from the fish. Try to hold back your reactions until the fish has clearly taken the lure. If he misses the bait and you don't jerk it away but keep it walking along, there's a good chance he'll hit again. If you

Cast a stick bait beyond the stump, then walk it up to the back of the stump, and half-step it around the side and the front, quickening the retrieve momentarily as the lure swims away from the front of this object.

jerk the lure clear away from the fish, you probably won't get a second hit. Then it pays to toss out another lure to the same spot immediately. A spinnerbait, floating minnow plug, or worm are good choices.

You'll find that it is important to cast a stick bait very accurately. In thick cover, you'll need to lay the line in such a way that you help direct a clear, desirable path of travel for the lure. If you've been fishing another type of lure for some time and then switch to a stick bait, you'll find it hard to cast precisely in close quarters until you get accustomed to the larger, heavier lure.

Pay close attention to the working action of every stick bait you fish. These are critically balanced lures, and though they may come from the same manufacturer, they are not identical. Some lures may need smaller treble hooks to perform well; with others you may have to fiddle with the line-tie screw to lower the angle. It's not uncommon to find one stick bait that works better than an identical one from the same manufacturer. Out of a dozen, it's a fair bet that one or two will have superior action. They're the ones you don't want to lose, lend to another fisherman, or leave in an open tackle box tray in the sun until they warp. Treasure and protect them.

SPECIALTY SURFACE LURES A few lures used by bass fishermen don't quite fit into the previous categories. The soft plastic frog is one such lure. Popular in usage, it fits into no category other than fishing grass and pads (which we'll cover in Part III). Two especially good lures of this nature that I can recommend are the Harrison-Hoge Super Frog (also called Bill Plummer's Super Frog) and the Snag-Proof Frog. I like these lures most in their natural frog colors, with white or yellow bellies, and in all-green and all-black versions. These baits are strictly for fishing the vegetation—the thicker the better.

In using the plastic frog, the two most important keys are fishing them extremely slowly and deliberately, and delaying in setting the hook. When I say to fish them slow, I mean slower than you can imagine. The man who invented the Super Frog takes up to 10 to 15 minutes to bring the frog in, sometimes longer. And he catches a lot of big bass. He'll twitch the frog, hop it off a pad, let it sit for what seems an eternity, then move it ever-so-slowly again. This type of fishing requires a lot of patience on the angler's part, and in fact it is best to work two such lures on separate rods at the same time, in different locations, alternating between retrieving them. When a fish hits, you have to delay your hook setting momentarily until you actually feel the fish with the lure. This is less of a problem with this type of lure than others because of its soft consistency, which makes it feel more natural to the fish and results in the bass holding it a bit longer than he might otherwise. When you do set the hook, it must be done hard.

Another type of surface lure out of the norm is the Burke Flex Plugs. There are popping, wobbling, and stick bait models of these lures, and they can be retrieved in manners already described here. The unique aspect of these surface plugs is that they are made of soft plastic and sport weedguards that make them extremely weed-free and snag-free. They do get hung up on occasion, but much less so than other lures. This type of surface lure can be fished in the thickest of cover, often with exciting results.

JIGS

As one of many dedicated jig fishermen, I feel compelled to endorse jigs as one type of lure I'd like to have on hand if survival by catching fish was at stake. Jigs have the simplest appearance of all artificial lures, the longest history, and an unparalleled advantage over other lures in their ability to appeal to nearly all species of gamefish. Jigs are particularly good in several forms and manners of presentation for largemouth and smallmouth bass.

Jigs are an anomaly in that, at rest, they don't particularly resemble fish, insects, or other aquatic forage. Also, for a lure-type that catches such a wide range of species, a jig is not the throw-it-out-and-reel-it-back-in-and-watch-the-fish-go-crazy-over-it kind of lure. For an item with such productive potential, many anglers have not or do not use jigs because they find working these lures hard to master. At the heart of such anomalies is the key to catching fish with jigs: success is directly proportional to your ability to impart action to the lure, effect a proper style of retrieval, and be able to detect strikes.

Although jigs can be fished in all types of situations and at all depth levels, for bass they are primarily fished on or close to the bottom. Though it seems academic to review techniques for establishing jig contact with the bottom, failure to reach and keep these lures on the bottom is the bane of many jiggers.

The simplest way to get a jig to reach the bottom is to open the bail of your spinning reel or depress the free-spool mechanism on a

Jigs will catch bass through all seasons of the year, but they are only effective if you are adept at detecting strikes, fish them in the right locales, and effect the right retrieval motion.

bait-casting or spin-casting reel and let the lure fall freely until the line goes slack on the surface of the water and no more comes off the spool. If the water is calm and the boat still, you can readily detect when you are on the bottom. If it is somewhat windy or if current is present, you have to watch the departing line carefully to detect the tell-tale slack and to differentiate between line that is leaving the spool because the lure has not reached bottom and line that is being pulled off by a drifting lure or boat. If you are fishing from a boat, a depthfinder can help you determine when your lure has reached the bottom because you will have some idea of the local depth.

The lighter the line and the heavier the lure, the easier it is to reach the bottom. The stronger the line, the greater its diameter and the more resistance it offers in the water. A ¼-ounce jig will fall quicker on 8-pound line than it will on 14-pound line, for example. The advantage here (the magnitude of which depends on fishing conditions), is that it is easier to get your lure to the bottom and keep it on the bottom with 8-pound line than it is with 14-pound line.

Once you are on the bottom, of course, you need to maintain contact with it. Assuming that you have cast your jig out, let it settle to the bottom, and are now retrieving it, you should keep it working in short hops along the bottom as long as the sloping bottom and length of line out, enable you to do so. If you are in a boat and drifting, the jig will eventually start sweeping upward and away from you and the bottom as you drift, unless it is very heavy, so you occasionally need to pay out more line until the angle of your line has changed significantly, then reel in and drop the jig back down again. When drifting, face the wind or current, and drop your jig out on the windward side of the boat. If you drop it on the lee side, the boat will soon drift over your line and you'll be in an awkward position for fishing.

Choosing the right weight lure to use is critical to most types of jigging. The ideal is to have a lure that gets to the bottom and stays there under normal conditions, but which is not too large to be imposing to bass. Most anglers who fail to reach bottom not only don't use the right retrieval technique or compensate for wind or current, but also use too light a jig for getting down to the bottom under the conditions that they face.

I once sat in an underwater observatory in Silver Springs, Florida, and watched a plastic worm being worked by a renowned tournament bass fisherman. This man was no stranger to jigs and worms, yet in the moderately flowing Silver Springs current, his plastic worm was being worked nearly 5 feet off a sandy bottom in 15 feet of water. Later he was surprised to find that his lure was nowhere near where he thought it was—he was sure that he was working the worm off the bottom. This can happen to anyone, particularly those not accustomed to fishing in moving water. Whether fishing a worm or jig, you have to take into account the effect of the current. This particular angler needed a much heavier weight to accomplish his normal retrieval under those conditions.

When fishing a jig in current, you should cast upstream or up-and-across-stream. Engage the line pickup system as soon as the lure splashes down, reel up slack, and try to keep the line taut by letting the jig drift or by reeling in slack (whichever is appropriate). You want to achieve a natural drift, not swim the jig up or toward you, and to maintain contact with it to feel a strike. Don't cast downstream; there'll be too much slack in the line as the jig sinks and the line is swept away. Fishing directly downstream won't allow you to work the jig for any distance or very naturally, and detecting strikes is difficult.

At times you won't want to fish a jig on the bottom. When bass are schooling and chasing baitfish, a jig is often a great lure to toss into the fracas. There you just need to effect a twitch-reel-twitch action, swimming the lure just under the surface. In vertical jigging, however, you may be prospecting for fish that are at any level between the bottom and the surface, or are suspended at a specific level well off the bottom.

If you know what depth to fish, you can let the desired length of line out and commence jigging, never reeling in any line and only paying line out if you begin to drift. Here's one way to know how much line you're letting out: reel the jig up to the rod tip, stick the rod tip on the surface, let go of the jig, and raise your rod tip up to eye level, then stop the fall of the jig. If eye level is 6 feet above the surface, your jig will now be 6 feet deep. Lower rod tip to the surface and do this again. Now you've let out 12 feet of line. Continue until the desired length is out. With a level-wind reel with a freely revolving line guide, you can measure the amount of line that is let out with each side-to-side movement of the line guide, then multiply this by the number of times the guide travels back and forth. If you use a reel that doesn't have such a guide, you can strip line off the spool

in 1-foot (or 18-inch) increments until the desired length is out.
Another method is to count-down the lure's descent. A falling rate
of one foot per second is considered standard and may be accurate for
medium-weight jigs, but you should check the lure's rate of fall in a
controlled situation first, to ensure accuracy.

For some vertical jigging you may need to let your lure fall to
the bottom, then jig it up toward the surface a foot or two at a time.
Bring the lure off the bottom and reel in the slack, then jig it there
three or four times before retrieving another few feet of line and jigging
the lure again. Repeat this until the lure is near the surface. The only
problem here is that you don't usually know exactly how deep a fish
is when you do catch one, and you can't just strip out the appropriate
length of line and be at the proper level.

Once you learn how to present a jig properly and can fish it where
it will be doing the most good, you're two-thirds of the way toward
success. The final step is detecting strikes, and here experience has
to be your teacher. Describing what a strike on a jig feels like is difficult.
To say that there is an almost imperceptible "tap" or light "tick" is
to be vague yet accurate.

JIGGING A LEDGE

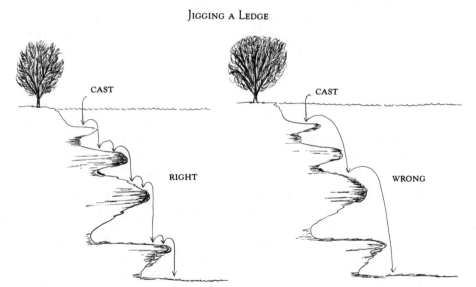

A vertical retrieve is essential when working a jig down a ledge. Short, slow hops
keep the jig crawling along. Long sweeps bring the jig swimming out and away,
causing the jig to miss most of the best cover.

Fish rarely hit a jig lying still, but grab it as it moves upward or falls downward, mostly the latter. As a result, it takes a knack for discerning that irregularity in the lure's movement that indicates a pickup. A sensitive rod with a fast-action tip is a plus for most forms of jigging, particularly when light line is used. Graphite and boron rods are particularly good for jigging. In jigging, unlike other forms of fishing, it is often necessary to keep your rod tip pointed upward to help detect strikes. (In other types of fishing it is best to keep your rod tip low to aid in hook setting.) This leads to not hooking a few fish, though well-sharpened hook points can be helpful in this regard. It is also advisable to fish a jig relatively slowly. Beginning jig fishermen in particular have a tendency to rush the retrieval of a jig. This not only results in swimming the lure too far from the bottom, but is seldom viewed favorably by fish.

The two basic categories of bass jigs are the jig and pork combination, and jigs with either bucktail or grub bodies. They are fished differently and have distinct characteristics and applications.

JIG AND PORK   The jig and eel, which is basically a jig with a strip of pork rind, is an oldtime bait. In recent years, however, jigs with pork have gotten a facelift and are being noticed for their versatility as well as their effectiveness. The new genre of jig and pork now includes the venerable and multi-dimensional jig and eel, plug jigs adorned with pork chunks (alias jig and chunk, jig and pig, jig and frog, etc.). Pork strips used with a jig and eel are made of pork rind that has been stripped of fat. Chunks have a layer of fat on them, giving them bulk and weight in addition to extra action. These baits are available from several manufacturers and in a variety of forms, to wit: with worm trailers, with twin-tail plastic or pork trailers, with pork frog chunks, with pork rind strips, with plastic lizard, with rubber skirts, with bucktails, with or without weedguards, and probably with some other garnishes that I've overlooked.

Whereas the jig and pork combination of yesteryear was principally thought of as a cold-weather, semi-deep bait, today it's a hallmark of versatility. Where do you fish the born-again jig and pork? Just about everywhere you want. With a weedguard it penetrates the most imposing tangles. Without it, try the open-water sanctums. Fish it deep, shallow, or in-between.

The most successful application of this jig is probably in the

The jig and pork combination is one of the most effective bass baits in use today.

bushes, brush, and submerged treetops. In the springtime, the shallow bushes along the banks often hold bass. The fish are deep in the middle of these bushes, which may be located in 5 to 10 feet of water. Few anglers toss a lure into the heart of these tangles, and, after all, a plastic worm, tossed from a good distance away, often only scours the periphery of the bush and may not be effective unless the bass elect to come out after it. By getting close to these objects, you can flip or pitch a jig right into this, work it through and out of the entanglement, and snake a hooked bass out with less difficulty than would otherwise be possible. The same is true for logjams and the roots of stumps or trees and other thick hard-to-fish spots. This is why the technique of flipping (discussed later) is so effective, and why these lures are part of that bass fishing method.

Rocky banks can be another strong jig and pork locale, particularly if they have a very steep dropoff and possess a lot of craggy, ledge-like formations. Bass will seek refuge in the crags and under the ledges but are often not susceptible to diving plugs or falling-away plastic worms. Here these jigs can be flipped or cast. In both cases, present the jig close to the edge of the rock and allow it to fall vertically close to the bank. Crawl it off each ledge, over each rock, swimming it along as unobtrusively as possible, and working it under the boat or as deep as your cast will permit. Always work the lure slowly, keeping light tension on the line, and be prepared to set the hook the instant a strike is detected.

Yet another prime application for these jigs is when bass are holding tightly in very dense cover, such as milfoil, hyacinths, floating mats of hydrilla and debris, grassy shoals, or bridge pilings and boat docks. The latter can be very difficult to fish with conventional casting techniques, but by getting close and quietly (and accurately) flipping a jig around them, you can achieve some highly effective results. In the thickly matted clusters, you should drop your jig in any hole that is visible, jigging it up and down repeatedly therein. In some cases you may even have to make your own holes.

The weight of the jig to use depends primarily on the depth of the water, but also depends upon wind and current conditions. For deep-bank work, a 1/4-ounce jig on light line might do the trick, but it is more likely you'll need a 5/16-ounce jig and may even have to go up to 1/2-ounce. For flipping the bushes and such, the jig size may vary from 3/16-ounce to as much as 3/4-ounce. The color is usually dark, with black, brown, or purple being the best bets. You'll need a weed-guarded bait (the forked style seems best) in the worst areas, so it's a good idea to have some jigs with and some without this feature. For pork chunks, a No. 11 Uncle Josh pork rind (which weighs 1/4-ounce and measures 1 by 2 1/2 inches long) is favored, in black or brown. The chunk, incidentally, can be trimmed with a knife to make it fall faster, if that seems desirable. Two-toned pork chunks are also available now. Although I haven't used them, I suspect that in some places, such as murky lakes, a black-and-orange or black-and-chartreuse combo might be the ticket.

To care for your pork baits, keep them in the container and brine they came in. After you are finished with a pork chunk, put it back in the manufacturer's jar. While fishing, keep the pork wet or it will dry and shrivel up and become useless. One way to keep it wet when it's not being used is to toss the jig and pork into your live well. Another is to leave the pork dangling in the water if you are fishing unobstructed areas. Still another is to use a Sav-a-Pig Grip-a-Lure folder; wet the inside so it stays moist, put your jig and pork in it, seal it with the Velcro closure, and leave it until you're ready to use the lure later. (I picked this up in a sports shop once and don't know who makes it, but I believe it's available from mail order tackle suppliers.)

By flipping or pitching a weedless jig and pork chunk from a short range, you can adequately probe this type of cover for largemouths.

To attach pork to a lure, locate the slit at the head of the bait and insert the hook point through it. To remove the pork, turn it sideways at a right angle to the hook point, grab the hook with one hand and the pork with the other and carefully exert pressure to pull the pork down while pulling the barb out.

These are, obviously, big baits. Even a 1/4-ounce jig with a twin-tailed trailer or pork frog chunk weighs closer to 1/2-ounce. Specifically what they represent is a bit of a mystery, though crayfish and sala-manders seem plausible. Unquestionably, these unobstrusive baits ring the chow bell in both cold and warm water for largemouth and small-mouth bass, and constitute one of the better big-bass baits in use today.

GRUBS AND HAIR JIGS Common bass jigs come in various head styles, either featuring bucktail or synthetic hair bodies, or soft-plastic grub bodies. The grub bodies may be flat-tailed or curl-tailed. The weight of the jig itself is the most important aspect in fishing it, and this may vary from ⅛-ounce to ½-ounce. Your choice should be dependent upon the depth of the water, its clarity, the wind conditions, and the lure you are using. This may sound involved, but it really isn't.

Use the lightest jig that you can under the circumstances. You don't want a jig to sink too fast, which would appear unnatural, yet you need the appropriate size to attain necessary depth. When fishing in a lake with current or when fishing in flowing water like a stream or river, you'll need to use a heavier jig than you would if the current were not present. Another influential factor is wind. The harder the wind blows, the more difficult it is for the unanchored fisherman to hold bottom with a light jig. Jigging depth is also influenced by the size of your line; the heavier the line, the greater its diameter and the more drag it has in the water, which obviously reinforces the fact that light jigs fall slower than heavier ones. Then, too, the clearer the water and the shallower it is, the more you should be using light jigs for less obtrusive presentations. This all adds up to interpreting the effects of the elements and selecting the best size lure according to the conditions.

Light hair jigs and grubs are usually better fished with spinning tackle than bait-casting. They cast better with spinning tackle, where the bail remains open and the lure falls relatively straight. With bait-casting gear, it is usually necessary to pay line out by hand after the cast to get the jig to fall straight.

Flat-tailed grubs should be placed on the shank of the jig in such a way that their tail rides flat, or horizontal, to achieve a good side-to-side falling action. For rigging curl tails, use the side seam as a guideline and rig the bait so that the curl tail rides up vertically in the same direction as the hook. The length of these flat-tailed or curl-tailed soft plastics varies from 1½ to 3 inches. The most successful colors for soft-plastic bodies are gray (or smoke), green, black, purple, white, and chartreuse. For hair bodies, the best colors are black, brown, yellow, and white.

These two types of jigs are good for all bass, but they are particularly successful on smallmouths, which generally prefer a more diminutive size meal. These lures also vaguely resemble crayfish and are more effectively fished in rocky areas, along rocky bluffs and dropoffs,

An assortment of jigs for largemouth and small-mouth bass.

ledges, sunken islands, shoals, points, and the like. It should be ob-vious, then, why smallmouths are most susceptible to these lures.

To work these jigs, you must first let them settle to the bottom wherever you've cast. When fishing a moderately sloping shoreline or point, you should slowly pull the lure a little bit off the bottom, let it settle down while keeping in contact with the lure, take up the slack, and repeat this. When working a ledge or a sharply sloping shoreline, slowly pull the lure over the structure until it begins to fall, let it settle, and then repeat. Don't hop the jig up quickly here, as it will fall out and away from the bottom, most likely missing a good deal of the important terrain. A good technique with grubs is to make them jump quickly off the bottom rather than make short hops. You can also swim a grub on the edges of cover by reeling it slowly across the bottom and giving it occasional darting movements with manipulation of your rod tip. The majority of your strikes while jigging will come as the bait falls back down, so be alert for a strike then, and keep both a good feel and an eye on your line to detect this.

SPOONS

JIGGING SPOONS   There are a number of spoons that can be used in open, deep-water fishing situations for largemouth bass. Usually metal or lead, and slab-sided, they are white, yellow, silver, or gold in color. They vary from ¼-ounce to ½-ounce in size and basically are used only for vertical jigging in situations where bass may be schooled or suspended. One of the best examples of this type of lure is the Hopkins spoon, which was originally a saltwater striped bass and bluefish catcher before being used inland in smaller sizes for black bass and now fresh-water stripers.

In vertical jigging you may look for suspended bass near specific submerged structures, such as rock walls, roadbeds, islands or humps, and even timber. To use these jigs, lower them either to the bottom or a specific depth, jerk your rod up, and let the lure flutter down. Repeat this procedure for a while at the same depth. The lure should rise a foot to a foot-and-a-half with each upward motion, then be allowed to sink back slowly as you keep gentle contact with it. Most strikes come on the fall back.

WEEDLESS SPOONS   These lures are quite unlike jigging spoons and are used in a totally different manner. Weedless spoons are used for fishing in and around thick vegetation, such as lily pads, bulrushes, sawgrass, and milfoil. They are generally not 100 percent snag-free, but they will usually get through most vegetation with the aid of a wire hook guard. Examples of good lures in this category are the perennially favorite Johnson Silver Minnow and the Strike King Timber King. Others are the Heddon Moss Boss and Rebel Moss Master, both of which are about as weed-free as you can get. The Johnson Silver Minnow and lures like it are best used with ripple pork rind, soft plastic curl tail, or rubber-skirt trailer to spice up their swimming action, and some anglers like to garnish this with a pork chunk. Good

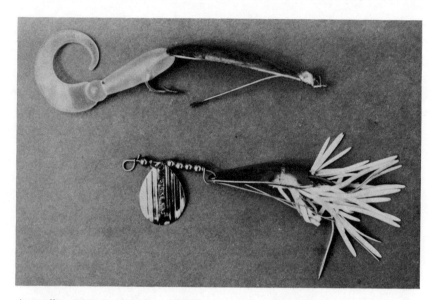

A weedless spoon (*top*) and weedless spoon with spinner (*bottom*) are good for working the salad.

colors are silver, gold, black, chartreuse, and frog-green, and best sizes are ¼-ounce and ⅜-ounce.

The basic technique for fishing a weedless spoon is to cast it far back into the vegetation and work the lure over and through it, allowing it to ease into and flutter down every little opening possible. In thick lily pad working, for example, you would cast back into the pads and slowly reel the lure up to an opening, let it slither off a pad into a pocket and ever-so-slowly bring it through that pocket, and then over or through more pads to the next pocket. Fishing grass and pads is discussed in Part III, but the important point to realize about weedless spoons is that you must fish them slowly and pick your way through the vegetation. Also, as with some other lures already described, you have to delay a moment in setting the hook when a fish strikes. Numerous missed strikes or "boils" by bass on these lures are due to the nature of the cover, so you must be sure a fish has your lure before you hook it.

A good innovation with this type of lure is the placement of a spinner blade in front. This is accomplished through a short wire shaft ahead of the basic lure, around which a small silver or gold blade revolves. This lure is typified by a long-time successful bass catcher, Hildebrandt's Snagless Sally; both Johnson and Strike King also have weedless spoons with in-line spinners ahead of them. This addition gives an added flash and attraction to this bait that will bring it to the attention of reluctant bass when the lure appears in holes or openings of thick grass or lily pad clusters.

SPINNERS

Spinners are not usually thought of as a bass lure by many anglers these days, particularly by those who chase largemouths exclusively or who never fish streams; however, spinners as a whole are one of the most popular lures in the world and in North America, and had more prominence on the bass scene in days of old. Fishermen currently use spinners to catch stream trout, pickerel, trout in lakes and ponds, panfish, muskies, walleyes, and smallmouth and largemouth bass. Plenty of other species—in fresh water and saltwater—also succumb to spinners every year under all kinds of circumstances. In this era of imitating prey, spinners continue to be effective even though they do not look anything like a fish. But in action, their wobbly flashy motion strongly suggests bait movement and offers an irresistible temptation to many fish. Though spinners are generally of minor value in largemouth bass fishing, they are quite valuable as stream smallmouth lures and are frequently successful for shallow-water, early-season smallmouth fishing in lakes.

Spinners come in many sizes and colors, and with various blade configurations. Spinners feature a freely rotating blade (or blades), mounted on a single, in-line shaft. Behind the blades are beads or bodies of lead or metal. Skirts of feather or hair, or plastic tubing, may be added to increase their appeal. They are available in weights from $1/32$-ounce to several ounces; with single, double, and treble hooks; with blade lengths from $1/2$-inch to several inches; and with assorted tail material. The $1/8$-ounce and $1/4$-ounce sizes are best for bass fishing.

The blade design controls the action and the angle of blade revolution. The lighter the blade, the faster the spin, which is why round, Colorado-bladed spinners are so popular. They are light, spin slowly, and work far from the shaft. The actual spinner blade is available in many colors, but the blade's color is not nearly as important as its visibility under fishing conditions. A good reflective quality is desired. Spinners also give some vibration when retrieved, a fact that is important to the fish and which probably accounts for the success of spinners when used at night and under very poor water-clarity conditions.

Factors of size and shape, such as blade design, weight, and surface area relative to weight, are related to how the lure is retrieved and how it casts. Like spoons, spinners are most commonly used with treble hooks, though single hooks are favored by many and are more

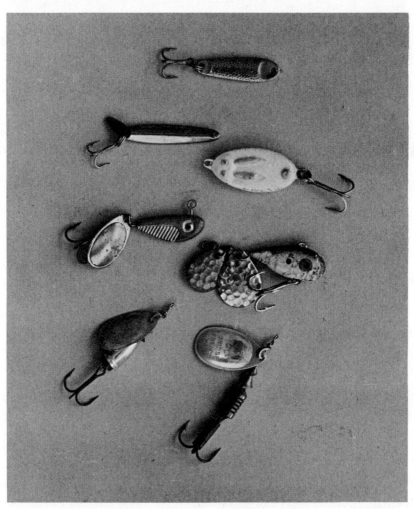

Jigging spoons (*top*), tailspinners (*middle*), and spinners (*bottom*).

desirable in some situations, particularly when single-hook-only lure use is required. A favorite single-blade spinner for bait fishermen is the so-called June bug spinner, which features a long shank hook and a single rotating blade, with beads along the shaft. Variations of this are popular for smallmouth bass fishing (and walleye fishing) on Lake Erie, using a Mepps Lusox spinner, an Earie Dearie, or similar spinners that are garnished with a live worm and drifted across rocky reefs.

In moving water, you generally don't fish a spinner downstream, but cast it upstream at a quartering angle (ten o'clock viewed from right, two o'clock viewed from left). The lure is tumbled by the swift water and also reeled forward at the same time. Fish them as slowly as you can under the circumstances; you should be able to feel the blade revolve with a sensitive rod. The depth of retrieve can be altered by raising or lowering the rod, or changing the speed of retrieval. Though spinners have received criticism for frequent hang ups, this is often a matter of misuse. In streams it is important to get the lure working the moment it hits the water. Hesitation often means hung spinners, particularly when casting across-stream in a fast flow.

One of the best times to fish spinners for smallmouths in lakes is just before spawning (provided the season is open, which it is not in some northern waters) and in the fall, when bass are just off rocky shorelines in 5 to 8 feet of water. You can cast parallel to the bank and allow the lure to sink to the bottom, then reel it in very slowly— just enough to rotate the blade and keep the lure swimming over the bottom. (This is also an effective technique for catching walleyes and northern pike, when they are found in the same lakes as small-mouths.) You also might be able to catch these bass at the same time by using jigs or crankbaits, but spinners may be as or more effective, owing to their slow retrieval rate and small, flashy appearance.

Spinners are best used with spinning tackle, though the larger sizes can be cast and fished adequately with bait-casting gear. For stream smallmouth fishing, though, light tackle, light line, and small spinners are the rule. Good spinners for bass include Sheldon's Mepps, the Blue Fox Vibrax, the Harrison-Hoge Panther Martin, Burke's Abu Reflex, the C. P. Swing, and Cordell's spinner.

TAILSPINNERS This type of lure is totally different from a spinner and perhaps doesn't even belong in this category. Nonetheless, I mention it here because the lure is known to all bass fishermen bythe designation of "tailspinner." A tailspinner is nothing more than a small lead-bodied lure with a treble hook under its belly and a revolving spinner blade at its tail. Typical lures of this nature are Mann's Little George, Cordell's Gay Blade, and Gapen's Slip (which performs the same functions but does not feature a spinner blade).

Tailspinners are at their best in schooling situations, when large-mouths are near the surface and feeding frenziedly. These lures are aerodynamically shaped and can be cast a country mile, particularly with spinning gear and light to medium line. They are then worked in a quick pump-and-go style, just under the surface. Tailspinners can also be fished deep, in vertical jigging style, for suspended bass in deep water near some particular structure, or they can be hopped off the bottom in fishing submerged islands, rocky points, and such. Effective colors are white, silver, and gray.

PLASTIC WORMS

Plastic worms are unquestionably *the* most productive bass lure. My guess is that more worms are sold each year than all other bass lures combined. No wonder they can claim productivity; there are so many in circulation they must catch fish.

What a worm represents is more of a mystery than why it is successful. Earthworms are not common to lakes and ponds, certainly not in significant numbers or at times other than after heavy rains or flooding. They could represent leeches, which are present in many bass waters, but these bloodsuckers are seldom more than 3 or 4 inches long and are usually smaller. Snakes do populate many areas, but I have worm-caught loads of bass in lakes where I have never seen a watersnake. And, though eels can be found seasonally in some lakes, this does not explain the appeal of worms at other times and in locales devoid of eels.

Not questionable, though, is why a worm catches bass. It looks like a fairly substantial morsel; it must have a realistic feel to a bass when it inhales it; it has good action and moves enticingly and rel-atively naturally through cover; and it is able to be worked effectively down at the level of the bass, which is to say, the bottom, and in its protected hideaways. Moreover, one of the pleasant effects of successful worm fishing is a sense of accomplishment. Some lures require little more than accurate casting and routine retrieval to be effective, particularly when bass are active. But a worm must be worked with your brain as well as your wrists; how you give it action, detect strikes, and react reflexively are major factors in its effectiveness.

Fishing a worm is more of a science than is the use of any other lure. We'll explore the many facets to its use and relate their importance to fishing conditions.

SHAPES, SIZES, AND STYLES

There are hard worms and soft worms, floaters and sinkers, straight tails and curl tails. They come in a whole spectrum of colors and may sport light tails, light heads, light bellies, stripes, and polka dots. They are made in small, medium, large, and huge sizes. Some are scented, some are oiled, some come pre-rigged. In short, there is a veritable smorgasbord of plastic worms.

The most important features of a worm, in descending order, are: softness, buoyancy, size, color, shape and tail design, and scent.

Softness is a very vital feature to any good worm. A soft worm feels more lifelike to a fish when he grabs it, and it aids the angler in setting the hook. Until the early 70s, before worm fishing became as ingrained as it now is, most worms were very tough. In fact, they weren't plastic; they were rubber. Today, all worms are made of plastic, and advances in the chemical composition of certain plasticizing agents allow for manufacturing control over the toughness of a worm.

A worm that is too soft is also fragile; it will tear when it comes into contact with objects and will barely hold a hook in it. A worm that is too hard feels unnatural and offers more resistance to hook point penetration, which at times is crucial in the timing of hook setting. Most worm manufacturers try to make worms that are tough enough to withstand reasonable use, but soft enough to aid fish catching. You can judge the comparative softness of different brand worms easily enough by squeezing them.

Another prominent feature of worms is their degree of buoyancy. The better worms have a light enough density to float on the surface of the water without a hook in them. Some will even float with a $1/0$ or $2/0$ hook in them, which is useful for fishing a completely unweighted worm on the surface over thick cover.

A worm that floats has a better appearance in the water because

Plastic worms are probably the single most effective bass lure of all and in the summer may account for more bass, including large bass, than all other lures combined. This photo of the author and a big bass that he caught in August on a plastic worm was a color cover of *Field & Stream*.

when it rests on the bottom, the tail section rides up. This accentuates both the behavior of the worm when it is moved and its stationary appearance. Some specialty worms, such as the very large and pre-rigged versions, understandably do not float and are not meant to float. But to judge the others, just drop an unweighted worm in the water, and you'll discover immediately if it floats.

The size of worm to use can vary with the fishing conditions and the size of bass that you expect to take in any particular water. Often there is a corollary between the size of the worm and the size of the bass that are caught, with small bass generally disdaining the largest worms. However, I have caught big bass on small worms and small bass on large worms, including some that were shorter than the length of the worm.

Your choice of worm size also depends on what you are seeking. If you are expressly interested in a trophy-sized lunker, then you should fish with nothing less than a 7-inch worm. In Florida, where 10-pound bass lurk in almost every body of water, an 8- to 12-inch worm is your best bet. In northern-tier states, where bass over 6 pounds are caught infrequently, a 7- to 8-inch worm is as large as you need.

Most bass fishing is done with 6-inch worms. All but the largest bass are good candidates for this bait, and in waters that are heavily fished, this size worm is relatively unobtrusive and unalarming to fish that are probably well conditioned to the presence of artificial baits.

In some locales, such as heavily fished, clear-water lakes, it is necessary to use 4- and 5-inch worms. On the other hand, if you have been catching small bass at a particular lake with a small worm, you might increase the size of your worm to appeal to larger fish.

Color is an important feature of worms as well. It is covered later in this chapter, since it is more appropriately discussed after we review the fundamental aspects of worms.

One feature of a plastic worm that has a debatable effect on success is its general appearance, in terms of shape and tail design. The basic body shape of most worms is round and moderately tapered from head to tail. Some worms are flat on one side, which I do not find as appealing as fully round models and which do not seem to have as good an action or object resistance.

Most worms have circularly molded indented impressions along their length, much like an earthworm, though a few are completely smooth. I don't believe it makes much difference to a bass or to the

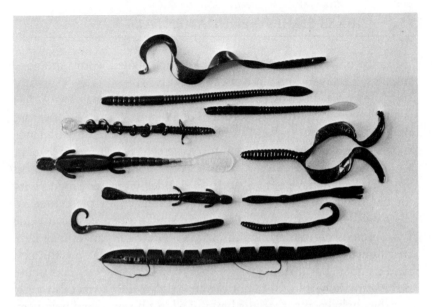

Plastic worms come in all sizes, shapes, and colors. This is a representative sampling of the products used for catching largemouth bass.

action of the worm whether it is smooth or slightly rippled, though there are few of the former available any longer. On the other hand, a few years ago some companies marketed worms with raised rings that trapped air between them. Air bubbles were released as the worm was worked. These worms did not appeal to bass any more than the standard versions and had a tendency to grab onto grass, pads, rocks, and limbs more so than other worms. This hampered their action and restricted their ability to freely move over objects. After being a fad, those products faded into oblivion.

Many worms come with straight tails, and an equal or greater number sport some type of curl tail. A few have beaver or paddle tails. The beaver-tailed models tend to be bulkier than other worms, and getting used to the different feel of fishing them takes a while. They produce more action and vibration than a straight-tailed worm, but I haven't had comparable success with them. They make a nice trailer behind a jig, however, especially when flipping.

Curl-tail worms include those with a simple J-bend at the end as well as those with opposite-curl features either at the end or two-thirds of the way through the body. I'm not convinced that they are more apropos than straight-tailed models. Their benefit, however, is that the curls produce a nice swimming action with only the slightest assistance on the part of the angler. Straight-tailed worms are good products, however, and I use them regularly.

It is worthwhile, then, to experiment with different designs, just as it is desirable to carry an assortment of different size and color worms in your tackle box. You will eventually develop the most confidence in one particular design and use it for 90 percent of your worm fishing.

Scent is also a matter of choice. Some worms are scented; most are just oiled. I have yet to notice a decidedly greater productivity out of any worm that came from the manufacturer prescented or lubricated, either with anise oil or some similar essence, or with one of the supposedly fish-attracting potions. These substances may help mask human odors that are imprinted on the soft plastic worms through hand contact, but it's hard to say that they of themselves contribute to the attraction of fish. I'm not convinced that they attract fish, only that they help keep potentially harmful odors off worms and help keep them soft. In my opinion, the most important factors for success are using a soft floating worm in the appropriate size and color and fishing it well.

RIGGING A WORM

The Texas rig has been the standard since suppliers stopped making worms out of hard rubber in preference for soft plastic. It can be used in almost any bass habitat, though it has limited value in really deep water and with heavy weights.

The Texas rig incorporates nothing more than a worm, slip sinker ($^1/_{16}$- to $^1/_2$-ounce), and hook ($^1/_0$ to $^6/_0$), with the hook point turned back and imbedded in the neck area of the worm so that it is essentially snag-free. To accomplish this, put a cone-shaped slip sinker onto your line, narrow end first, then tie the line to your hook. Take the point of the hook and imbed it into the center of the head of the worm up past the barb, then bring the point out the side of the worm. Pull the shank of the hook through this passage and rotate it 180 degrees. Bring the shank all the way out until the eye of the hook is secured in the worm head. Slide the point into the body of the worm so that it is firmly imbedded in it, yet has not pierced through it. Do not curl or rotate the worm but be sure that the hook and worm are aligned and that the worm is straight and not bunched up.

The slip sinker will slide freely on this rig, but there are times, such as when you are fishing in thick cover, when it is advantageous

Illustrated are the steps for rigging a plastic worm Texas style. The worm on the far right is improperly rigged because it is kinked, which leads to twisting.

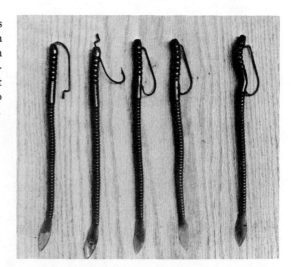

to prevent the sinker from sliding freely (and getting hung up). To do this, jam one end of a toothpick in the head of a sinker as far as it will go, and then break it off. Jam the other end into the back of the cone, and break it off.

The biggest problem experienced by users of the Texas rig is getting the worm curled or bunched up. This causes the worm to spin when it is retrieved, producing an unnatural, unappealing action and contributing to line twist.

The theory behind the unpegged Texas rig is that when a bass grabs the worm, he does not feel the hook and does not detect the weight, which slides up the line. Theoretically this gives the angler an extra moment in which to react and set the hook. When he does set the hook, it should freely pierce the worm, one of the reasons why the worm should be relatively soft.

The size of sinker used varies from $1/8$-ounce to $5/8$-ounce and depends on depth, wind, and the general activity of the fish. Hooks vary from $1/0$ to $6/0$, depending on the length of the worm. A general guideline for their use is: $1/0$ or $2/0$ with 4- to 6-inch worms; $3/0$ with 6-inchers; $4/0$ with 7-inchers, $5/0$ with 8-inchers; and $6/0$ with larger worms.

If the size of the hook seems large to you, rest assured that it isn't. Big, strong hooks will stand up better under the force of hook setting and the strain of very large bass. It doesn't require a big hook to land a bigmouth bass; after all, plenty of fish, including large trout and salmon, are routinely landed on extremely small hooks. But in

The worm at far right is properly rigged, Texas style, with sliding slip sinker. The middle worm illustrates a spawning rig, with hook midway along the worm and without a sinker. The worm at left is rigged Texas style, but a toothpick is jammed into the sinker at the top and at the bottom and broken off to peg the worm and prevent the sinker from sliding along the line.

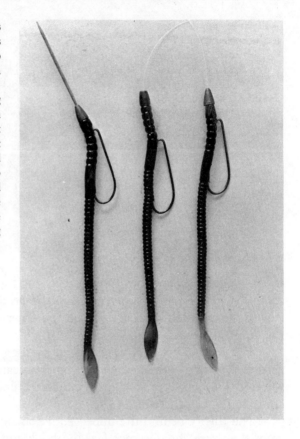

worm fishing, a large hook with a large bite is needed to keep the worm from balling up and impeding hooking. A bass usually has its mouth closed, with the worm inside, when you set the hook. The force of that setting brings the barb forward, pushing the head of the worm down the shank, where it balls up. If the hook is small, the worm balls up so much that it impedes the direction of the point into the fish's mouth, slowing the hook-penetrating process. As a result, the angler misses the fish and retrieves a fully balled-up worm, with a hook point that has barely pierced the body of the worm. Large hooks minimize this problem.

A number of worm hook styles are popular with fishermen. I particularly like a keel hook and have predominantly used an Eagle Claw 295 JBL style. Similar designs, with curved shafts that I also like and use are the Messler hook and the Colt .45, both of which are supposed to rotate to help improve hooking efficiency. Tru Turn hooks are similar and also come highly recommended. These are all good worm hooks, and you should try them and see if one works better for you than others. Another style, popular with some anglers, is the Childre Keeper hook, which has a small barbed shaft that you stick into the head of the worm and which attaches to the eye of the hook. I've had fair success with this but don't like the way it chews up worms or how easy it is for worms to slide down the shaft when they confront an obstruction.

The Texas rig may be the most popular plastic worm-rigging method, but it is not the only one. The Carolina rig, especially good for deep-water bottom fishing, features a floating worm that rises up unweighted. This rig sports a medium-weight sinker, followed by a barrel swivel, an 18- to 36-inch leader, and a hooked worm. The hook is generally no more than $1/0$ size to give greater buoyancy to the worm and is usually exposed, though it can be imbedded into the worm Texas-rig-style when there are obstructions present. The sinker,

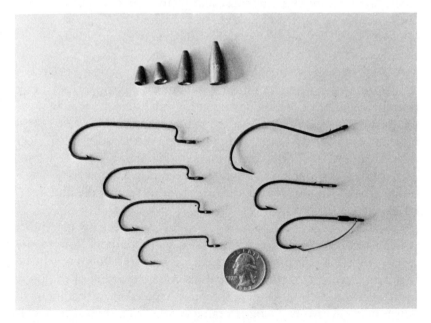

Shown are different sizes and styles of plastic worm hooks and an assortment of slip sinkers.

which can be barrel-, egg-, or cone-shaped, weighs ¾-ounce to 1 ounce and slides freely to the swivel, so a fish can take the worm and move off without feeling resistance. The length of line between barrel and worm is somewhat arbitrary; 18 to 24 inches is the norm, but some anglers like to go with as little as 8 inches for swimming the worm through weed beds.

Another variation on this rigging method that is useful for unobstructed open-water fishing is the so-called Do-Nothing rig. It features a heavy (½- to 1½-ounce) sliding slip sinker ahead of a barrel swivel, 3 to 5 feet of line between the swivel and worm, two panfish-size hooks, and a short straight worm. The hooks are rigged in tandem and are exposed; the worm is roughly 4 inches long. Some anglers use a small plastic bead between the sinker and swivel to prevent knot abrasion. A little tough to cast, this rig is fished in a slow, reel-cranking manner without any special rod or retrieval action. Despite its name, it is good enough to interest reluctant, bottom-dwelling bass.

The manner of hooking worms is often subject to experimentation. Setting the hook into the bony jaw of a bass is often hard, especially if the hook point must first pierce the worm body; that's one reason why super-soft worms are preferred by Texas-rig users. Hooking variations, therefore, are usually directed at improving hooking efficiency.

Some anglers put the hook through the head and leave the point exposed for fishing on the surface (without a weight), or they hook it in the collar or near the midsection for weightless, extremely slow, free-swimming simulation. A variation on the latter, with Texas-style hooking, is to thread the hook from the top of the worm down near the midsection, then bring the point out and imbed it into the worm. This is fished without a weight and has been called a spawning rig for bedding bass, which normally take a worm in the middle and swim off to remove it from the nest area.

Multiple hooking is another possibility, especially for short-striking fish. Small worms can be rigged with one hook toward the rear by using a long, thin sewing needle to bring the line through the body, then tying it to the hook and inserting the shank of the hook in the worm and either leaving the hook exposed or imbedding it to be weedless. A two-hook rig, in tandem and using snelled hooks, is a little tougher to execute, but many anglers prefer this. Such a rig enables anglers to catch bass that strike either the head or the tail of the worm.

Worms can also be attached to jig hooks; many anglers have summer-bass success with 4-inch worms behind small jigs, fished on light line.

THE IMPORTANCE OF SINKER SIZE

A plastic worm is meant to be fished slowly and hopped or crawled along in a natural, unalarming fashion. The slip sinker plays a vital role in the worm's performance, dependent, of course, on how the angler actually accomplishes his retrieve.

The lighter your sinker weight is, the more likely you are to have success. Sinker weight must be matched to the terrain and fishing conditions, but using the lightest sinker you can, and still correctly fish under those conditions, brings the best results.

The primary reason for this is that the heavier the sinker, the larger it is and the more detectable it may be to a bass. This is particularly true when fishing pressure is intense or when the bass are sluggish. Another important reason is that the worm is moved more naturally with a light sinker than with a heavy one, where its actions are more dramatic and pronounced. A worm with a light weight swims more convincingly than one with a heavy sinker. Light weights don't hang up as much as heavy ones, and they aid in detecting strikes. For these reasons, I prefer to use the lightest slip sinker possible for the conditions.

My most-used slip sinker size is $1/8$-ounce, with $3/16$-ounce running a close second. I will go down or up in size if necessary, usually to no more than $5/16$-ounce, unless flipping a worm, when I may go to a $1/2$-ounce sinker. Sometimes, strong winds or current make worm fishing very difficult, and you have to use a larger-than-customary weight to gain casting accuracy and to maintain a feel for the bottom. In shallow water you can usually get away with a light sinker, but as you fish deep, you may need to increase the weight of the sinker. You can cast small worms and light weights more effectively with spinning tackle than you can with bait-casting equipment. Also, the use of light line is conducive to light sinker use, since it does not offer as much resistance as the larger diameter, heavier line.

WHERE AND WHEN TO FISH A WORM

You can fish a plastic worm anywhere. *When* you fish it might vary. I generally don't use a worm much in the spring, when the water is cool and when bass are very energetic. In the spring, bass are usually very responsive to spinnerbaits and crankbaits, which can be worked quite fast. When you want to cover a lot of territory fairly rapidly, a worm is not the best bait to use. If, however, in doing this, you catch a couple of fish in one area, it may pay to switch to a worm in order to fish that area more thoroughly and more productively.

Summer is traditionally the best time to fish a worm, when the bass are well secured in or near some type of cover, and you need a worm to work that cover extensively. This is one of the true benefits of worm fishing: you cover the area well, and you fish it on the bottom, where the bass are. Though swimming a worm over cover may at times have merit, primarily you fish it on the bottom.

A plastic worm rigged in weedless fashion is at its best when used around typical bass-holding objects like stumps, fallen trees, grass, pads, hyacinths, hydrilla, docks, milfoil, and the like. When bass have left the shallows of the reservoirs for the breaklines, worms are very effective.

When making a cast to a particular object, such as a stump, for example, cast beyond and to one side of that stump (such as the shaded side) initially, working the worm slowly up alongside and then past the stump. Bait-casters should take care to cast beyond the area they want to fish a worm, as the worm does not drop straight downward, but usually falls on an angle toward the caster due to tension on the line. With a spinning reel, keep the bail open to allow the worm to fall relatively straight down from the place where it hits the water.

Sometimes a worm can be employed to catch a bass that has missed another lure. For example, when a bass strikes but does not get hooked on a spinnerbait, surface lure, or shallow-running plug, he may not hit that same lure again if you throw it back. But there is a good chance that he'll hit the less obtrusive worm if you cast it out in that area quickly afterward.

Bass are receptive to worms in relatively warm water. In warm water, worms are softer and feel more natural. In really cold water, I think plastic worms harden and thus are more quickly rejected by bass. In temperatures below 55 or so, worms don't seem to appeal to bass;

A tangle of brush and limbs is a good place to work a pegged plastic worm, slithering it over each limb and letting it fall into each cavity.

from 55 to the mid 60's, they have some appeal: from the mid 60's on up, they are in their best range. I have caught bass on worms in water temperature as low as 50 and as high as 92.

Worms work well at any given time of the day, particularly during the summer, and at night. I don't often use a worm early in the morning. It can be effective then, but at that time bass are more likely to be on the move and feeding, and other lures can be as or more effective before the sun rises and bright light forces the bass to seek deep shelter or cover.

RETRIEVAL TECHNIQUES

The two most difficult things for a beginning worm fisherman to master are how to retrieve the worm most effectively and how to detect strikes. Mastering hook setting rates a distant third in difficulty. These are also the three most basic components of worm fishing techniques.

It would be helpful to understand how a bass strikes a worm. I have read research by two different authorities who have observed bass behavior extensively, and both observed seemingly contrary methods. One said the worm was inhaled from the rear, the other from the front, head first. Perhaps it doesn't matter. What is known is that when a bass really wants that worm, he will suck in the whole thing.

The strike of a bass on a worm has often been related as feeling like a double tapping at the end of the line. This is so, and I believe that the first tap is what you detect when the bass makes the motion to inhale it, and the second is what you detect as it enters the fish's mouth. If you feel a third tap, the bass is probably expelling it.

Learning to detect a strike or rather to differentiate a strike from contact with underwater objects is the most difficult aspect of worm fishing. There is no shortcut to learning this. An ability to detect strikes and learn the "feel" of a worm comes through experience. The more you fish with a worm, the quicker you'll develop this feel.

One trick I've suggested to beginning worm fishermen is to practice in their backyard or in shallow water where they can see the worm. Drag it over rocks and logs and tree limbs. Crawl it on gravelly surfaces. Watch it work in a clear pool. Simulate fishing conditions.

Another key to detecting strikes is to watch your line. In the most radical instances, an eager bass may pick up a worm and immediately run with it, in which case your line noticeably moves off to the side or away. Sometimes you'll see the line move like this before you feel the strike. Usually, however, there is a barely perceptible flickering of the line, particularly the section nearest to the water, which is a result of the bass inhaling the worm and drawing it (and the line) toward him. In time, you'll come to see and feel the strike at the same instant.

To retrieve a plastic worm, you should begin with your rod butt and arms close to your body, with the rod held perpendicular to you and parallel to the water. Raise the rod from this position (we'll call it 9 o'clock) upward, extending it between a 45-degree and 60-degree angle, which would mean moving it from 9 o'clock to 10:30 or 11.

As you raise the rod, the worm is lifted up off the bottom and swims forward, falling to a new position. Make this motion slowly, so the worm does not hop too far off the bottom and swims slowly. When your rod reaches that upward position, drop it back to its original position while at the same time retrieving slack line. Keep your motions slow. When you encounter some resistance, as would happen when crawling it over a log or through a bush, first gently try to work the worm along; if this fails, try to hop the worm along with short flickers of the rod tip.

Sometimes the slip sinker gets hung up under rocks, and if you jiggle your line, the sinker falls back and becomes free. Other times, the sinker will fall over a limb and slide down the line while the worm stays back behind that limb. This makes detection and retrieval difficult and can be solved by pegging the slip sinker with a toothpick and breaking it off, thus preventing the sinker from sliding up the line. The sinker remains directly in front of the worm.

Pegging a worm is useful for fishing brushy areas, lily pads, hyacinths, moss, and grass as well as amidst stumps and trees. I seldom fish an unpegged worm in such areas and find that this technique makes retrieval and strike detection easier. It goes against the theory of having a freely sliding slip sinker so a fish can pick up the lure and run off with it without detecting the weight, but this is minimized by a quick hook-setting reaction, a sensitive rod, and a sensitive line to detect strikes more readily.

However you develop your style of retrieval, it is important to remember that the worm should be on the bottom, or right near it, at all times. Sometimes wind and current work to hamper bottom scratching, and you should be aware of this.

The time to set the hook on a bass is usually as soon as you can after detecting a strike. Remember that since the worm is rigged weedless with the hook imbedded in it, you can't simply rear back when you feel a strike, as you might when fishing a lure with exposed hooks.

Here's how to set the hook when using a plastic worm: as soon as you detect a strike, lower the rod tip and extend it out and point it toward the fish. (This momentarily gives the bass slack line and helps keep it from detecting the falsehood.) Quickly reel up the slack, and as the line draws tight, set the hook. Continue to reel in line to counteract the effect of stretch and to ensure that no slack is present.

It is important to retrieve a worm slowly, raising the rod from a 9 o'clock position up to about 11 o'clock, then lowering the rod and retrieving slack line. You can crawl the worm along, or slowly hop it with very short strokes.

When I set the hook, I bring the rod butt up into my chest, not high over my head, and I constantly maintain pressure on the fish. The whole maneuver is accomplished in an instant and appears to be one fluid motion.

Remember that removing slack line is critical, since your hook must penetrate not only the balled-up worm, but the cartilaginous mouth of the fish as well. Take notice of where your worm-caught bass are hooked, and you'll find that many are hooked in the upper part of the inside of the mouth, near the lips, and that many are hooked on the sides of the mouth, again near the lips. In some cases, where an eager bass has quickly swallowed the worm, he will be stomach-hooked. But most times the fish is hooked near the edge of the mouth, and this is ample evidence that you barely got him and that in another fraction of a second or with a little hesitation, tension on the line, or too much slack, you'd have missed the fish.

There are some variations to the standard worm fishing technique that I've detailed here, and you may want to try these if conditions warrant. One thing that is very difficult to do with a worm is to fish it properly in wind. If you have a specific place that you wish to fish and it is buffeted by wind, you may choose to anchor your boat in such a way that you can fish directly upwind or downwind of that spot. At other times you may elect to drift and fish.

A few places that I regularly fish are weedy bays with depths of 3 to 7 feet and grass that covers most of the bottom. There are bass throughout these areas, and when the wind is severe I position myself to drift with the wind over as much of this area as I can, while using my electric motor to either slow the drift speed or keep a desired position. Depending on the force of the wind, I'll cast with it or work against it. You can quickly run your batteries down by working constantly at a high speed and headed into the wind, but that may be necessary. If you have to drift, fishing in the direction the boat is headed is difficult, but may work because it allows you to fish a spot before the boat drifts over it. Drifting with the wind is a common smallmouth fishing technique on Lake Erie (though not with plastic worms); only there, where deeper water is often worked, it only makes sense to drift behind the boat. The key here, of course, is getting down to the bottom and staying there.

Fishing against the wind can almost be like trolling and can be effective, provided your boat is not moving too fast and that your sinker is heavy enough to keep the worm down. One trouble with slow-trolling a worm is that bass strike and reject it quickly, because the worm is always moving and there is little or no slack.

Occasionally, you may find it beneficial to swim the worm slowly just off the bottom. This works best in lily pads, in moderately thin grassy areas, and in similar spots. Though I am not much for fishing an unweighted worm, some anglers do so in thick vegetation. It is difficult to cast an unweighted worm with most bait-casting equipment (though it can be done with the magnetic-spool models), though not too difficult with spinning tackle.

One trick I employ when I am doing a lot of worm fishing is to cut down on the length of my retrieve. Many times I do not fish a worm all the way back to the boat. Rather, I work it through and along all the necessary cover, and if nothing is present between that cover and the boat, I'll reel the worm right up and make another cast, since I know there is little likelihood of a bass being away from the cover in open water.

COLORS

I am not inclined to recommend one color very strongly over another, though I will note that dark-colored worms are far more popular and successful than light ones. I am personally partial to black and purple worms, though I carry and use red, blue, grape, and motor oil as well, plus the two-toned shad colors. Water color and visibility play a part in worm-color determination, and at times one color outperforms another because it stands out better in that type of water. At other times, several colors are equally productive. More important than color is having confidence in your lure, fishing in the right places, and utilizing proper fishing techniques.

Some worms are better known by flavors than by colors. There is nothing to the flavor gimmick other than the fact that the impregnated smells help mask human odors, which may be imparted to worms when touched. Most worms are coated or otherwise treated with anise oil or some similar licorice-like smelling agent that keeps them moist and soft. Salt worms, which are impregnated with salt (put the worm in your mouth and you can taste it) are popular in some areas and are thought to induce bass to retain them longer than they might otherwise, but I think this advantage is merely psychological.

I do a fair amount of fishing with firetail worms and recommend them, especially when fishing success is slow. Firetail worms are merely those with a light color blended into the tail section. I particularly like black, grape, blue, and purple worms with either a light pink or lime green tail. Unfortunately, firetail worms also attract the attention of other species, including pickerel, bluegill, and rock bass, even more so than one-color worms. These fish can be a nuisance at times when you're using these color combinations.

TACKLE

My recommendation for worm fishing is to use a good quality rod that has an even taper, with a strong butt and backbone and a "fast" or relatively limber tip. The disadvantage of a rod with a stiff tip is that it casts a worm poorly and is not sensitive enough for detecting strikes. Having a special "worm" rod to fish plastic worms is not necessary. A graphite or boron rod is strong and sensitive and is an advantage to a fisherman skilled at detecting pickups. I like to use a 6-foot bait-casting rod, but the popular choice is a 5 ½-footer.

Spinning rods are not used as much for worm fishing as are bait-casting and spin-casting rods, but they are perfectly acceptable if you have a fairly stiff rod that allows you to detect even faint strikes and

Dark-colored worms are most popular with fishermen, plus rods that have backbone for hook setting but a "fast" or relatively limber tip for sensitivity.

to set the hook. Most people who fish worms on spinning rods use a rod that is too limber, and they are unable to set the hook.

There are no special criteria for reels where worm fishing is concerned. Line is also a matter of personal preference, but in plastic worm fishing the elements of stretch, abrasion resistance, shock resistance for hook setting, and basic strength are all factors.

In cover-free, open-water fishing, you may use between 8- and 12-pound test line for worm fishing, the lighter in particular for clear waters and wary fish. For fishing heavier cover and especially where big bass are found, heavier line is needed. I see no reason to use more than 20-pound-test line for bass fishing, no matter how tough the conditions, though some who flip in heavy cover and who seek big bass use 25- and 30-pound line. My thinking is that good line and proper drag settings are as important as basic breaking strength. Using more than 20-pound-test line on a freshwater fish like a bass (most of which are small, anyway) is like using rope, and, in my opinion, it takes away from the sport. I use 12-pound-test line for 95 percent of my worm fishing (and those who know very little about bass fishing think that's pretty heavy), and I go up to 17 or 20 under the worst conditions.

Because setting the hook with a plastic worm is such a punishing experience and because worms are fished in all manner of cover, the line you use should be high quality and particularly resistant to abrasion and able to withstand sudden shock-loading. I've found the latest cofilament line to be particularly beneficial in worm fishing because of its low stretch and high sensitivity values, which aid strike detection and hook setting.

I am not too concerned about line visibility for worm fishing. I use only fluorescent line, which makes line watching and strike detection a bit easier because of its high visibility. I once experimented with fluorescent yellow line and didn't have any trouble catching bass on worms while using it; however, I prefer to fish with clear, light blue, or light green lines because I use the same tackle for other types of fishing and in instances where having a less visible line is an advantage.

The only other point about worm tackle that needs to be stressed is that of keeping your hooks sharp. You can get by with hooks fresh out of the box, but it pays to hone them, giving them a razor-sharp edge. A sharp hook gets through the balled-up worm fast and enhances your fish-hooking ability.

Although it seems intricate, worm fishing is really not too difficult. It does take time, practice, and patience to become successful. Beginning worm fishermen often become discouraged by failure to receive strikes, by missing a fish, or by setting the hook into objects that they thought were fish but weren't. Don't be discouraged. Even experienced worm anglers miss strikes or set the hook falsely. Beginners also have a tendency to give up on the worm, or fall back on previously successful techniques without using the worm enough. I suggest that learners go out bass fishing a few times with nothing but worms. That is the way I finally became satisfied with my abilities with a worm. Don't bring any other lures or bait, just a supply of different color worms, hooks, and sinkers. By forcing yourself to stick with this, you'll get the experience—and the fish.

LIVE BAIT

Live bait can be very effective in the hands of a good fisherman, but the key to success with it is principally the same as for success with any type of artificial lure: knowing the habits of the fish and selecting the right habitat in which to work your lure or bait. Live bait can be fished anywhere that lures can, including the perimeters of and underneath dense matted vegetation.

The kinds of live bait that catch bass are the same that would be found naturally in their environment, as well as some that are not. This includes worms, minnows, crayfish, large shiners (and occasionally shad or alewives), frogs, salamanders, leeches, waterdogs, and a few other creatures. Sometimes it pays to select your bait in accordance with the type of food most prominent in the particular habitat of the fish, such as minnows or crayfish. At other times the best bait may be creatures that are not abundant in that water or that do not constitute a major part of the bass' diet, such as earthworms and frogs. Determination of what to use depends on the availability of bait, its importance in the diet of bass, and especially where and how it is to be fished.

The tackle preference for live bait fishing usually runs to spinning and spin-casting equipment with the small- to medium-sized bait offerings, since it is easier to cast and position them with this gear. Bait-casting tackle can be used with larger, heavier bait. A lot of bank fishermen and some boat anglers still use cane poles. Live bait is fished with a variety of hooks from No. 6 for smaller bait to ⁵/₀ for the largest; although single hooks are usually used, sometimes treble hooks are preferred, particularly in open water. Split shot is needed with small bait to keep it at the proper level, and unless you are live-lining the bait, some type of float or bobber is necessary. Largemouth bass are not too shy about snatching bait, so line size usually isn't too critical as long as it isn't too heavy in relatively clear water. Smallmouths, however, are more finicky and are often found in much clearer, deeper water than largemouths, making lighter line for bait fishing a little more appropriate.

Smallmouths are considerably different in respect to live bait fishing than largemouths. They have a decided preference for crayfish, in any area where they are found. I witnessed a most phenomenal exhibition of live crayfish success for smallmouths a few years ago on Lake Ontario with charter boat Captain Charlie DeNoto, who has perfected a technique he calls "center-line drifting." He fishes near-shore areas that have a softball-size cobblestone bottom, in depths that range from 20 to 30 feet. He baits his hooks with softshell crayfish (locally called crabs), which ring a smallmouth's dinner bell like no other form of food.

The key to his technique, besides using softshells and knowing the prime locales, is drifting a 40- to 50-pound weight along the bottom. DeNoto uses an iron or steel block that doesn't snag up, and secures it via heavy rope to the gunwale amidships, allowing the boat to drift sideways with the wind. The anchor drags bottom fairly close to the boat, stirring up rocks and leaving disturbed crayfish in its wake. A chum line of sorts is created, and DeNoto claims that smallmouths are not only attracted to the free chow but even follow the dragging anchor. He applies a No. 1 or 2 split shot about 18 inches above a No. 4 hook, uses light line, and drifts the softshell in the trail of the anchor.

Four of us fished DeNoto-style one morning, and in 4½ hours we used ten dozen softshells; *every* crayfish meant that a smallmouth was caught or stole the bait. There were several times when everyone

Centerline drifting with live bait produced this Lake Ontario smallmouth.

had a fish on the line, and there were also moments when a bass was hooked every time a crayfish was put out. It was remarkable small-mouth action, and since every fish was taken on 4- or 6-pound-test line, it was outstanding entertainment.

Just as remarkable as the fishing was the fact that we could not duplicate the results using any other method. DeNoto and I both caught bass on hair or grub jigs worked behind the anchor, but were outfished by the bait anglers. He says the success rate while using jigs is about a quarter to a third of the rate with softshells. He also says that hardshelled crayfish are quickly rejected in preference to softshells and that worms are half as effective and minnows even less so.

There's no doubt that live crayfish make excellent smallmouth bait. Softshells are hard to obtain, however, and in most areas fishermen use hardshells of varying sizes. When still-fishing, leave your bait open, hold the line in your free hand, and periodically give a light tug to the line to keep the crayfish from burrowing under rocks. In drift fishing, close the bail and keep the rod tip high to detect a strike.

Peculiarities pop up everywhere, of course. For instance, live leeches are a popular smallmouth (and walleye) bait in the spring in the upper Midwest, but I don't find fishermen using them extensively anywhere else. I regularly hear about fishermen who have tremendous success in Ontario lakes with live frogs, though I have no experience with such fishing.

An old axiom says that big bait catch big bass—that certainly has validity for largemouths. In Florida, it's common to fish with 9- to 12-inch shiners for trophy-size (over 10 pounds) bass. Remember that a largemouth has an enormous mouth, capable of consuming fairly large prey. If you are using small minnows for panfish, you may catch small bass, but you'll probably have to move up in size to appeal to the heartier appetite of bigger bass. Smallmouths don't often succumb to very large baits; small or medium-size bait are likely to work with all sizes of smallmouth bass.

Live bait must act naturally to get the attention of bass. A crayfish that rolls instead of crawls or a minnow that doesn't swim lessens your chance of success. You can hook live bait in a variety of ways. Nightcrawlers and large angleworms can be hooked singly through the collar, or through the collar, midsection, and tail. Smaller worms can be hooked together to form a squirming, tail-hanging gob. Minnows are best hooked through the back just in front of the dorsal fin, as are large shiners, though trolled baitfish are sometimes hooked through the lip. Frogs are best hooked in the forward, meaty part of the leg, salamanders in the forward part of the tail behind the rear legs, and crayfish through the forward part of the tail. For leech fishing, use a small hook (about size 6) through the head and tail sections. Crickets, too, have been known to catch an occasional bass, though usually while employed for panfish.

Bait must be lively to be productive. Bass aren't interested in dull or dead bait, so keep your bait as fresh and lively as possible. Change baits whenever the one in use seems to be losing its vitality. If you can keep your bait cool and well aerated, it will stay in good condition.

Crayfish are one of the premier live baits for bass.

When fishing with a float or bobber, it's easy to tell when a fish is mouthing your live offering. But that isn't the case when live-lining (letting bait run freely). Then, it is often difficult to know if a fish has picked up your offering or if your bait is hung on brush, rock, or grass. Keep a light hold on your line to detect gentle strikes, and when in doubt, pull ever-so-softly on the line. If it moves off vigorously, you've got a fish.

Determining what depth to fish is an important aspect of bass angling, too, but gettting your bait to that depth is just as critical. Most of the time you need to fish bait on or near the bottom, whether you are fishing a lake, pond, or river. You must be able to detect, by feel, when the bait has reached bottom. When still-fishing with a float or bobber and a sinker, you must allow for the distance between sinker and hooked bait when setting your rig out; the bait should be slightly above, not resting on, the bottom.

Don't be in a rush to set the hook when live bait fishing. A bass needs time to consume his quarry. Often he takes the bait cross-wise in his mouth and swims a short distance away with it before swallowing it. By waiting a short time and by not putting tension on the line during this period, you stand a better chance of hooking the fish.

Live bait anglers should realize that bass with hooks in them may survive. If you've hooked a bass that you can't keep (perhaps because the season isn't open or the fish is under the minimum size limit) or that you don't want to keep, and you leave the hook in the fish, there is a good chance that the bass will survive. Clip the line off above the hook. The hook will deteriorate within a few weeks if it is not stainless steel or cadmium-tin. If it is not bleeding profusely and if you have been careful to handle it as little as possible, the fish should survive.

9

BOATS

I've had the opportunity to fish from almost every type of craft imaginable, excepting sailboats and racers, and have owned seven different bass boats, plus other craft, in the past twelve years, so I feel qualified to expound on the merits of various boats for bass fishing.

There is really no such thing as a "bass boat." What we call a bass boat is simply a good fishing boat that is particularly useful where a lot of casting is required and where presentation and boat positioning are especially important. I frequently use my so-called bass boat for muskie, pike, walleye, trout, salmon, shad, pickerel, panfish, and striped bass fishing, and it is very functional for all these activities.

Almost any boat can be used for bass fishing. Your fishing conditions, interests, and budget should mandate the type of boat you use. The most popular and useful boats for bass fishing are the fiberglass models, the aluminum vee-bottom and flat-bottom rowboats, and canoes. At one time, I owned one of each of these and used them all in different ways.

I use a fiberglass or aluminum "bass" boat almost everywhere I can because they are well-outfitted, comfortable vessels with lots of room. A vee-hulled, fiberglass boat is especially suitable for large lakes, ponds, and rivers, where rough water dictates sturdy craft and where a big boat with a lot of engine muscle can help cover a lot of distance quickly. Aluminum bass boats can also be used under these conditions, but the flat-bottomed models do not handle rough water well. Some of these boats, pounded by hard running through rough water, wind up with loose rivets, so bear this in mind. The vee-hulled aluminum boats take rough water a little better, but still not as well as a fiberglass boat. They sit up higher in the water, and because they are lighter,

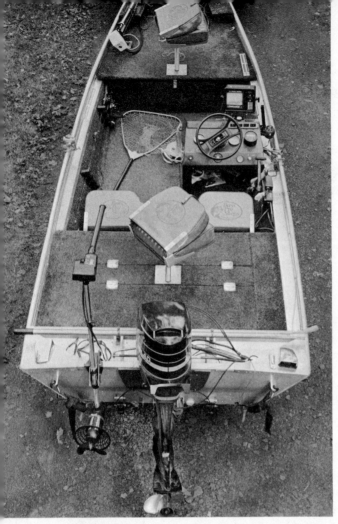

You can fish for bass out of many different types of craft, depending on your needs, interests, and budget. Johnboats (shown top right and in many other photos in this book) are excellent for relatively calm, small waters and streams. Fully equipped aluminum bass boats, such as this 16-footer (top left), are economical and suitable for most waters that don't get too rough. Fiberglass bass boats (bottom left) are very popular and suitable for large and small waters. Small boats can be taken from a bare hull and made into a fishing machine (bottom right) that allows you to pursue bass.

they are more susceptible to being blown around in the wind, making electric motor control difficult. I use these large boats any place I can. With my four-wheel-drive Jeep, I can put them in most places, even where access is meager.

A smaller aluminum or flat-bottom boat is very functional for bass fishing on small lakes, rivers, and ponds, where it is not necessary to cover a lot of territory and where adverse conditions are seldom present. I use a johnboat on small private water where either motors are not allowed or the sight of big boats might create ill feelings with local residents. Small aluminum vee-bottomed boats can be used in the same manner, except that they are less suitable for small river fishing than a johnboat and more suitable to moderate-size lakes, owing to their deeper draft design (meaning that they draw more water, which makes them less suitable for shallow, rocky water, such as rivers, but more suitable to small lakes).

I seldom use canoes for bass fishing. They are too unsteady and too difficult to position. They are influenced by current, the force of wind, or even the working of some lures. If you fish by yourself in a canoe and toss out a deep-diving crankbait, watch what happens: it pulls the canoe in the direction you cast. Canoes become moderately useful for bass fishing only when you put an electric motor on them for positioning.

Whatever boat you have or that interests you, think of it as a fishing tool. It has to get you where the fish are. It must weather the necessary water conditions for a range of places and it must be reasonably comfortable to allow you to put in long hours. It must be versatile to handle a variety of angling pursuits. It must be designed or modified to allow you to fight and land fish (especially big bass). And it should have readily available fishing and boating accessories.

In considering a boat for bass fishing, ask yourself: Where will I be using my boat? What type of boat matches my needs and the place(s) in which I expect to use it? What does my bank account allow?

BUYING CONSIDERATIONS

Most bass boats look pretty much alike to the average angler or would-be boat buyer. One may be lighter than another. One may be faster. One is made of some new material. And so forth. They all feature many options and sport assorted claims. Most folks are at a loss to evaluate the products they see, particularly if they have never before owned a fishing or pleasure boat.

There are some guidelines to help you. Some may seem rudimentary, and some apply to all boats, but they are all important considerations, especially when you realize that "bass boats" have only been around for about 15 years and that bass boat buyers and users are generally a new, young generation of boaters and fishermen.

As you might expect, safety is the most important consideration in buying a bass boat, especially since many of the latest high-powered craft can fly in excess of 60 (even 70+) miles per hour. I want to digress here and note that speed is important primarily to tournament fishermen and race jockeys, and that I have no use for such boat operation. Nonetheless, even moderately powered bass boats will go 40 mph, and that's pretty fast. I suggest you disregard speed capabilities and concentrate on other features of a boat in making your evaluations.

Since 1978, all new boats have been required to possess upright flotation, meaning the boat will stay afloat if capsized or swamped. Most boats manufactured prior to '78 did not have this feature (although some, including Rangers, did), and you should bear this in mind if you are thinking of acquiring a used boat.

One indication of dubious flotation characteristics in a boat can be noted by checking to see if foam flotation has been injected into and fills all nonusable space except the sump area. Not injecting foam into all areas saves money and lowers the cost of the boat, but possibly at the expense of safety. Ask the sales representative if a recognized, independent testing agency has verified the manufacturer's flotation claims.

To check construction, look for reinforcement (with marine-grade plywood) of critical areas where weight will be applied, such as the bow, the gunwales (on fiberglass boats), compartment and livewell lids, the electric motor support, and the console. In some cases you cannot see these, but you can knock on different places and determine any change by the resulting sound.

Look for areas that wobble or buckle when pressure is applied; this is an indication of the thickness of material used. Also, look for good gauge wiring; often marine dealers have to replace the electric motor wiring in bass boats to accommodate the high-powered electrics. And check for workmanship by examining the finish, smoothness, and general appearance of decks, gunwale, and sides. Also observe the type of screws, locks, and fasteners to see if they are made of good quality material to withstand abuse.

Some hidden construction features you should investigate in fiberglass boats include the use of fiberglass to reinforce areas and to bind joints. In some boats you can see the woven cloth strands. They should be on the bottom and continue up the sides; some boats only have it on the bottom. Also, sometimes the storage compartments are not laminated to the hull. You can take a pocket knife and push the blade under to determine this. Look to see if the upper corners of the livewells are completely sealed; if not, water will splash in the corners when the boat is running and the livewell is full, and water will get into the adjacent dry storage compartments.

Check to see if the storage areas are really going to be dry; if there is a pedestal seat base above a storage area, that compartment will be wet. See if water can seep into a storage area when the bilge or sump is full (if it isn't sealed off, you'll get water into it). Look for proper ventilation in the gas and battery compartment, and make sure that batteries and gas cans or tanks are (or can be) firmly secured so they don't bounce around when riding on the water or when being trailered.

Every prospective buyer should look for a solid one-year warranty from the manufacturer. Also, look for a detailed owner's manual; many do not have these, yet this is an indication that the manufacturer stands behind his product and that he wants the consumer to obtain maximum use and satisfaction from it.

It's a good idea to look for brand-name manufacturers in bass boats. Once scores of companies built bass boats, but a poor economy a few years back put many of these (including many lesser quality manufacturers) out of business. Ranger, one of the first in the bass boat business, may currently be the largest and makes excellent fishing boats. I've owned six Rangers and can attest to their quality. Also, Skeeter and Hydra-Sports bass boats are of good repute.

Conferring with owners of the brand or model of bass boat that you are considering purchasing is a good idea. You can get a perspective on the good and bad points of the boat (motor and trailer, too) and the dealer who sells and services it. In the past, many dealers who sold runabouts and ski boats were not familiar enough with the needs of fishermen to adequately rig boats for serious angling. This brought problems in installation of electric motors, electronics equipment, propellers, and the like. Today, most of the larger dealers and suppliers of the better-known products are pretty savvy when it comes to installation and rigging, and there are not as many problems as there used to be. However, you should thoroughly discusss installation and placement details with a dealer before any work is done to be sure you get things installed where and how you want them.

Much of the dissatisfaction with certain bass boats stems from anglers themselves as a result of their not knowing what they really needed or wanted when they first purchased and equipped their boat. So it's important to determine what your *real* needs and requirements are. Many bass boat owners started small and worked their way up to more elaborate, more sophisticated, and more costly equipment, when they needed the latter all along. If they had correctly judged their wants and needs in the first place, they would have saved money and time by buying properly, initially. The converse is also true. Many bass fishermen have far more boat and engine than is practical for their needs. Therefore, honestly evaluate your situation before you buy.

More can be said about boat care, trailering, and so forth. I'm not going to detail that here, however, as information about boat care, maintenance, trailering, and the like is readily available from other sources, including books, manufacturer's literature, etc. For information on boating-related equipment for bass fishermen, however, see the next chapter.

10

ACCESSORIES

The bass fisherman, like every other angler, is a gadget-conscious and accessory-conscious consumer. He thinks he must have one of every item that is manufactured and that is claimed to make his fishing or boating activities easier.

The range of accessories available to anglers today is greater than it has been at any other time. Many of the accessories do aid better fishing and better boating; however, all you basically need to catch bass is a hook or lure, some kind of line, something to put that line on, and a place to fish. On the other hand, you can become as elaborately equipped as you like. I'm going to detail a lot of accessories here, a few of which have already been mentioned in other chapters, however briefly.

Many of the accessories mentioned here I personally have and use, but I don't recommend that you purchase any of them in order to become a successful bass angler. Some accessories are more useful than others. My intention here is to point out what is available and give my thoughts on how it can be an aid to bass fishing.

One of the most important and useful items for any boating bass fisherman is an *electric motor*. An electric motor, called a "trolling" motor by most of the angling fraternity, allows you to maneuver and position your boat in the proper angle for casting and to make the type of presentation that is required for the fishing circumstances, all as quietly and carefully as possible. Electric motors essentially take the place of oars and sculling paddles, but are quieter and interfere less with fishing activities.

All electric motors are battery powered. Some run off a single 12-volt battery; others run off 24 volts, requiring two 12-volt batteries;

still others have the capability of running off either one or two 12-volt batteries. Not all electric motors are alike. Some produce considerably more thrust than others, meaning they are more powerful. There is sustained thrust and initial thrust, the former being the power generated while underway and the latter being the initial startup power. Initial thrust is greater than sustained thrust. The amount of energy (designated as amperes, or amps) consumed per hour by electric motors varies, and this figure, when known, will tell you how many hours of continuous use you can get out of a battery at varied speeds.

This gets pretty technical, so the best thing to do is check the specifications of these products and determine how much power you need and for how long in normal fishing circumstances. Generally, the heavier your boat and boat load, the more thrust you need. Another factor to consider is how much fishing you do in areas of substantial current or wind—both drain the reserves of a battery quicker than calm-condition operation.

On most fiberglass and on many aluminum bass boats, the electric motor is mounted permanently on the bow, with the bracket support installed on the starboard to put a little weight on that side and counterbalance the console and driver weight on the port side. On small boats such as rowboats and johnboats, electric motors can be mounted on the front or back. I have used them both ways and recommend bow mounting. Boats move with greater ease when pulled rather than pushed; plus, with bow mounting you can see where you are headed and know when to avoid objects.

Small boats usually only require a single 12-volt electric motor, though you can employ more than one motor at a time. Some anglers who fish reservoirs where no outboards are allowed rig up two or three electrics in unison. I once had two small electrics of relatively low thrust on a johnboat, and they worked marvelously (they were hooked to two batteries). Small-boat electrics feature a turnscrew-clamp transom mount, which makes them adjustable and removable. With some, you can leave the bracket installed and remove the rest of the motor. Some of these models can also fit on the front of a small boat, but it pays to check your boat out first and then see if the motor you may buy will fit the design of your bow.

Permanent-mount electrics are used on conventional bass boats and large craft and can be operated manually or remotely, depending upon the unit. Remote units are operated via a foot-control pedal that is on the bow deck. Manual models do not have a foot control pedal or cable running to the motor and are steered by foot or by hand. I am currently using the Motor-Guide Magnum Perfector on my bass boat. It has a remote on-off/speed control bracket that sits on the deck; you can start and stop the engine with your foot by stepping on the switch, but you have to manually steer the motor. This system is good for those, like me, who prefer to stand up and be right on top of the motor, controlling it carefully at slow speeds.

Many anglers prefer the manual type of electric and use their feet, hands, and arms to control positioning, because in the past they've experienced cable breakage with the remote-operated units. Cables are much better these days, however, and aren't the problem they used to be. Where you may have problems is in the foot control unit itself. The cable on a Minn-Kota 565 electric that I used to have broke several times where it connected to the pedal, and I spent precious fishing time taking it apart and fixing it.

One feature to look for in an electric motor is a breakaway bracket, where the shaft of the motor can slip back if it collides with an

This particular bow-mounted electric motor has a remote on/off switch and is manually steered with the help of an extension handle. It also has a tilting feature that allows the shaft to swing back if an object is struck. Note the bow-mounted depthfinder and tiedown rein.

immovable object. This will save you from having bent shafts, damaged lower units, and extraordinary stress on the mounting bracket. Motor Guides have these, as did the Silvertrol (no longer made) electrics.

Another important feature is a good armature and easy-release/take-up system for getting into and out of the water with minimum effort. Different motors vary greatly in this regard.

Silence is another important feature. Some electrics are considerably noisier than others. Two Mercury Thruster Plus electrics that I had were extremely noisy. Silvertrols were on the noisy side, too. The Minn-Kota was fairly quiet, as was a Johnson electric I once had, but these and the Mercury were also pretty weak. If electric motors are new to you, shop around and compare features as well as price. Operate a few different models to compare all of their performance aspects.

You should also look into the new battery-energy-saving and variable-speed control systems recently marketed by Minn Kota and Motor Guide. The Minn Kota model works on any manual- or remote-operation electric motor. These devices are economical, provide a wide range of power, and extend battery life.

Electric motors cannot be used without a *battery*. This is a seemingly obvious fact, yet one that many prospective first-time electric motor buyers overlook. You don't just buy an electric motor. You also need one or more batteries, plus a means of recharging the battery. An electric motor does not automatically recharge the power source, and in the course of a full day's fishing, you will probably drain the energy of a battery considerably; therefore, it is necessary to frequently recharge it with a *battery charger*.

The best products for powering electric motors are deep-cycle batteries. Deep-cycle batteries are often called marine batteries, but not all "marine batteries" are deep-cycled, so you should check to be sure that the batteries you obtain for electric motor use are deep-cycle products. These are constructed with special plates that allow them to be regularly drawn down and recharged; standard batteries are not meant to do this and do not have nearly the life of deep-cycle batteries when used for electric motor operation. I've used Gould Action Pak and Sears Marine Diehard deep-cycle batteries with good results for many years. For maximum performance, you are best off with the highest-amperage batteries that you think you can use (I've used 80 amps, but prefer 105), and a high-amp-capacity battery charger (at least 10 amps; more if you'll need to fully recharge dead batteries in several hours). For starting the outboard motor, you don't need a deep-cycle battery. A conventional automotive battery will do, but opt for a non-deep-cycle marine battery. I've had good use out of Gould Super Crank, Sears Diehard, and Interstate products.

Remember that the batteries are the lifeline to your boat's operation. Clean the terminals and connections regularly for good contact. Check the fluid level and adjust as necessary. Signs of a weak battery include low electric motor propulsion, weak depthfinder or graph recorder signals, low temperature gauge readings, low tachometer and speedometer readings, and weak fuel gauge indications.

Batteries on a full charge last longer, so keep your charge level high at all times, even through the winter. If you are charging directly to a battery, you can use the clamp-type terminal connectors, being sure to place the positive and negative wires properly and keeping the battery compartment ventilated. If your boat is wired for automatic charging, you need a three-prong adaptor that is attached to your charger's lead wires and that merely needs to be plugged into the boat receptacle with the system switched into the charging mode.

Electric motor batteries need regular recharging, which can be done using a charger with wires that clamp directly to the battery terminals or by an automatic charging system wired into the boat.

Another valuable accessory is a *depthfinder*. As you have learned in other sections of this book, one of the basic keys to catching bass is locating them and fishing appropriate lures at the proper depths. If you are not familiar with the particular lake that you are fishing, chances are that without a depthfinder, you will be largely unaware of the depths of the various areas in which you are fishing. This does not mean that you can't or won't catch bass. It does mean, however, that at times you may not be aware of certain characteristics of that body of water which might greatly aid in your fish-finding and fish-catching efforts.

For example, suppose you're fishing a shoreline where it is obviously shallow close to shore and where there is a gradual dropoff. As you move down that shore, suddenly it is not so shallow any more against the bank, and you're not certain how deep it is. You could be 50 feet from shore and be in only 10 feet of water. You could also be in 60 feet of water. If you were tossing a crankbait into shore that ran about 7 feet deep and the shoreline had a gradual slope as described, your lure would not be in a bass zone throughout its retrieval because

A flasher-style depthfinder, mounted on the bow for instant reference and reading on a scale from 0 to 30 feet, is extremely useful to bass anglers.

you could not hope to get the lure down to where fish may be along this steep drop. Furthermore, you wouldn't know that dropoff existed unless you were using some type of sinking lure that you kept bouncing off the bottom, or unless you had a weight attached to line, which you periodically dropped overboard to pinpoint depth at various areas.

A depthfinder is not necessarily used to find fish. It is used to determine depth, to ascertain the characteristics of the bottom and anything between the bottom and the surface, and to guide you in learning the contours of any body of water so that you may best locate the type of habitat that is suitable to the fish you seek.

The simplest type of electronic depthfinder is the portable unit commonly referrred to as a "fish locator." Powered by two 6-volt lantern batteries, this instrument flashes the depth readings on a calibrated scale. These work well on small boats used for bass fishing. You can shoot through the hull (not carpeted, though; place transducer flush to flat bare metal area), use a bracketed or suction cup transom mount, or use an electric motor mount, depending on what is most convenient and what type of transducer is employed.

A permanent bow-mounted depthfinder is particularly helpful for bass fishermen, who spend much of their fishing time in the bow, casting and running the electric motor that takes them along likely fishing areas. You can get by with a bass boat that is equipped with only a console-mounted depthfinder but you have to look constantly back at it to check the depth. You can flip the unit over to read it upside down from the front, or you can place it on an adjustable swivel to turn it toward the bow. Neither situation is as desirable as having a unit on the bow right in front of you. Ideally, the transducer for this unit should be located on the bottom of your electric motor to give you readings directly below the front of the boat. If you can't afford to buy two depthfinders, you should consider buying two transducers—one for transom or through-hull use for the console and one for electric motor mounting for bow use. You'll need two brackets or swivel bases for the depthfinder, too, to switch the unit back and forth as necessary.

Conventional bass boat operators like to have another sonar instrument in or on top of the console for use while underway with the outboard motor. These include flasher and digital-style depthfinders, liquid crystal display recorders, and graph paper recorders. I'll elaborate on the functions, usefulness, and operation of these for

On conventional bass boats, the console is the operations center. Note how graph, LCR, in-dash flashers, temperature gauge, compass, and other devices are positioned in these Bass Tracker (right) and Ranger (above) boats belonging to the author.

bass fishing, as well as the all-important matter of transducer installation, in the following chapter.

One item used frequently in conjunction with sonar equipment
is *marker buoys*. Many fishermen find these helpful. When you come
upon a place that you would like to relocate, to fish more thoroughly,
or to boat over and examine more closely, you can pinpoint it by
using one or more marker buoys. You can make your own marker
buoys but good products in bright colors are available from Lowrance
and Humminbird. These are nothing more than plastic floats and
heavy weights, with strong line attached to those weights. It is best to
get a flat type of marker rather than the round barbell version because
the former is more resistant to the effects of current, wind, and waves
than the latter. Round markers can get blown quite a distance from
the specific site they were supposed to identify; such drifting does not
happen with the square marker buoys. Incidentally, you might want
to put your name on these buoys with a dark indelible marking pen;
I've had curious pleasure boaters and sailors pick up mine.

An accessory that I don't like to be without, but with which
many bass anglers are not equipped, is some type of *temperature gauge*.
I have a surface temperature gauge on my boat, and I also carry a
hand-held thermometer that I keep in a tackle box and carry with me
everywhere. The boat gauge only reads surface temperature, but it is
most valuable, particularly in the spring and fall, when water temperature conditions are changing on a sometimes daily basis, and where
surface water temperature, particularly when it is warming up, is a
strong indication of where you might expect to find fish and under
what conditions the fish might become more active. The other temperature gauge that I use is simply a pool thermometer. It's a sturdy,
reliable thermometer that I purchased from a pool equipment supplier
for less than ten bucks. It's hardy enough to be bounced around in
my boat or tackle box, and I use it to check the surface temperature
of the water or the temperature at any particular depth (by tying it
to the line and dropping it down).

In addition to a temperature gauge, there are other water-reading
devices available to anglers. An *oxygen meter* is a device that analyzes
the oxygen content of the water. I have never used this type of
instrument nor am I convinced there is much reason to do so; therefore, I cannot offer any constructive advice regarding it. There was a
move toward using this device a few years ago and toward explaining

the importance of fishing in high oxygen-content water for bass. This was espoused by some writers and paid professional fishermen as an important tool, but hardly anyone is using them today.

Similarly, the *pH meter* has gone through its up-down-up periods. The first of these devices, one of which I used, had an extremely delicate probe and needed tender loving care to operate properly. Mine never worked right. The pH meters from Lakes Illustrated of recent years, however, have been improved dramatically, and no longer pose such problems. A pH meter measures the relative alkalinity or acidity of the water. Highly acidic water (which has low range values) is not conducive to most fish life and aquatic organisms (which we've learned in recent years from the acid precipitation dilemma). The theory is that if you find the water that has the optimum pH for bass, then you will not waste your time by fishing in the locales that must necessarily be devoid of bass. I'm not convinced that pH meters are vital to bass fishing success all or part of the time and today don't use one. In time, as acid precipitation becomes an ever greater threat to our environment, some bass waters may become acidified, and the use of this device may be worthwhile. Those who have the money to spend on this and the time to experiment with it may find it to be a small help in the overall bass-catching puzzle, but don't look for it to be a miracle-worker.

Currently looming as an interesting product for bass fishermen is a device that helps you *select lure colors* by analyzing the clarity of the water. Called the Color-C-Lector and manufactured by Lake Systems Division, this 9-volt battery-operated handheld meter sports a probe that is lowered into the water and which correlates the most visible colors to the clarity of the water. This device differentiates between muddy, stained, and clear water, and registers the colors (and shades) that are most visible to fish under those conditions.

I've had several months' experience with this device as of this writing, and I'm sure that it will be a hot item in the future. Many manufacturers are coordinating their lure colors to the spectrum that was devised for this Color-C-Lector, and tackle boxes separating lure colors and holding this unit are available.

This may have even more application in deep-water trout and salmon trolling than it does for bass fishing. I've used it in both applications, and my experiences have been interesting. The colors it has suggested using have often been those that make a lot of sense (red, for instance, in super-clear water), while others are those that you cannot quite duplicate with lures in your box. I've been using colors nearest to the one suggested if I don't have the exact color.

There's no doubt that the Color-C-Lector gets you thinking more about the color of lure you choose and why you choose it. To make your use of this instrument more meaningful, follow these guidelines:

1. Determine which scale to read by lowering the probe into the water. If you can't see it beyond 2 feet, the water is muddy; if you can't see it beyond 4 feet the water is stained; if you can see it beyond 4 feet the water is clear.

2. If you don't have the nonfluorescent color lure that the needle points to, use a color next to it; that will still be in the range of high visibility.

3. When the needle rests in the middle of a fluorescent band, that fluorescent color is dominant and the nonfluorescent colors below it are secondary.

4. Mixing colors of high visibility can be very beneficial. If you have stained water and the needle points to the middle of chartreuse, try using a lure that combines purple (the secondary nonfluorescent color) with chartreuse.

5. When taking a reading on the bottom, don't let the probe keel over. The sensor is on top of the probe; lift the probe so that just the tip touches bottom.

Essentially this device tells you what colors are most readily observable under the conditions to a fish. It's important to realize that readings (and colors) will be different in shade than in sunlight and when natural conditions change, so you need to check the C-Lector periodically. Bass are not motivated to strike prey by color alone, so don't use this device as the last word in lure color selection, though it can help keep you aware of water clarity conditions and possible colors to try.

An important accessory for those who get back into densely vegetated areas is an electric motor *propeller guard*. The Weedguard (Weed Master) is a plastic basket-like covering for the electric motor propeller that protects it and keeps weeds from snarling in the prop. Most electric motors manufactured since 1984, however, possess a weedless-style propeller that cuts through all but the thickest vege-

This battery-operated device measures what colors are most visible to fish based on the clarity of the water and light conditions, and may point you toward using lure colors that will improve your success.

tation. You can install these propellers on most old electrics, too.

A great accessory for anglers who fish shallow rivers or venture into uncertain waters is an outboard prop guard. OMC makes them for their 9.9 and 15 hp motors. The guard protects the lower skeg as well as the propeller. In appropriate situations, the motor is operated in the tilted shallow-water-drive position so it will kick up when it hits an object. Some anglers have devised homemade guards. I cut the fork from a pitchfork and clamped it around the lower unit of a 7.5 hp motor; this worked well as a guard but the engine performance was impaired during top-speed operation.

Getting your boat safely to the fishing grounds and out of the water is a critical aspect of boat ownership. You should check the condition of your *winch* and rope periodically. I've had to replace most of my polypropylene winch ropes with steel cable, because the rope broke or frayed badly after a full season. A few winches were replaced with heavier duty models when the originals broke or the teeth were stripped. Fishermen unable to hand-winch large, heavy boats onto a trailer may need to employ a steel-cabled electric winch. Use a safety chain to restrain the boat in case the cable snaps while the boat is towed at high speeds, and use some good transom tiedowns.

(Incidentally, if you have the time and ability, you can take an ordinary boat and build wooden platforms, install a rod storage box, add pedestal seats and a bow-mounted remote-control electric motor, create a console, or install a livewell. Enclosed and lockable storage compartments are fairly easy to add to many boats. Don't put high seats on top of bench seats in small boats, as this makes the boat tipsy. Be careful about removing bench seats to build platforms, as you need side support and under-the-seat flotation.)

A lot of fishermen like to have some type of *anchor-pulley system*, and you can select from manual and electric models, which may be mounted fore or aft. Anchoring from the bow is preferable under all but still-water situations and especially under windy or strong current conditions. You should remember this if you are considering a permanent anchor mount.

Livewells are important to have if you want or need to keep fish alive during the fishing day or to keep large bait alive. They are not practical in many small boats, however, because they take up a lot of room and, when full of water and fish, add a lot of weight. You can utilize a 48-quart cooler with an aeration pump as a livewell if you'd prefer, as long as you have a battery to power the pump.

Bass fishermen who cast all day often stand up or find standard pedestal seats too low for them. Long *pedestal seats* are available from several sources (including Nautical Interiors and Bass Pro Shops), as are bicycle-seat-type butt rests so that you can lean against these while standing up to take some pressure off your legs and back and be a little more comfortable.

Aluminum fishing boats should have some type of floor covering. Outdoor *carpeting* is best, particularly if you can get the fabrics used by boat manufacturers. These not only stand up better to weather but allow easy hook removal. Carpeting deadens the "tinny" boat noises as well as the inevitable fish-alarming sounds made by anglers. In lieu of carpeting in both flat-bottomed and semi-vee-hulled aluminum boats, however, wood floors can be installed.

Fishermen who don't want to put lures away while fishing or who want certain lures readily available yet free from entanglement in their boat should consider installing one or more *lure holders*. The Weed Master Snatch Box is a good one, with a lid that locks lures in place, plus a storage area inside. Berkley's Outdoorsman lure holder is a simple strip of foam and plastic. Yet another model is the Action lure holder from Nautical Interiors.

Not too many bass boaters have *rod holders* on their boats. I do because I use my boat for many other types of fishing, some of which require rod holders. A rod holder can even be functional for live bait bass angling. There is a variety of rod holders on the market, most of which are generally functional. I highly recommend the Down-East rod holder, which is made of corrosion-resistant metal. There are models that mount on the gunwale or handrail, as well as clamp-on models for aluminum boats.

Another accessory that can be useful is a *push pole*. I carry a Johnny Reb collapsible model with Y-shaped feet, which can be stored in the rod box or mounted along the gunwale or stern for easy access. It sometimes comes in handy for those exasperating moments when you get stuck on a sand bar or stump and can't rock the boat free. It is also useful at times for fishing in thick vegetation where electric motor propellers get hopelessly bogged down.

Several other boating accessories should be carried in your boat, including spare fuses, engine oil, electrical tape, needle-nosed pliers, WD-40, and required boating paraphernalia. Having a Type III (keeps an adult floating upright with head out of the water) *life preserver* for each person onboard is extremely important. The vest-like models are best and should always be worn when the boat is moving at fast speeds.

Because safety is a top concern for every boater, a feature that all bass boats should have is an *ignition safety cutoff switch*. Also known as a kill switch, this device shuts the motor off if the operator is thrown out of the boat or away from the steering wheel. This can happen when you are traveling fast and strike an unseen obstacle that violently jerks the steering wheel out of your hand and tosses you out of the boat. It can also happen on that rare occasion when the steering wheel cable breaks while the boat is under fast speed. A neighbor of mine was killed on a local lake last year while testing his boat. The steering cable snapped, he was thrown from the boat and run over by it; he didn't have a kill switch. In these instances, the torque of the engine will send the boat into a sharp right turn. It will go in circles, shortly coming back and running over the person who was thrown out of the boat. Generally, this occurs on lakes where there are a lot of obstruc-

An ignition safety cutoff switch is attached to a lifejacket or clothes via a lanyard and automatically shuts the engine off if the operator is thrown away from the throttle.

tions, such as submerged timber, and where fast boat travel is common. Accidents like this can be prevented with a kill switch, which is fastened by a lanyard to your life vest, jacket, or pants belt loop, and which stops the engine when the cord is pulled.

Turning our attention away from boats, one accessory item that I don't like to be caught without is *rain gear*. I believe in bringing rain gear with me at all times to avoid becoming soaked, cold, and uncomfortable. When you're dry and warm, it's easier to concentrate on fishing. Buy the best rain gear that you can afford and that is large enough to fit over your normal clothing. I like two-piece rain suits rather than ponchos. I use a chest-high suspender-type of pants, which keeps dripping water out of the pants when I bend, and a jacket with Velcro wrist enclosures, a large drawstring hood, and double-sealed front closure.

Clothing for bass fishermen differs little from that for other outdoor activities. Wear what is comfortable and be prepared for cool weather. It's colder on the water than on land; it's colder when it's windy; and it's colder when it's windy and rainy. Use the layered-garment approach. Wear a jacket, a sweater over a shirt, and so on. You can always take off some clothing items, but if you don't have them and you're cold, there is little you can do. I've worn longjohns while bass fishing on many occasions and usually try to be prepared for the worst in spring, fall, and late winter. At times, such as when covering long distances in a fast open bass boat in cold weather, I wear a snowmobile suit (make sure your life vest will fit over the snowmobile suit, heavy jacket, or rain gear). Ski goggles help your eyes and visibility at that time, too.

Obviously, you need to have some kind of *tackle box* for your lures. The type of tackle box for your needs depends on how much fishing you do, how many lures you have, and what kind and size they are. If you only wade or shore-fish, you don't need one of the mammoth tackle boxes that holds everything except a 12-volt battery. On the other hand, if you have a broad tackle inventory (as most avid bass anglers do), then it won't do to have a small box.

There are a number of good quality tackle boxes on the market today. Their most important features are: compartments that are large enough to fit the average size plug into; storage area for jars of pork baits; racks for spinnerbait storage; tray composition that prohibits chemical interaction between plastic products (these used to be called worm-proof; most good boxes today withstand such problems); and sturdy handles, latches, and the like.

I used to like a fairly large tackle box that would hold an enormous

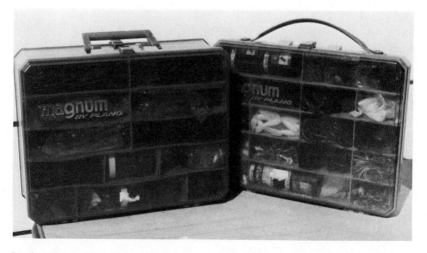

Single- and double-sided tackle boxes with adjustable compartments and see-through lids store a lot of items, keep lures well segregated, and are portable.

amount of equipment, but I have gradually gotten away from that for traveling convenience and better bait arrangement by going to the use of one- and two-sided flat Plano Magnum boxes with adjustable compartments and amber see-through lids. These are not only functional and easily accessible, but they hold more lures than you might think and are great for traveling when space is a premium (including airline travel). I keep a two-sided box full of plastic worms, hooks, and sinkers; a two-sided box full of plugs and spinnerbaits; and a one-sided box for jigs, pork baits, and related tackle.

There are many other accessory items, that I haven't touched on, here. These include such serviceable items as a stringer, fillet knife, hook sharpener, ruler, net, scale, compass, spotlight, fluorescent night light, and sunglasses. Most of these, and some other products I haven't mentioned, have some merit for bass fishing (and other types of fishing, too). What you should have depends to a large extent on what you can afford, what your fishing activities and circumstances are, and just how well you can get along with (or without) any particular item that might (or might not) make your angling life a little bit easier.

PART III

SKILLS, SAVVY, AND TECHNIQUES

11

PRACTICAL BOAT
AND SONAR USE

How you fish for bass is as important as when, where, and with what you fish. Included in this category of "how" is what you fish from and how you fish from it. Very often the most crucial factor in success or lack of it will be the way you use your boat and boating equipment to cope with the fishing conditions.

What kind of boat you have is not as important as whether it suits your fishing needs and whether you can use it effectively to meet the conditions. Some boats, understandably, are better designed for serving multiple needs. Although I discussed the features of boats and boating equipment in the previous section, I did not cover the fundamental aspects of their application. Understanding some of these aspects may make you a more successful bass angler.

BOAT POSITIONING AND LURE PRESENTATION

One element of successful bass fishing is boat positioning—keeping your boat in the proper position for the time required to fish an area thoroughly. The most regularly fished area of a lake is the shoreline. When there are a lot of objects such as fallen trees, stumps, and rock piles, it is advantageous to position your boat 30 to 40 feet from shore and cast perpendicular to it. However, sharply sloping shorelines are better fished by casting forward over the bow of the boat, when the boat is positioned close to and parallel to the shore.

There are times when you need to position your boat close to the bank and work parallel to it, and other times, such as when there is a lot of cover present between your boat and the bank, when it is best to stay out from shore and cast perpendicular to it. Boat positioning greatly aids bass fishing efforts.

If two anglers are in the boat, both can be casting forward, and their lures will be in the fish-catching zone a greater portion of the time than otherwise. Once fish are located, it might pay to back out from shore and thoroughly work the area from all angles, especially by fishing meticulously with a plastic worm or jig.

Another time when you should get close to shore is when there is thick brush and grass at the edge, and an immediate dropoff of three or more feet is present. Jigs can be worked vertically in this brush as you move along, or floating/diving plugs can be "jiggered" zigzag fashion in, out, and around the shoreline with a long rod. This is very effective and something that cannot be accomplished adequately by perpendicular positioning.

Keeping your boat close to shore and fishing outward is another tactic. Stump beds or rock piles or other objects that are far enough away from shore that they might be under the boat can usually be worked if you are positioned between them and the shore, especially if the water beyond them—away from shore—increases in depth. Deep-diving lures would probably be best here. Even if you do not see or locate underwater objects away from shore, it pays to cast deep-diving plugs out the other side of the boat occasionally.

If there are specific objects along the shore that can be seen and cast to, then fishing at right angles from a boat moving forward and parallel to the shore is acceptable. However, where the shoreline does not have such obvious structure, but drops off at a good rate, plastic worms can be "trolled" by working the boat in close and drifting or maneuvering with an electric motor to keep the worm bouncing along at the 10- to 15-foot zone. Rowboat anglers can do this quite well by drifting and occasionally working one of the oars to maintain position.

Working a visible straight line of grass beds is another example of how it is worthwhile to fish close and parallel. However, when the grass is punctuated by cuts, channels, pockets, and the like, it is advisable to keep the boat out a bit and cast in, concentrating on the irregular features and the holes in the interior of the grass patches.

Points, always a good fishing location, should be fished more thoroughly than other areas. Three basic boat positions—on either side of the point and straight out from it—should be taken, and a range of casts should be made from each location. If you have a depthfinder, you should watch it as you work around the point; concentrate on the break area where the point tapers off to deep water.

A depthfinder is a substantial aid to all bass fishermen anywhere on a lake, regardless of the type of boat used. In most cases, proper boat positioning over areas likely to hold bass but not visible to fishermen can only be accomplished through the use of a depthfinder. By watching this instrument and following the contours of a promising spot (such as a mound, rock pile, deep grass bed, etc.), you can keep your boat on the fringe of the likely area and your lures in the fish-catching zone.

Working not-so-readily identifiable bass habitat is where many fishermen fail to operate to maximum potential. Take, for example, a situation where a deep weedline exists off a bar or point adjacent to deep water. Some anglers, intent on the immediate shoreline, may not discover the grass at all or not work far enough out from shore. Others will only give this spot a few quick casts enroute to other places. Since bass will hang in the deep weedline and at the end of points where they break to deep water, a prime location combining both of these attributes should be thoroughly worked, approached from all angles, and covered with a range of lures. Keep watching the depthfinder while maneuvering the boat back and forth and in and out of such an area.

There are many fish-holding locales that should be fished thoroughly and for which various boat positions are advantageous. These include pilings, docks, fallen trees, bushes, and so forth. The important point always to consider is how to present a lure most effectively and how to position yourself for thorough fishing.

The one natural condition that thwarts the best positioning and presentation efforts of many bass fishermen is a strong wind. Casting

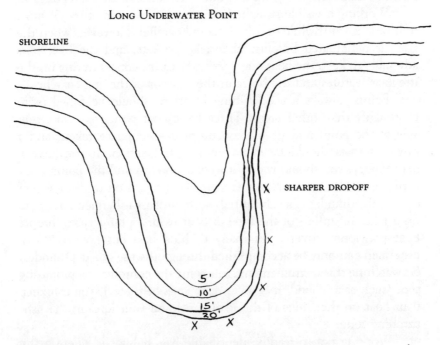

This representation of an underwater point shows why it is necessary to approach such a location from several directions and to cast in many places. Points often taper off abruptly. Breaklines and sharper dropoffs are the best locations when bass are deep, and they can be pinpointed with a depthfinder.

is very difficult (particularly into the wind), strike detection and lure working are impaired, and effective boat positioning is seldom possible. Sometimes you can use the wind to carry you past the areas to be fished. More often you have to run the boat into the wind to maximize the time you spend in desirable areas.

SITTING VS. STANDING

There is no doubt in my mind that you can see fish and fishing holes better, can set the hook better, can play a fish better, and can cast better while standing then you can while sitting down. The time-honored safety practice has been not to stand up in small boats, and I admit that this can be risky in cluttered boats, unstable craft, and in areas where a boat may collide with obstructions in the water. But in many boats, and especially the modern breed of bass boat, you can stand up reasonably comfortably and safely.

Because of their raised pedestal seats, sitting in most bass boats is almost akin to standing anyway. Sitting anglers, however, have a tendency to become complacent and lose their attention and concentration. Also, fishing from a low point, as when seated in a john-boat, rowboat, or aluminum vee-bottom, can be a hindrance when working some lures, where it is necessary to keep your rod nearly horizontal with the surface and where, while working the lure, you may bang the side of the boat. The higher elevation afforded by standing or sitting in a raised seat gives you more freedom of movement and better vision.

I stand up while bass fishing in nearly every craft but canoes. I even stand up in small johnboats provided my companion is not constantly fidgeting around and is careful about his movements. I don't, however, stand while river fishing. In small boats I usually position my legs on either side of the seat and may lean a knee against the transom or gunwale for stability and support. I place a lot of importance on visibility, better fishing positions, and general aware-ness, and I think standing up provides this. Standing, of course, is not for everybody, nor is it practical in many types of craft or in very rough water. Use your best judgment, and if you do stand up in dubious circumstances, wear a life preserver.

The higher elevation afforded by standing in a stable boat is a benefit to nearly all aspects of bass fishing.

FISHING FROM THE BACK OF THE BOAT

Most of the articles I've seen on bass fishing and bass boating and that give constructive fishing advice seem to imply that every bass angler is necessarily up in the bow of the boat. Obviously, however, many bass anglers fish from the back of the boat. I've got a few comments that might be helpful to anyone who has occasion to be behind another angler.

In my experience and observation, a fair to moderately skilled bass angler, fishing behind a good angler, will do poorer during the course of a day than his companion. Yet a good angler fishing behind a fair or moderately skilled angler, will do as well as, if not better than, his companion. A good angler who fishes at a moderate pace will generally get first crack at most of the better bass cover. I believe the first cast to a likely bass hole is the most important one. That's why I emphasize the importance of accurate casting and good presentation. A good caster can conceivably hit every prime spot along a particular section of cover or shoreline. Where you are positioned in the boat is less important than your skill in casting and presentation.

There are two attitudes to consider in this subject—that of the boat operator and that of his guest. If the operator, or forward angler, is incapable of precision boat handling and positioning, he can unintentionally make fishing more difficult for his companion. If his attitude is not one of fairness and fellowship, then he is likely to try to hog every fish-catching opportunity. When I have friends in the boat with me, I try to take into consideration their general fishing skill and their casting abilities. It's not necessary to tell good anglers what to do. When we work a shoreline, for instance, I'll cast to every other good spot, leaving my friend good fishing opportunities, which he recognizes. With some anglers, I may deliberately not cast first to a good spot, but point it out to them and give them first opportunity. If you're friends and you're interested in a good time, fun fishing, and success for both of you, I think this is the way things should be.

If you're the guy in the back and you're not satisfied with the opportunities you're getting, say so. Simply ask to have the boat positioned the way you need it (e.g., closer or further from shore). I've been in this situation many times, and sometimes it's not a bad idea to give the guy in the bow a subtle message by casting up ahead of him or by going right up to the bow and casting shoulder-to-shoulder. Sometimes, in fact, such as when flipping in close quarters, it is best for both anglers to be in the bow, or the stern angler will never get a chance at the right spots. In my opinion, two anglers in a boat should be working with, not against, each other. In addition to getting equal opportunities, they can be using different tactics and different lures, trying to figure out where the fish are and what they'll take. This complementary approach can mean better fishing for both anglers.

This back-of-the-boat angler took a nice bass from that blowdown in the background. Stern anglers can have good success if they are attentive to what they are doing and if the better opportunities are not hoarded by the bow angler. Fishing savvy, good casting skills, and a considerate angling partner are the keys.

In the end, this matter boils down to individual attitudes, skills, and a sense of fairness. Many times I'll invite someone to fish in the bow of my bass boat when conditions warrant it. Or I'll work the boat so they can have the proper angle for a cast at a particular spot. I expect they'd do the same for me. If someone wants to hog everything or complain all the time, then I won't fish with him.

One last important point, regarding shoreline fishing from the back of the boat, concerns how you work a shoreline, or weedline edge, or in general follow a straight path along some type of cover. The angler in the back should not fish parallel to or behind a moving boat. Let's say you're working parallel to the bank, bow on the left and stern on the right. You're in the stern and the boat is moving slowly down the shore in the direction the bow is facing. As you face the shore, you have a casting range that arcs roughly 180 degrees. Your best fishing chances, best presentation efforts, and best lure working occur in the first half of that arc. A lure cast up ahead will cover more ground than will one cast perpendicular to the boat or behind an imaginary perpendicular line. It will work more naturally; a lure cast behind a moving boat leans sideways and runs erratically. And you will generally cast it more precisely. This fact applies equally to anglers fishing in the front or the back, but for some reason back-of-the-boat anglers seem to ignore it more.

SONAR USE

Graph recorders and depthfinders are some of the best tools for anglers who fish from a boat. An outgrowth of sonar (short for sound navigation and ranging) applied by the military in World Wars I and II, today's electronic depth-finding and fish-locating equipment is helping anglers enjoy their sport and become more learned and proficient. The use of these devices has become so widespread in the last two decades that finding a creditable guide who does not possess at least one of these instruments is difficult. They would no sooner think of fishing without such tools than of driving an auto at night without headlights.

Why? Because sportfishing sonar is the bass angler's magic underwater eyes. With it, he can find concentrations of migratory, suspended, schooling, and nomadic fish, plus he can locate unseen habitats that may be attractive to bass. With sportfishing sonar devices, he can become accurately acquainted with the beneath-the-surface environment of a body of water in significantly less time than without it. In addition to these benefits, the use of sportfishing sonar allows an angler to navigate better, more safely, and quicker than he might otherwise.

Locating fish with sonar is no guarantee that they are the kind of fish you seek (on Lake Erie they could be sheepshead when you think they are bass; in a southern impoundment they could be channel catfish when you think they are stripers) or that you'll be able to catch them. There still is no substitute for angling savvy, skillful presentation, and knowledge of fish behavior and habits. This notwithstanding, there are many times when even the most skillful anglers can find bass but not catch them. And many fishermen are only moderately successful anglers despite their collection of electronic wizardry. What you have may be important, but less so than what you do with it.

How sonar instruments do what they do is immaterial to most fishermen. A few technical points, however, will help you understand and use these machines to the fullest.

Sound travels at 4800 feet per second through the water, which is four times faster than it travels through air. Sportfishing sonar instruments issue signals (pulses) at extremely swift rates, in some cases as many as 20 per second. The greater the distance between transducer (the object that sends the pulse out and receives them) and bottom, the longer it takes for the pulses to bounce off it (or other objects between it and the bottom, including fish) and return. Nonetheless, the speed of operation is amazingly swift.

Transducers send out their pulses in a three-dimensional cone-shaped wave, not in a narrow band. Cone angles range from 8 (most narrow) to 50 degrees (extremely wide). The diameter of these cones influences how much detail will be seen. An 8-degree cone has a 2-foot diameter when the water is 15 feet deep, 4-foot at 30, and so forth. A 20-degree cone, which is more or less standard in freshwater, has a 6-foot diameter in 15 feet of water, and 12-foot at 30. A 45-degree cone has a 13.5-foot diameter at 15 feet, 27-foot at 30.

I've had transducers that ranged from the least to the greatest cone angles on different boats I've owned and have found that the narrowest cones are most useful in extremely deep water, such as 150 feet or more; the widest cones enable you to see a lot more of what is beneath you and are especially useful for downrigger trolling and fishing directly below the boat, and work only at slow boat speeds; the medium-range cones are less specialized, have all-around functionality, and are best used in less than 100 feet of water. For bass anglers, the most functional cone angle is in the 16 to 22 degree range, since most of their sonar usage is relegated to fairly shallow water.

Many first-time users of sonar and those who have switched from one brand to another have difficulty getting their machines to provide optimum results, especially graph recorders. Most problems result from improper transducer installation and operator misuse.

Misuse usually centers around the control functions, particularly sensitivity and suppression. The sensitivity control (also called gain) is akin to volume. Many inexperienced sonar users keep this turned down too low, either because they are experiencing electrical interference or because they think a low setting is adequate. When the sensitivity is too low, sonar may fail to register key bait, fish, or bottom readings. When extremely low, only an indistinct bottom may be registered. On some units, a high sensitivity setting prompts a lot of false signals and distorted images, primarily due to the inadequacies of the machine.

On a flasher-style depthfinder, the sensitivity should first be turned up just enough to indicate bottom depth. Then it should be increased till a second reading, double the depth of the bottom, is recorded. This is an echo signal, resulting from the sonar pulse going down to the bottom, bouncing back to the surface of the water, returning to the bottom, and bouncing back again. Adjust the sensitivity control so the echo signal is faintly distinguishable. As you move into deeper or shallower water you'll have to respectively increase or decrease sensitivity.

An echo signal on a graph recorder can be confusing and isn't practical for shallow-water use. With these instruments it is best to turn the sensitivity up high, usually at a two-thirds to three-quarter setting. Increase it till you have a strong, well-defined bottom marking. If you turn it too high you may get black marks all over the paper or interference signals; turn the sensitivity down slightly to avoid this. If you are getting no marks (good machines can detect algae, debris, tiny baitfish, and severe water temperature changes) between the bottom and the surface, or the bottom is indistinct, the sensitivity setting is too low. As you increase or decrease depth, or if water conditions change markedly, you may have to alter the sensitivity slightly.

Suppression is a control function used to block unwanted and interfering noises from being registered. I rarely use any suppression on my sonar equipment, wanting to get the maximum "view" of what is below. The higher the suppression setting, the more you will block out fish signals. Suppression is best used when operating a boat at high speed when engine noise or boat movement over choppy water may result in distorted or wild signals. If you experience interference in normal, slow-boat operation, it could be due to a problem with the sonar instrument itself, improper transducer installation, or electrical interference from other objects in the boat.

Although there are other controls on some of these instruments, including depth or fish indication alarms, variable depth scales, and surface clutter suppression, graph paper speed is the most notable. Although slow paper speed conserves paper, it sandwiches details, making it more difficult to determine what is below. When you know what to expect or are continuously going over the same ground, or are only interested in depth, a slow paper speed is fine. When it is important to see the maximum amount of detail, run the paper at high speed.

I've had about six Lowrance graph recorders, including all of their microprocessor models and the current X-16 version, and have always found that the best results come from a mid- to high-sensitivity setting, little or no suppression, and medium to high paper speed. These graphs are excellent products, and I'm often disappointed when comparing the performance of other brands to the Lowrance graphs. Whatever graph recorder you have, experiment with the sensitivity and suppression controls and the paper speed, at various depths and boat speeds, to get the most out of your machine.

Sonar devices may seem magical, but there is nothing magical about interpreting their signals. Flashers are harder to read than graphs because signals disappear quickly, and at times flashers produce so many signals that you cannot digest the information quickly enough to interpret it. A flasher can tell you almost as much as a graph recorder, but you have to watch it all the time and need practice to confidently determine what every signal is.

Depth is gauged by watching the innermost part of the signal band. Often the bottom signal covers a range, say from 24 to 28 feet.

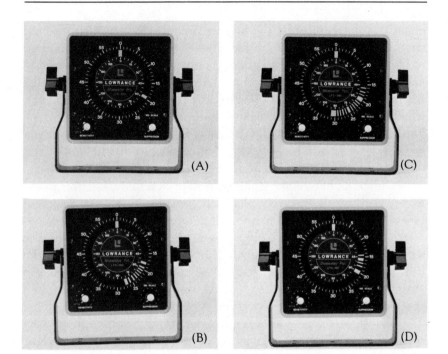

Illustrated here are: (A) a flat, solid bottom at 19 feet with nothing between the surface and bottom; (B) a sharp drop-off from 18 to 27 feet, perhaps a rocky ledge; (C) a sharp drop-off with brush, perhaps a creek channel location; (D) a brush pile in 20 feet of water. (*Photos courtesy of Lowrance Electronics*)

The shallow edge of the band, in this case 24 feet, denotes the depth directly underneath. A hard bottom typically gives off a wide signal, because it reflects transducer pulses better. A soft bottom produces a weaker signal and a narrow band. A hard bottom enhances the echo image while a soft bottom weakens it. A dropoff will appear as a wide series of signals, which is actually the transducer receiving several signals (remember the cone diameter) of varying depths at one time. A rocky bottom appears choppy and broken up, while a sandy bottom is solid. Even a sandy bottom can appear choppy if the boat is moving through substantial waves, which cause the boat (and transducer) to bob up and down. Weeds return a thin, pale signal; fish in weeds show up as brighter signals. A school of baitfish produces a flurry of short-duration signals. This is just a sampling of what to expect, but understand that you can become fairly adept at interpreting signals as long as you pay attention to the unit.

On a graph recorder the bottom is easily distinguished, and the strength of the impression on the paper is often indicative of the type of bottom, just as it is for flashers. Trees, stumps, boulders, dropoffs, and the like, are all readily observed, without having to watch the monitor continuously. Most graphs have a gray- or white-line feature, which issues a light band below the bottom that helps distinguish bottom terrain features (a lump that is filled in, for instance, might be grass, weeds, a fish, etc., in direct contact with the bottom and ordinarily indistinguishable from the rest of the terrain).

Unlike flashers, some graphs can show you minute matter in the water, such as algae, heavy plankton concentrations, and sedimentation. Readily observed in the upper layer of freshwater impoundments in the spring, these appear as small specks. Some graphs also show the depth of the thermocline (a layer of water separating the warm upper and cold lower sectors) when this is well established in summer and fall in large lakes. This appears as a faint gray band (often speckled) and remains at a constant depth.

Fish signals appear on a graph as an arc, unless the fish are very small, the paper speed is very slow, or the boat is moving very fast. This is because a fish is first picked up on the outer edge of the cone, then directly underneath it (the strongest pulse area), then on the outer edge, as the boat passes over it. The strongest reading of the fish is seen as the center part of the arc. A partial arc means that a fish was moving either in or out of the cone when you passed by. A school of bait shows up as a big pod, which may be vertical or horizontal, depending on the species. Sometimes you can decrease the sensitivity on a graph to separate individual fish.

Knowing the specific size of fish detected with sonar is very difficult, because this varies according to the size of the fish, the speed of the boat, paper speed (on a graph), and the sensitivity setting. If you catch a fish out of a school that you've just marked on a flasher or graph, you may have some idea how fish size compares to signal size, but if any of these factors change as you continue fishing, it's a new ballgame. Remember that on a flasher small fish produce less intense signals of short duration and big fish produce wide signals that last longer.

Although determining size of fish is somewhat possible, determining species is not, although educated guesses based on extensive experience and knowledge of individual species behavior and certain environments can be accurate.

You can tell if fish are active or not and, thus, potentially susceptible to angling. With some species, suspended fish are likely to be inactive, while others, situated on top of a stump or edge of a drop, may be waiting in ambush. At times you can watch fish hit a jig worked vertically below the boat, or see fish follow a lure (on graph recorders). I've watched fish come off the bottom, follow a lure, strike it, then be played out of the cone angle up to the surface.

The newest sonar devices on the market and catching on with increasing and surprising popularity are the liquid crystal display recorders (LCRs). Many bass anglers have recently gone to these in

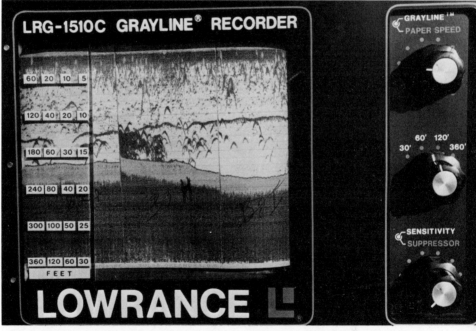

A test paper run by the author on Oklahoma's Tenkiller Lake shows the characteristic inverted V-shaped marks of respectable-size fish (probably white bass or stripers) suspended in 20 to 30 feet of water, with small baitfish and plankton dispersed through the upper layers. The line at 22 feet could be a downrigger weight, but is a large deep-diving plug that was being trolled by another boat. The ability to detect and record small items such as this, even within mere inches of the bottom, is a tremendous feature of these machines.

preference to flashers and graph recorders. Their appeal is based on an economical price, no installation or expense of graph paper, and no need for constant monitoring. Thus, they are supposed to meld the good points of graphs and flashers without their disadvantages, though few anglers who depend on a graph are forsaking them for LCRs. However, many bass fishermen who don't need a graph recorder like an LCR for its graph-like screen information.

With LCRs, signals appear at one side of the screen as you go over them, cross the screen, and disappear at the other end. Some of the better models have a screen update to recall a full screen's worth of information, a zoom feature that narrows down the area being observed, an automatic depth-determining mode, and forward and reverse displays.

I've got a Humminbird LCR 4000 on my boat and am still learning to thoroughly use it, though I've had experience with a Vexilar LCR in the past. One disadvantage to LCRs is the difficulty of reading them in bright sunlight or from particular angles, and it is often necessary to rotate or tilt them to be able to view the screen information adequately. Some anglers have difficulty distinguishing bottom characteristics (soft versus hard bottom), interpreting the signals (is that brush or small fish clustered together?), and distinguishing between large and small fish or groups of small gamefish and baitfish. This is because LCRs transfer signals into dots, most of which look like one another, and are hard to interpret when they appear on or close to the bottom.

These units are going to become more sophisticated in the near future and will be more popular as anglers learn to use them. It took awhile for fishermen to learn to interpret flasher-style sonar (many people still use them merely to indicate depth and are not good at interpreting the signals they produce), and the same pattern is emerging with LCRs, though such matters as transducer usage, transducer installation, sensitivity, and suppression functions are roughly the same.

Most sonar devices used by bass fishermen are permanently mounted on boats. But some manufacturers have pack housings that make certain stationary units portable. To make other units portable, you'll need to purchase (from the manufacturer) a spare electrical connection, to which you can attach alligator clips for battery terminal connections. (Be sure you'll have a 12-volt battery where you're headed.)

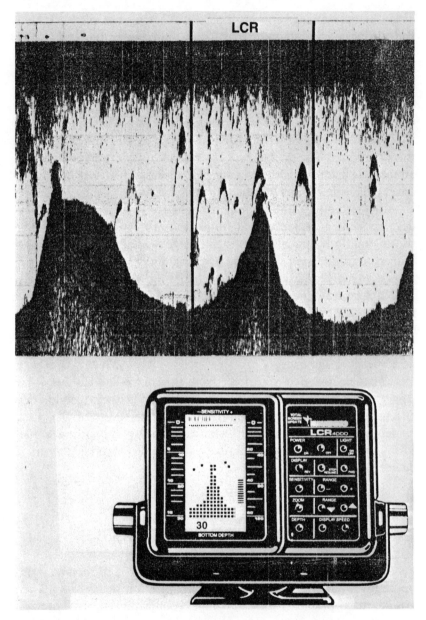

Illustrated here is a graph paper interpretation of signals produced by a liquid crystal display unit. The LCR is on the 30-foot scale. An underwater ridge is depicted at 18 feet. Fish are suspended on top of the ridge and nearby from 12 to 16 feet deep. (*Courtesy of the Humminbird Division of Techsonics Industries*)

Take the appropriate transducer off your boat (or use another); lay it flat on the floor (aluminum boat) or in the bilge of the boat for non high-speed use, or use a transducer bracket (sold in some stores and in mail-order catalogs) that clamps to the transom or gunwale of the boat. If the battery is strong and you only use it to power the flasher or graph, it will work for many days without needing recharging.

I've used this method for taking graph recorders with me to places that had no means of recharging batteries. Another option is to find the appropriate-size tackle box, fit the electronic unit, a wet cell motorcycle battery, battery charger, transducer bracket, and transducer all inside for ease of use and transportation.

In learning to use sonar equipment, it is imperative that you develop some confidence in it from the start. After you've digested the instruction manual, take the time to experiment with it over known terrain. Bring your boat over shallow water in shore, where you know the depth, and check to see that the sonar reads accurately. Find a stump several feet down, and see how it registers on your machine. Go over a sandy bottom, a mud bottom, a rocky bottom. Go out to deeper water and check the depth measurements against a handline or measured fishing line, if you are wondering about the depth-reading accuracy.

Rest assured that you don't have to employ sportfishing sonar devices to catch fish. Anglers survived for years without depthfinders and fish locators. If you only fish one or a few bodies of water and already know them thoroughly, you can probably do without sonar. In shallow ponds, streams, and rivers, there may be no need for these devices.

TRANSDUCER INSTALLATION

Getting good readings from your sonar gear is important to interpreting what the machines read. Improper transducer installation leads to many problems and can hamper your fishing efforts. Through-the-hull transducers are best for fiberglass boats and should be installed in the sump on a smooth surface, without air bubbles in the epoxy bond, and hopefully in a locale that is free from any irregularities in the hull. Large aluminum boats require transom-mount transducers installed midway between the hull strakes to minimize the effects of turbulence when the boat is underway. I like to use kick-up brackets with these, which allow them to be installed below the hull line (they would be at the line on other brackets); this bracket puts the transducer deeper to minimize the possibility of interference from air bubbles and also lets the transducer swing up if it contacts a rock, stump, etc.

Because improper transducer installation is the cause of much unit malfunctioning, plus angler difficulty in learning to use these devices, here are some tips on how to correctly install transducers:

1. Position a transom-mount transducer so that no air bubbles will trail below it. Strakes, weld lines, rivets, etc., give off a bubble trail, especially at high speed. Find a location that permits clear water to flow below the face of the transducer (such as between strakes on an aluminum hull). The closer you are to the centerline of the hull, the better. It may be necessary to point the transducer up slightly; if pointed down, the flow of water may emit a bubble trail beneath. If there are heavy bubbles below a transducer, you'll get no readings.

2. When epoxying a transducer in the sump for through-hull shooting, keep it close to the centerline (to be sure it will read in heavy seas) and away from struts and supports. Place it at least one foot in front of the transom in small boats and several feet in large boats, due to the possible extra fiberglass layers that are applied in the hull-transom bondage.

3. In many fiberglass boats it is best to have the transducer laid into the hull in the manufacturing process. I've had five boats that were so arranged. However, boats with an air space, foam, or balsa core are not conducive to through-hull mounting, as sonar cannot pass through these substances. Transom-mounting is best for aluminum boats. Wide-angle transducers are not recommended for through-hull mounting, but I had good results with a 45-degree transducer (for a Lowrance X-1550 computer graph) that was installed in the fiberglass of an 18-foot boat during construction.

4. To tell if your boat and transducer are suitable for through-hull transducer mounting, put water in the bilge and take the boat out to 30 or 40 feet of water. Place the transducer on the hull in the bilge and turn the sensitivity of your flasher or graph back until you faintly receive a bottom signal. Move the transducer around to different locations until you get a better (stronger) signal. When you get a good spot, turn the sensitivity back again till you barely detect bottom

View of transducers mounted on the transom of an aluminum bass boat. The outer transducers are mounted with kick-up brackets in case they contact an obstacle and are situated just underneath the transom. The middle transducer is on a permanent bracket mount and is flush to the bottom of the transom. All are located midway between strakes to be free of turbulence.

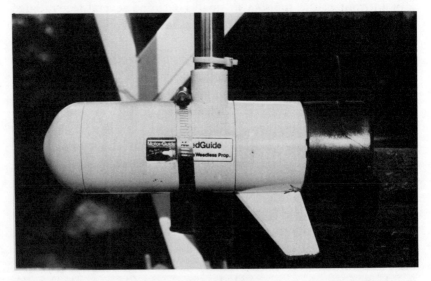

The transducer for bow-mounted sonar should be attached to the bottom of the electric motor or to the shaft, with the wire clasped in several spots around the shaft.

and try to find a better location. When you have the best possible spot, take the transducer out of the sump and place it overboard in the water and compare this signal with the one you received from shooting through the hull. If the signals are the same, you can shoot through the hull. If the through-hull signal is significantly different, you should not shoot through the hull. If it is only slightly different and your usage will be primarily in shallow water (or in freshwater up to 150 feet), then you'll still get good enough results when shooting through the hull.

5. Though manufacturers are loathe to suggest or approve it, you can cut a hole in the hull of aluminum or fiberglass boats and install the transducer so its face makes direct contact with the water (this may invalidate the manufacturer's warranty). One method of doing this is to fiberglass a 2 × 4 to the inside of the hull, then cut a hole the size of the transducer through the hull and wood, and epoxy or fiberglass the transducer in place.

6. If you are experiencing continual electrical interference, it may be caused by an untuned engine sending extra electrical energy through the tachometer cable that is placed alongside the transducer cable. Try relocating the transducer cable.

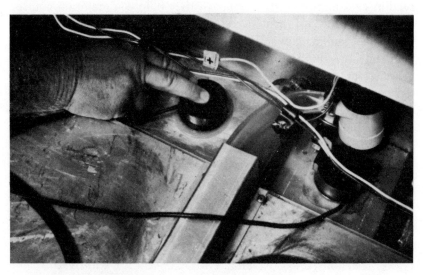

Epoxying a shoot-through-the-hull transducer in the sump.

FINDING AND USING LAKE MAPS

Every angler who fishes a large or unfamiliar body of water should have a good map of that place with him. Maps, especially those that show underwater contours and hydrographic features, will help you navigate without getting lost or possibly running into obstructions, and will help you find areas that may provide good fishing. By pinpointing the location of islands, mounds, shoals, reefs, dropoffs, roadbeds, channels, river and creek beds, and other forms of structure, you can fish the particular places that are most likely to harbor bass.

An attractive feature about such maps is that they allow you to devise a plan of attack in your own home, days before an outing, for fishing an unfamiliar lake. Once you have acquired the knack of reading an underwater contour map or a navigational chart that details bottom features, you are certain to find some areas where bass are located.

Underwater contour (hydrographic) maps and navigational charts are distinguished from topographic maps. The latter seldom denote water depth or the location of reefs, rocks, shallows, and such, while the former do, and are preferable. Underwater contour maps are available for many lakes, and these can be particularly useful because their high level of detail pinpoints important hydrographic features. When used in conjunction with a compass, they help you maintain course, especially in fog or low-light conditions or at night.

Topographic maps and navigational charts are produced by American and Canadian federal agencies and are available at some sporting goods stores, marinas, and major-city map stores, and cost a few dollars apiece. Dealers usually stock local area maps and can order others for you. To order maps yourself, obtain a map index from the appropriate government agency.

For U.S. topographic maps of areas east of the Mississippi, write: U.S. Geological Survey, Branch of Distribution, 1200 S. Eads St., Arlington, VA 22202. For areas west of the Mississippi, write: U.S. Geological Survey, Branch of Distribution, Box 25286, Denver Federal Center, Denver, CO 80225.

For navigational charts of U.S. waters, contact: National Oceanic and Atmospheric Administration, National Ocean Survey, Distribution Division (C44), Riverdale, MD 20840 (301-436-6990).

For Canadian topographic maps, contact: Canada Map Office,

A paved road once crossed this section of a large impoundment. Note the fence row disappearing into the water on the left, and the row of trees that lined the road on the right. Somewhere this road may have a stone wall that parallels it and one or more bridges that spanned a tributary. By using an underwater contour map and some type of sonar device, you could locate this road, that bridge, and perhaps other features that exist here, and conceivably find a place where bass are hiding to ambush prey. These and other types of bass-attracting cover are particularly likely to be found in manmade impoundments.

Surveys and Mapping Branch, Department of Energy, Mines and Resources, 615 Booth St., Ottawa, Ontario K1A 0E9 (613-998-9900).

For navigational charts of Canadian waters, contact: Chart Distribution Office, Department of Fisheries and Oceans, P.O. Box 8080, 1675 Russell Rd., Ottawa, Ontario K1G 3H6 (613-998-4931).

These agencies do not charge for a map index or chart catalog. Order maps long before you expect to depart on a trip. Remember that the larger the scale, the more detail is provided. Other maps of big waters may be available from jurisdictional agencies such as the Corps of Engineers or TVA, although their maps are rarely detailed enough to give you more than general information.

Maps supplied by private firms are often geared to fishermen's interests and provide a great deal of underwater contour information. Their size and scale level will determine how helpful they are as boating and fishing aids. The Sportsman Series of maps, for instance, gives

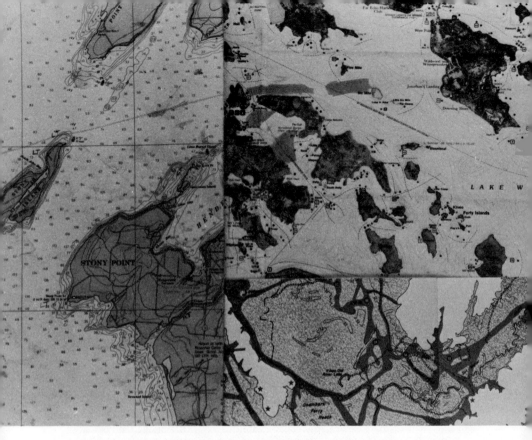

Look closely because there are three different types of lake maps here. At lower right is a section of an underwater contour map of a manmade lake (Toledo Bend in Texas) depicting old river beds and submerged creek channels and flats. At upper right is a section of a navigation map of a natural lake (Winnipesaukee in New Hampshire) showing reasonably good depth and shoal information. At left is a section of an NOAA navigational chart of the eastern end of Lake Ontario in New-York, providing very detailed contour, shoal, and reef data. The larger the scale of the map, the more detail it will show and the better it is for navigation and locating bass structure.

detailed information about many southwestern impoundments, including the popular Lakes Sam Rayburn and Toledo Bend. They're available from A.I.D. Associates Inc./Publishers, 3300 Royalty Row, Irvine, TX 75062 (214-438-6277). A good private source for Southeastern waters is Southern Guide Fishing Maps, 500 Gulfshore Dr., P.O. Box 1326, Destin, FL 32541 (904-837-2519). The Alexandria Drafting Co., 6440 General Green Way, Alexandria, VA 22312 (703-750-0510), produces fishermen's maps of the Mid-Atlantic and Southern regions, including the Santee-Cooper region of South Carolina.

Many good maps are available at tackle shops, sporting goods

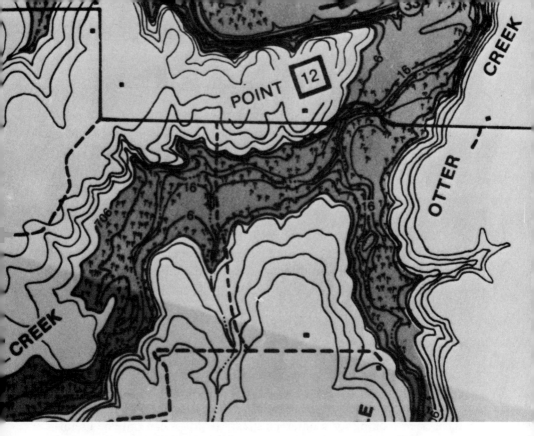

This is a close-up view of an underwater contour map, and it depicts just one small section of a large impoundment. The shaded area is the level of the water at normal pool elevation. Two creeks merge here and then enter a main river arm of the lake. The path of the creeks and the location of timber, flats, shallow coves, and steep shorelines can be observed by studying the map. Steep shorelines are found where contour lines bunch together. The place where a channel bends near the shore or comes close to a steeply sloped shoreline (meaning deeper water nearby) can be a prime place to find bass. By analyzing a map, you can pinpoint prospective bass areas or find new places similar to those in which you have found success.

stores, and marinas near popular waterways. In addition, state fisheries agencies often have contour maps (ranging from large-scale to reduced size on an $8^1/_2$ × 11 sheet of paper), particularly for smaller lakes and ponds, and you should check with these agencies for such availability.

Not all of the information on lake maps is necessarily 100 percent accurate, and it is not uncommon to find particular structures not indicated on underwater contour maps or navigational charts. But these products are substantial aids to fishermen who know bass habitat and behavior and can identify areas that are likely to be productive. This is particularly so where big lakes are concerned and where it would take an inordinate amount of time to explore for bass and bass habitat. These maps are used not only to help find your way around, but to locate the types of seasonally preferred habitats that have been mentioned earlier in this book. Moreover, once you have had success at finding bass under certain conditions, it is possible to refer to your map in search of other areas that may be similar to that in which you found fish.

People have suggested to me that I write about how to read and use these maps, but I don't think there's any great secret about how this is done. The features of a map are evident once you've read the symbols chart. What you should look for depends upon the type of habitat in that water and the time of year. This past spring, for example, I used a contour map of Truman Lake in Missouri to direct me to feeder creeks. Once I fished a few, and found that bass were nearly ready to spawn in the backs of coves and feeder creeks, and caught some nice fish shallow along sharply sloped banks adjacent to deep water, I used the map to point me to other creeks and coves with similar features, then started exploring. In summer or fall, I would have been looking for a different situation. Maps can only be useful when used in conjunction with your knowledge of bass behavior and a little fishing savvy.

It's a good idea, incidentally, to store maps in a large, clear, sealable plastic pouch or to treat them with a waterproofing material to help them last in marine environments. Color coding the different contour levels or marking certain areas with indelible markers is also worthwhile.

12

THE FINE POINTS

Just as there are practical considerations in the use of your boat and accessory equipment, so, too, are there many fine points of tackle usage and angling technique that can make you a better bass angler. Most of these fine points are understood but not often expressed by experienced anglers, and they tend to be lost in the usual fundamental reviews of bass fishing information. Aspects of angling savvy gained by veteran bass fishermen are often overlooked or undervalued by beginning or relatively inexperienced anglers. This is not to the embarrassment of the latter, since many of these elements are particular, yet key, details that are often only learned through ample experience or the teaching of others. As stated earlier, how you use your tackle is as important, and sometimes more important, than what you are using. Now that we have considered the tackle itself, let's look at technique.

PRACTICAL CASTING TECHNIQUES

Casting technique is something that all anglers should master fully. Most fishermen know basic casting procedures. However, the finer points of casting, as related to bass fishing applications, often need sharpening.

The first cast to a likely bass hole is often the most important one, so it pays to be able to make each cast count. This requires practice, but it also helps to use fish sense while casting. Every cast should have a purpose, directed at a particular spot because it is a likely looking bass hideout, and that spot should be fished in a deliberate manner.

If, for example, you are fishing crankbaits along a rocky shoreline that drops off dramatically, you won't have success if your lure constantly lands 6 feet out from shore. The fish could be hugging the bank or be on bottom 12 feet down. No matter how deep your lure dives, it will have missed a prime area right from the start.

Make every cast count by knowing what visible cover bass prefer and then by casting to the position likely to do the most good. Make casts to all sides of likely places. And learn how to feather your casts so that the lure doesn't come crashing down on the water's surface like a bomb.

With spinning tackle you should use your index finger to control the cast and water entry. With bait-casting gear you do the same with delicate thumb control on the reel spool. Raising your rod tip at the last moment helps soften lure impact, but is not reliable as a means of controlling accuracy. Sidearm or underhand loop casting, where it can be accomplished, is an effective method of making a soft presentation.

Another point to understand is that short casts are as worthwhile as long ones and are probably better much of the time in bass fishing. Forget about long-range casts for most bass fishing, with the exception of certain crankbait fishing circumstances. Short- to medium-distance casts are adequate. Most long casts waste time because they require you to make a retrieve over a lot of barren water. If the bass are within the first 15 feet of shore, don't sit 100 feet out banging away unless the water is especially clear and the fish are spooky.

By covering a lot of water through most of the retrieve, you ultimately squander a lot of fishing time during the day. You also risk losing a fish that strikes your lure at long-range distances, because distance and line stretch (more of a factor with nylon monofilament than with cofilament line) may keep you from setting the hook properly or controlling the fight.

Many times I've been asked to move the boat out from shore or from grass or weed patches by anglers who are so used to making 70-foot overhead casts with spinning tackle that they can't cope with 30-foot flips into brushy, weedy spots. But the end result is that you have much more control over a fish on a short length of line than you do over one on a long line.

The first cast to a likely bass hideout is usually the most important one, so you must be accurate and make your first opportunity your best one. Learn to feather your casts so that the lure drops softly, and don't make overly long casts.

As in all forms of angling, the basic casts used in fishing situations are the overhead, sidearm, and underhand casts. In other types of fishing, the overhead cast sees perhaps 75 percent usage, while the other casts are infrequently employed. However, in bass fishing, because of the nature of the cover in which these species are found and because of the necessity of accurate lure placement, there is a regular need to use all three casts. Therefore, you must become proficient enough with these to make accurate, quiet lure presentations to various objects and cover.

The overhead cast is probably the most used cast in bass fishing. Here, the wrist and forearm do all the work, using the top section of the rod for thrust. The cast begins with the rod low and pointed at the target. Bring the rod up crisply to a point slightly beyond vertical position, where flex in the rod tip will carry it back; then, without hesitating, start the forward motion sharply, releasing the lure halfway between the rod's vertical and horizontal positions. The entire casting action should be a smooth, flowing motion; you are doing more than just hauling back and heaving.

FISHING A STUMP

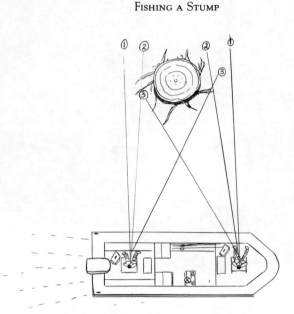

When fishing any isolated object, such as a stump, don't aim your cast to land directly on it or in front of it. That usually spooks a bass. Make your first cast beyond and away from the stump, a tactic that may draw out a fish. Make the next one beyond it also, but bring the bait as close to the stump as your lure will permit, even bumping it. Make sure that you and your partner have covered all angles.

The sidearm cast is essentially similar in motion to the overhead, except for horizontal, rather than vertical, movement. The sidearm cast can be dangerous if performed next to another angler in a small boat, so you must be mindful of the position of your companions at all times. To cast underhand, hold the rod waist-high, angled halfway between vertical and horizontal positions. The rod must be flexed up, then down, then up again to gain momentum for the lure through the flex of the rod. Most boron and graphite rods, incidentally, are too stiff to permit this kind of casting, though some composite rods and most fiberglass rods are adequate.

Another cast that I employ in tight quarters or for short ranges is a flip cast, which is something of a cross between the sidearm and underhand cast (different from flipping). It starts with the rod horizontal to your side, but you only bring it backward a short distance and then make a loop with the tip so that the tip springs around in a 270-degree arc and flips the lure straight out and low. This cast is used for short-distance (under 20 feet) work in areas where you can't bring your rod up or back for a conventional cast. This cast is almost impossible to accomplish while sitting down in a boat.

SETTING THE DRAG

I've met so many anglers who have told me exciting but sorrowful tales of losing monster bass—in some cases, surely world records—because the fish broke the line, that I have identified the same pattern in nearly each experience. It amazes me how many 8-pounders break 17-pound line, how many 12- and 15-pounders break 30- (even 40!) pound line, and how the hapless and harried victim doesn't even realize the incongruity of this and the fact that it was his own fault.

Let's be honest; a 10-pound bass swimming at maximum speed can't possibly apply 30 pounds of pressure to your tackle. Technically, on a dead weight basis you should be able to hang that 10-pounder from 12-, 14-, 17-, or stronger pound line without the line breaking. So why does that fish break it in the water while fighting to get free? Let's analyze the possibilities.

First, you could have bad line, a portion that is in a weakened condition. That's possible, and the line is always the first place that anglers place blame. Seldom, though, is this blame deserved, particularly if the line was a premium-grade product from a recognized manufacturer. Secondly, the line could have been cut or frayed or poorly knotted. This is more likely to be the explanation than is the first possibility, especially if you are angling in areas with many abrasive obstructions, and you don't check its condition periodically. Cut or frayed sections can be only half as strong as the undamaged portions. If the knot slipped or didn't hold up, you should be able to tell by examining the line. If the line is curled then your knot slipped out; portions of a broken knot may still remain on the line. Thirdly, the line might have broken because it took more pressure than it could absorb, even if it was strong line. This is often the main reason for breakage; however, it is not due to the brute force or sheer weight of the fish so much as it is due to the angler's failure to properly employ one of the primary features of his fishing reel—the drag.

The purpose of the drag is to let line slip from the reel at varying pressures when force is applied to the line. It serves as a shock absorber, or clutch. The looser it is set, the less force is required to strip line off. If the drag is set properly, a strong-pulling fish may be able to take line from the spool by applying less pressure than would be required to break the line or knot (this is determined according to the breaking strength of your line and the efficiency of your knot, as detailed in Chapter 7). Thus, the drag acts as insurance, as a buffer between you and the fish. Properly set line drag is most useful when playing strong, hard-fighting fish, when using light line, and when reacting to sudden surges by fish. The latter is a very crucial time in playing a fish. Such surges may occur at the beginning of the fight and especially as you bring a still-green fish alongside the boat.

The reason so many big bass are lost due to line breakage is that the angler tightened the drag, so there would be no slippage. In effect, he did not use the drag. When the big fish made a sudden surge, there was no shock-absorbing effect other than line stretch (assuming he was using monofilament or cofilament line). It would be like pulling at one end of a tightrope. The impact of this rush was more than the line could withstand, so it broke.

In defense of anglers who use very tight drags, it should be noted that most do so because of the habitat in which they are fishing. Thick grass, hyacinths, timber, and stump fields leave little margin for error when you hook a big bass among them. The fish usually tries to get to cover, where he may break off or pull free, and you have to muscle him away from it. This can't be accomplished easily with light line or if the drag is too loose, so you have to compromise in these situations.

The most accurate way to set the drag is to bring line off the spool through the rod guides and attach it to a reliable spring scale. Keep the rod up as if you were fighting a fish and have someone pull on the scale to watch the dial so you know at what amount of pressure the drag began to slip. Lighten or increase tension accordingly. I set the drag tension at between 30 and 50 percent of the breaking strength of the line for normal bass fishing conditions. In heavy cover I'll raise the tension to roughly 75 percent. If you think about drag tension in terms of the breaking strength of your line, you'll realize that 50 percent of 12-pound line is still 6 pounds of pressure, and few fishermen exert 6 or more pounds of pressure even when setting the hook. I think most anglers would be fooled if they were to pull line off their drag and guess the tension setting.

An important point to realize about drag tension is that the less line you have on your spool, the greater the tension will be. As the diameter of the spool gets smaller, more force is required to pull line off it. In bass fishing, as I've mentioned, line capacity is seldom much of a factor, so this item about drag doesn't usually come into play. Nonetheless, if you use your tackle for other species of fish that may take a lot of line, such as striped bass, you need to be aware of this and to compensate accordingly by not having too tight a drag at the outset.

With a lot of experience, you can set the drag by hand, adjusting the drag control and pulling line off by hand until you reach what "feels" like a good tension setting. I do this and have no trouble, but it is imprecise. Another, better technique is to catch your lure or bait hook on some solid object, like the underside of an oarlock or on a handrail, and pull back on your rod to approximate the surge of a fish. Adjust the drag while doing this to achieve what feels like a suitable setting.

I like to set a drag somewhat on the loose side when using light and ultralight tackle and particularly when fishing for smallmouth bass, though not so loose that line slips when I set the hook (which impairs hook-setting efficiency). In open water a loose drag gives the fish a little more chance and adds to the fun. And you can apply extra drag tension if need be. By cupping the palm of your hand over a spinning reel spool or by putting your thumb on a bait-casting reel spool, you can apply some amount of tension in addition to that which your drag is applying.

Be aware of the importance of proper reel drag usage. Check the drag on your reel periodically. Drags have been known to freeze when kept too tight for long storage periods (they usually are hard to free initially and provide a jerking flow of line), so keep the pressure loose when storing a reel and adjust it at the start of each day's fishing.

MASTERING THE RETRIEVE

The art of retrieving may be the most underrated element of bass fishing. Working the lure is an intrinsic part of the fishing process, and any angler who has refined his retrieval techniques is the one to bet your money on. We detailed specific retrieval methods in each lure category in Chapter 8, but there are some points to cover that are basic to all types of lures.

The keys to successful retrieval of most lures are depth control,

How you fish a lure is every bit as important as what you fish. Keeping your rod low on the retrieve is vital to hook setting and lets you better work most surface lures.

action, and speed, all of which vary in importance depending on the situation and the lure. It should be obvious to most anglers that achieving the proper depth is perhaps the most important factor, since you can't hope to catch fish unless you are getting your offering down to the fish's level. Only an extremely aggressive bass will go far to catch bait not in its area.

If you are not catching bass, it may be because you are not fishing deep enough, even though you are fishing in the right territory. One of the reasons that plastic worms are the single most effective type of largemouth bass bait is that they are fished on the bottom 99 percent of the time. On the bottom, whether it is in 2 feet of water or 12, is where the bass usually are.

The ability to achieve a certain depth is a function of the design of the lure and the way in which you use it. A plastic worm or jig must possess enough weight to maintain contact with the bottom for the length of the distance covered in the retrieve, when it is used in such a manner and not (as in the case of a jig) fished vertically in open water. But, of course, you first have to let that bait hit the bottom and not retrieve it too fast.

Don't rely on the diving ability of plugs as stated in the manufacturer's packaging. You can easily test this feature yourself by tying on a lure and casting it over a known depth. When you retrieve it a few times, if it doesn't scratch the bottom where you are fishing, bouncing off obstacles and pulsating the rod tip as it contacts the underwater terrain, then that lure is not diving deep enough for you. And if it's a new plug, you should be able to see the scuff marks on the bill or lip.

Another factor related to depth and diving lures is your line. A plug will dive deeper on light line than it will on heavy line. Light lines have a smaller diameter and offer less water resistance than heavy lines, allowing the lure to reach greater depth. Sometimes the difference is minute, but the difference between a diver retrieved on 17- or 20-pound-test line versus one retrieved on 8- or 10-pound-test might be enough (1 to 3 feet) to bring success.

It is no accident that most of the better quality reels today possess high-speed retrieve features (4.7, 5.18, and 5.3 to 1). This enables you to make rapid retrieves and to gain line quickly when fighting a fish. And it is good because you retrieve a greater amount of line for each turn of the reel handle, whereas an angler with a slow-speed reel puts less line on the spool with each turn, requiring more effort to retrieve the same amount of line. In some fishing situations an angler with the right lure but a slow-retrieve reel is at a disadvantage to another angler with the same lure but a higher retrieval speed capability. Yet when the fish are sluggish, the reverse may be true. On the minus side, a high-speed reel lulls some anglers into retrieving too fast, dwelling more on fast fishing and covering a lot of territory than on proper presentation.

To some extent, speed is a factor in the retrieval of all lures. Moderate speed for plugs catches the least fish, with more succumbing to high- or low-speed retrieves. Some lures can be retrieved too fast, at which point they lose their tight action and run off to the side. Keep that lure coming directly back to you with a maximum amount of action.

FISHING DEEP

One of the primary reasons why bass fishermen are unsuccessful is that they fail to get their lures or bait down to the level at which their quarry is located. Exactly what is deep? This varies among lakes and among fishermen. Anything over 10 feet is relatively deep. Yet in some areas (like Florida), few lakes have water over 15 feet deep. In others, most of the lake is over 20 feet deep; bass have been caught as deep as 80 to 100 feet in some places. Getting your offering down to these fish is often more of a problem than getting them to strike. Here are some considerations, then, for fishing deep.

Very few of the standard variety of crankbaits will go deeper than 10 feet on a cast-and-retrieve. Often, bass fishermen working a bank will find that the fish are 10 to 20 feet deep along the shore, but their plugs will not get there or will only reach the right level if they stick their rod tip deep in the water. The few plugs that will dive deep are usually very large, meant to be cast or trolled, and used for such fish as stripers and muskies (there are some large-lipped outsize crankbaits that will dive 15 to 25 feet).

Remember that line diameter affects the depth attainment of any lure and the way in which it works. The bigger and heavier the jig, the faster it will fall. In really deep water, most jigging is done straight below the boat. In less deep, shoreline areas, jigs can be retrieved to cover a lot of bottom terrain. Worms, too, will go as deep as you like, but they are best fished on the cast-and-retrieve, rather than vertically, and are of limited value beyond 20 feet.

Any lure that sinks, of course, will achieve the depth you desire. The drawback here is that it takes time to get them to the desired depth. You can determine the sinking depth by counting until your lure reaches the bottom (as signified by slack line), trying to maintain a drop of one foot per count.

There are other ways to get lures deep, the primary ones involving the use of weights. Sometimes small weights, such as split shot or rubber-core sinkers, will be enough of an aid, though they may influence lure action. One of the better types of weights, especially for river trollers, is the bead-chain sinker. This is available in weights ranging from $1/4$ ounce through 2 ounces, and it features a long, barrel-like weight on a snap-swivel assembly. The device prevents line twist from occurring, does not get hung up too readily, and works with all types of lures. A leader is utilized to connect the weight to the lure.

Another device is the Gapen Bait Walker. This is a rig shaped like an open safety pin or a spinnerbait, with a lead body on the

SHORELINE DROPOFF AND BREAKLINE

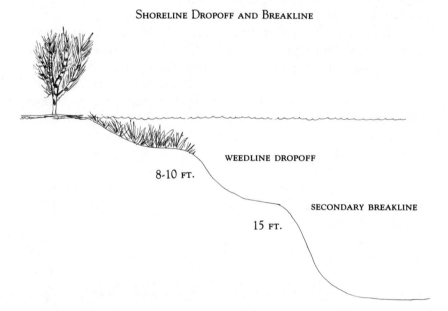

WEEDLINE DROPOFF

8-10 FT.

SECONDARY BREAKLINE

15 FT.

Bass may reside in the grass, at the edge of the grass, or on a dropoff. They may move upward (or inward) to feed, holding in deeper water in bright light and in the summer. You should attempt to locate the point at which the sloping bottom drops off more noticeably than the rest of the terrain. Concentrate on the primary and secondary breaklines, especially if there are rocks, stumps, or timber at such points. These are principal feeding areas and good places from which bass can ambush bait. Whatever your lure choice, you must be able to get it down to the proper level and effectively fish it there.

bottom and a swivel at the end of the top arm. Your fishing line is tied to the midsection, and a drop-back leader 18 to 48 inches long is attached to the swivel. This rig comes in a wide range of weights and can be used to cast (it's not easy, but manageable if you use the smaller sizes) or troll lures. It is also remarkably snag-free, due to the shape of the lead weight and the angle of pull. A good use for this is in casting or trolling small crankbaits, so that they will get down to a depth that it is impossible for them to reach unaided.

I use these occasionally to catch smallmouths in 20 to 25 feet of water, primarily using floating/diving minnow-imitation plugs or shallow- to medium-depth crankbaits in crayfish and shad patterns. The Bait Walker keeps the lures right near the bottom and is good at avoiding hangups. Several other devices work along the same principle, and they are good systems for getting deep and covering a lot of potentially productive ground.

Although it is far from being among the standard tools of a bass fisherman, a downrigger certainly can be used for bass, particularly smallmouth bass. One of the best pieces of graph recorder paper that I ever ran was on Lake Ontario one summer while smallmouth bass fishing with downriggers. We trolled small crayfish plugs and spoons at 30 feet over a cobblestone bottom and watched smallmouths come up from the rocks, look at the downrigger weights, and strike the lures that were trailing a short distance behind the weights. In large, clear lakes where bass are found very deep (such as Ontario, Erie, Lake Champlain, Lake George in New York) fishermen equipped with a downrigger may have some action using this gear to get light lines down to specific levels.

FISHING CLOSE: FLIPPING

A few, formerly obscure, methods of catching bass have almost no relation to standard retrieval techniques, but are successful chiefly because they offer quiet presentation and close-to-cover fishing. These methods include jiggerpoling, wherein a plug and short length of line are attached to a long canepole, and a fisherman in the bow of a boat jiggers the lure in and around grassy banks and stumps; yo-yoing or doodlesocking, wherein a small clearing is made (with a pole or paddle) in a clump of thick moss, milfoil, or other grass, and a jig or worm dropped into it; and flipping. Flipping has become popular with some fishermen in recent years and is the most popular of these techniques. Some form of flipping has been around for years and was called dabbling or pitching until the marketing wizards latched onto it.

Flipping, a fairly simple method, is a controlled short-casting technique used in close quarters for presenting a moderately heavy jig or plastic worm in a short, quiet, accurate manner to cover that cannot be properly worked by a lure cast from a long distance away.

Imagine that you are looking at a bank with a sharply sloping shoreline. Within half a foot of the bank are some bushes, the base

Bass will hold on the edge or in the midst of this sawgrass, and the only way to make an effective presentation to them is to flip a worm into every nook and cranny.

of which may be in 2 feet of water. Any plug pitched at such a target will land directly in front of it and will be on its way without getting very near the fish. A worm might do the trick but the first cast would have to be extremely accurate; most likely the worm will fall too far in front of the bush to entice the bass out. But when flipping, you could position your boat 15 to 18 feet from the bush and use a long rod to swing a jig or worm so that it lands in the most opportune place without smashing down noisily on the water's surface. A lot of bass inhabit very thick cover, and flipping is a surefire way of getting your bait literally in front of their mouth.

At a time when bass are probably more attuned to the ways of man and more skittish and aware of outside influences, flipping is a good technique to use with such cover as brush, standing timber and stumps, logjams or debris-filled flotsam, heavy lily pad and vegetation clusters, steep craggy ledges, docks, and boathouses. Flipping will reach the bass holding close to such cover.

The tackle required is a long rod, heavy line, and a jig or worm. The rod should be between 7 and 8 feet long, with a long straight handle. It must be stout, because bass are often violently jerked out of heavy cover on a short length of line, and the bigger the bass the greater the stress and the greater the degree of difficulty. Most flipping rods are one-piece bait-casters, with an upper section that telescopes down into the handle for easy transportation and storage. Most flipping is done with bait-casting rods, but some anglers prefer spinning gear. The same rod features, however, are applicable. Flipping takes a toll on your arm muscles if you do it for a long period of time, and because of this, a graphite rod, weighing considerably less than fiberglass, is very beneficial.

The reel used on a flipping rod can be the same that you use for other bass fishing applications, but it is best if it has a narrow spool (line capacity is not a factor) and is light. It should also have a clear sideplate (no knobs sticking out to catch line on). A reel that allows one-handed operation is a big plus. Several manufacturers now have reels that are solely for flipping or that have features applicable to flipping. I prefer the latter, as such a reel can be useful for conventional fishing as well as flipping. The ABU-Garcia Ultra Mag II Plus, which I've been using the past few seasons, is one such product. With it, you can depress the Thumb Bar to instantly cast, plus, in its flipping mode you can depress the Thumb Bar to let line out and not have to turn the handle to engage the gears. This makes a difference in convenience when flipping, as you often have to strip off more line but don't have to take time to crank the handle to engage the gears.

Most flippers use 25- to 30-pound-test line, and some even use 40. They go to such strengths because of the lack of stretch, less effect of abrasion (you often fish in abrasive areas), and need to horse big fish out of thick cover. I've been using 17-pound-test monofilament for flipping and haven't regretted it, though I've been waiting for the day when I had to change because a huge bass took my bait in thick cover and I couldn't handle it. However, with the new cofilament line, 17- or 20-pound-test should give the advantage of less stretch, plus provide greater sensitivity and improved lure action. This new line may cause more anglers to drop down a bit in line strength.

Black or brown jigs, primarily in $\frac{1}{2}$-ounce sizes, but also a little lighter and a little heavier, are the most popular flipping baits. These should have fiber weedguards when used in all but rocky ledge areas and sport a "living rubber" type of skirt and a large hook. They are adorned with all manner of enticements, including worms, curl-tail grubs, pork strips, and the like, but pork chunks (No. 11 Uncle Josh in black or brown) are the most popular.

I prefer to flip a plastic worm, however, and usually do until someone fishing with me proves that jigs are doing it and worms are not. I use a 7- to 8-inch worm on a $\frac{5}{0}$ hook for this, and a heavy ($\frac{1}{4}$- to $\frac{1}{2}$-ounce) slip sinker that is pegged to prevent it from sliding up the line. This seems to get hung up less frequently than a jig, and when you have a strike you can hesitate for the slightest moment to get a firm hook-set.

To flip properly, you must remember that your goal is to make a pinpoint bait presentation to a particular object within 10 to 20 feet of your boat and to do so in a quiet, splash-free manner. Seldom are you able to flip while sitting down; this is a technique that requires stand-up work, occasionally with two fishermen close together in the bow of a boat (as when working every nook and cranny of a stump- and blowdown-filled stretch of shoreline). To begin flipping, let out about 7 to 9 feet of line from rod tip to lure. Strip line off the reel until your free hand and rod hand are fully extended away from each other; this will give you 5 to 7 feet of line at your disposal in your free hand. Considering the length of line out and the length of your rod, you're now able to reach a target 20 to 22 feet away (a few more if you count the length of your arm).

To flip your bait out, raise the rod tip and swing the jig back toward you under the rod. The motion demands wrist action, not elbow or shoulder movement. The bait swings back toward you, and when it reaches the top of its pendulum-like swing, flick your rod-holding wrist to direct the lure toward its target. Lower the rod tip, and let line flow through your free hand. Extend your rod arm if necessary to reach the target, and keep the line in your hand until it reaches the target. When you retrieve the lure to move it to another spot, lower the rod tip and point it toward the lure, grab the line between reel and first guide with your free hand and strip it back while lifting up on your rod (similar to the hauling technique used by fly casters). Swing the lure out and back and send it forward again to the next object.

When the lure is in the water, you may jig it up and down or crawl it along after it has fallen freely to the bottom. Climb it up, over, and through all of the cover. Closely watch the line for the slightest movement, and be attentive to the softest strike. Don't keep it in any one place long, and try to nudge it through cover instead of ripping it. When you set the hook, you may do so in the conventional manner, with one hand on the reel handle and the other on the rod handle, and play the fish out of the cover (easier done with a worm). Often, however, a strike occurs when you are holding line in your free hand and the rod in your other hand and there isn't time to grab the tackle conventionally, so you strip the free line back, jerk the rod tip up sharply, and hope you've not only gotten hook penetration but can yank the fish out, all in the same motion. It doesn't always happen, and a lot of good-sized fish are lost while flipping, so you have to work fast and try to out-muscle the fish through the cover as best as possible. At times you'll stick a small fish and yank him clear out of the cover

To flip, let out about 7 to 9 feet of line from rod tip to lure; strip line off the reel and hold it in your left hand (figure 1). Point the rod tip up and out and swing the jig forward (figure 2). The bait will come back toward you, and when it reaches the top of its pendulum-like swing, direct it toward the target (figure 3). Lower the rod tip, and let line flow through your free hand; extend your rod arm if necessary to reach the target, and keep the line in your hand (figure 4). (*Illustration courtesy of Mariner Outboards.*)

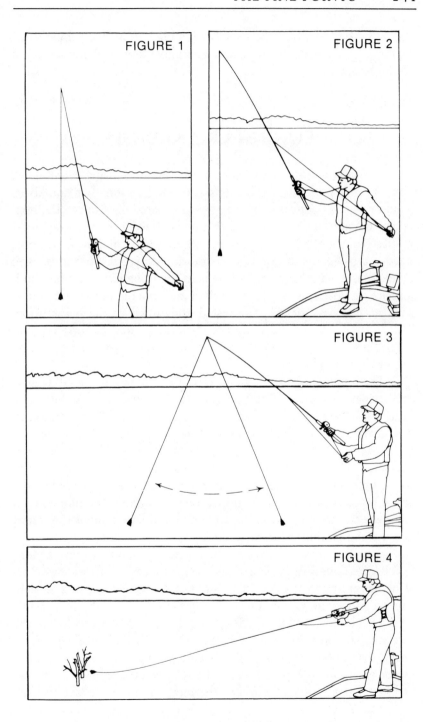

and over the boat, but when you hook a big bass in thick cover while flipping, you'll have an excitingly fast and furious bulldog scrap out of the happening.

TUNING CRANKBAITS

Considering the advanced state of manufacturing technology, plus the hefty retail purchase price, it would seem that crankbaits would not need adjusting in order to be fishable right out of the box. Alas, 'tis not so. Not every lure can be freed from its wrappings, knotted on your line, and run true, cast after bass-catching cast. Some need extensive modification, and, unfortunately, a few never run well at all. Many manufacturers have refined their quality control methods and are producing lures that essentially run true out of the box (a few, such as Rapalas, are all tank-tested and tuned at the plant before distribution). Nonetheless, even good-tracking lures can run awry after catching fish, so you need to know what to do to get the best action out of these products.

The majority of crankbaits have clear plastic bills of various lengths and shapes for diving. Line-tie screws are attached to these bills, and all running problems center on these little screws. When a crankbait runs awry, it is the fault of the line-tie. The line-tie screw must be placed vertical to the mean horizontal plane of the bill of the lure, but since this screw eye is positioned partially by hand at the manufacturing plant, the element of human error can be introduced. If the screw is placed a fraction of an inch out of position, the lure will not run perfectly true, and occasionally an assembler misaligns the screw, causing the product to need tuning.

A well-designed crankbait should have a good wiggling action. Some lures have a tight action, and some have more of a wide wobble. Whichever action it exhibits, a lure should come back in a straight line to you while swimming or diving. The body of the lure should be vertical, not canted off to either side. It is important to get the lure running perfectly true; if it runs even a little bit off, it has an unnatural action that will probably cost you fish. It is a good idea to check each plug before you fish it; tie it on your line, drop a few feet of line from the tip of the rod to the lure, then run the lure through

A long, beefy rod and heavy line are needed when flipping because it's a chore to tangle with big bass in heavy cover.

the water a few times next to you. If it does not run properly, adjust it immediately.

To adjust a crankbait, you need only a pair of pliers, preferably needle-nosed, to bend the line-tie screw. If, as you watch the path of retrieve head-on, the lure is running to your right, you must bend the line-tie screw to the left (again, looking at it head-on). If the lure runs left, bend the screw right. Adjust the screw in stages, bending it slightly, then casting and retrieving once to see the change. Keep adjusting and changing until the lure runs true. In radical cases you may have to bend the line-tie screw far from its original position. When bending the line-tie screw, be careful that you do not loosen it. The screw is merely epoxied in place, and loosening may render the plug unusable (sometimes you can take the screw out and re-glue it using clear five-minute epoxy).

With a pair of pliers you can tune a crankbait to run properly by bending (not twisting) the screw eye in the opposite direction from which the lure is running astray.

Before you tune a lure that seems to run awry, make sure you are not retrieving it too fast. All plugs have a top working speed, beyond which they will not run properly. This speed is not the same for all lures. With today's high-speed-retrieve reels, you could be reeling your lures faster than they will run effectively. Also, make sure you are not working the lure against the movement of the boat, which will cause it to run improperly. Check it when the boat is not moving, or put the lure in the water next to the boat and watch its action.

Most crankbaits will not run very well if a tight knot is tied directly to the screw eye. For this reason, it is best to use a split ring or rounded snap (not snap-swivel) for connection. Most crankbaits are supplied with split rings or snaps, and your knot should be tied to this. Snap-swivels may alter the action of these plugs, making perfect tuning a difficult task. A lure that is already tuned to work without a snap-swivel may have to be re-tuned to work with it. Moreover, a snap-swivel poses another possible problem point when fighting fish, and the least possible number of things that can go wrong, the better. The only advantages to using a snap-swivel are that it facilitates lure changing and prevents twist. Crankbaits don't induce twist, and snaps will ease the job of lure changing. Most of my lures don't have snaps; I take them off and replace them with split rings. I prefer to tie my line directly to the lure and, in a rush, can tie an improved clinch knot to a crankbait in about 30 seconds, which is seldom a significant loss. Moreover, a foot or so of line about the lure is sure to get abraded with a bit of use, necessitating regular line inspection, clipping, and re-knotting.

Sometimes crankbaits can be sensitive to the slightest adornment. If you pull a plug through weeds and get a tiny confetti trailer on your hooks or line-tie, you'll feel the action of the lure change. Tie a new knot on a bait that was running fine and the action may just be off due to the position of the knot. This is corrected by changing its position and realigning the knot or by retying the knot and snugging it tight. You may also find that some crankbaits work best if you use a loop knot. Deep-diving minnow-shaped plugs, such as the Rebel Spoonbill Minnow (an overlooked largemouth lure, incidentally), as well as some surface lures are this way.

Some crankbaits seem to need more frequent tuning than others, and some small lures need more frequent tuning than large ones. Some never get tuned exactly right. It is not uncommon to make many casts and retrieves and modifications of a new lure before you get it running to your satisfaction. So when you have a finely tuned, regular fish-catching crankbait, you should treat it with respect and give it a special place in your tackle box.

Ideally, you should tune all your lures before they are put to the ultimate fishing test. On some trips where I didn't want to waste any time tuning lures, I've gone to a lake beforehand to check the action of every crankbait that I planned to bring along. This is possible if you have a pool or beach area in which to work leisurely. A swimming pool would be especially good because you can see how the lure works and how deep it dives. If you want to observe action and depth of retrieve, don goggles and get into the water while a friend casts. An up-front observation of what a lure does is better than relying on what you think it does.

PREPARATION AND VERSATILITY

There are a lot of little practical points related to bass fishing that any angler can use to improve his odds. Yet, with all the present emphasis on fishing techniques, habitat identification, and fisheries knowledge, too often the simple subjects get neglected.

A big oversight of many fishermen is that they have not prepared any of their tackle before starting the day. The time to rig tackle is not when the sun peeks over the trees and the mist rises off the water. That's a poor time to be running line through the guides and tying knots onto hooks and lures.

For most bass fishermen, especially the occasional angler, and particularly during summer months, the early morning is a very pro-ductive time. Every moment you lose then is a vital one. Don't be readying equipment at lakeside when you could be fishing. Rig your tackle, even to the point of tying on a lure you expect to use, the night before you're going fishing. You can always retie a hook or lure for the conditions in the morning. And get all your lures and accessory equipment shipshape prior to actually fishing.

Having a well-organized tackle box is a step in the right direction. This means you should have a tackle box (or boxes) that allows you to group lures by types and categories, yet prevents the extremely annoying entanglement that results when several treble-hooked lures are placed in the same compartment. You ought to organize your lures in such a way that when you need something, you know where it is, and you can get it out and tie it on fast.

Something that adds to your preparedness and versatility is having several fishing outfits on hand and ready to use on any given outing. But even better is to have one or more additional rods prepared for fishing. A different type, style, and color lure for each rod makes sense.

Some words about versatility: fishing conditions can change from day to day and lake to lake. The most consistently successful bass fishermen are those who can adapt to these changes. This necessitates being proficient with different tackle, fishing techniques, and lure presentations. The one-lure fisherman is in for a number of fishless days if he doesn't develop a rounded angling temperament.

Having several rods at the ready is not a sign of overeagerness. It makes good fishing sense. I fish with four or five rods in the boat most of the time and see the looks this draws from casual fishermen. I use only one rod at a time, of course, but I have the capability of switching instantly if necessary. This pays off most when a bass strikes but misses a lure. Such a fish frequently will not come after the same lure a second time, but if you pick up another bait immediately and throw it out, he'll probably hit that one.

Several rods are also a benefit when a feeding fish or school of bass surfaces nearby, and you can drop the rod you are fishing with and pick up another with a surface lure on it, and whip out a cast to the action spot. Also, having rods with different strength line can be of immense value if you have to go to heavier or lighter tackle than originally planned.

Aside from tackle and tackle-related equipment, lack of boat readiness is another factor that hampers efficient fishing operations. Fueling up in the morning is probably the worst offense (though better to do this than run out of gas halfway across the lake).

If you are new to a lake or will fish it for the first time, try to find out as much as possible about it before you fish there. This will save a lot of time when you are ready to fish. Also, minimize your chances of squandering fishing time by trading stories on the dock; by tinkering with boat, motor, accessories, or tackle on the water; by running needlessly back and forth over the lake; and by spending too

By having an extra rod or two handy, you can be prepared to switch baits or tactics instantly if conditions warrant. Often you can catch bass on another lure after it has just missed a different one moments before. The author saw this smallmouth swirl after and miss his crankbait. He picked up another rod with a floating minnow plug, cast back out, and caught the bass.

much time in unproductive areas or in repetitive situations. One of the hallmarks of the better fishermen is that they have an uncanny knack of knowing when to change, when to do something different, when to go to a new locale. This adaptability, or versatility, and preparedness are good traits to cultivate for savvy bass fishing.

CONFIDENCE

Bass fishing is a sport with many intangibles, all of which have some influence on the angler's success. Some anglers are more astute than others; some are plain luckier than others; some are blessed with more natural talent. Yet, every angler can improve himself if he desires to do so and is willing to make the effort.

One intangible factor is confidence, an elusive quality that is particularly lacking in new or inexperienced bass anglers. Confidence can't be bought in the tackle shop or acquired from a successful and experienced compatriot—it is earned through experience.

You acquire confidence by learning and doing—by developing an understanding of the habits and habitat of your quarry, by mastering the intricacies of your tackle, and by slowly putting together the pieces of the bass fishing jigsaw puzzle. I hope that this book helps upgrade your fishing proficiency; if so, your confidence will soar.

Just going out and catching a couple of bass is a big boost to the neophyte's confidence. So is having and knowing how to use good equipment. When I first started getting seriously involved in fishing, I got a top-quality spinning rod and reel. It was one of the best outfits then available, and the mere possession of that equipment made me feel like I could be more successful by using it. Sure, that's a psychological ploy, but for some people it works—the very fact that they have good equipment instills in them the desire to achieve and the motivation to learn and become more skillful.

I also remember how frustrated I was when I began fishing on those days when I caught little or nothing. And there were many. I used to wonder when I'd catch more than two keepers each outing. Then, that progressed to wondering if I'd ever catch a limit. And that changed to wondering about a big-fish limit. But I stopped wondering a long time ago (well, I do wonder if I'll ever catch the world record bass, but that's another story). As you learn and as your abilities grow, your level of bass fishing competence rises, and you become more successful. Success breeds confidence, which in turn may foster greater success.

Every move that a good bass fisherman makes is related to confidence: in the selection of which lure to use; in the selection of an area to fish; in the placement of his casts; in judging when to stay in, or leave, a particular spot; in determining what type of retrieve to employ; and so on. Because he is confident, he concentrates harder on what he is doing and is generally more attentive to the nuances of bass fishing. At the same time, he realizes that not every cast will produce a fish, nor will every day be a good one. He realizes that bass are unpredictable creatures and that he can't always figure them out, which is probably why he likes the sport in the first place. Yet, every top-notch bass angler I know is convinced that there's a bass hiding by the nearest ambush point and that he's going to catch it. That's confidence.

Don't overlook the effects of feeling positive about your abilities and about your understanding of the world of bass fishing. Well-placed confidence may be the best tool in your repertoire.

13

BASS HANDLING TECHNIQUES

Bass fishing has many varied aspects: the pleasures of preparation and anticipation, the enjoyment of the outdoors, the pursuit of the unseen, and the challenge of outwitting a game quarry. The ultimate thrill for most anglers, however, is in hooking and fighting the fish. Therefore, knowing how to play, land, and handle bass and how to care for those that you keep is especially important.

PLAYING BASS

With heavy tackle and relatively small bass, what you do to bring that fish to net doesn't matter too much, because the odds are in your favor. But when you begin to match your tackle to the quarry, making the fight more balanced, or when you latch onto a particularly strong or large bass, your skill at handling that fish from hooking to netting will be tested. How you choreograph the fighting of a fish under these conditions is critically important and is a technique that can be mastered through experience, provided you understand the fundamental elements.

The first step in fighting a bass is to be prepared for what is about to happen before it happens. Start by keeping your rod tip down during the retrieve. With the tip down, you're in the best possible position to respond to a strike. If there is little or no slack in the line, you can make a forceful sweep up or back when you set the hook and then be in immediate control of the bass to begin playing it. (When working a jig or plastic worm, however, it is necessary to keep the rod tip up to feel the lure and readily detect a strike.) When setting the hook, you can compensate for a high rod position by bowing the rod slightly toward the fish while reeling up slack; this enables you to get a positive sweep and be in the proper position for the beginning of the fight.

Hook setting is always a quickly accomplished maneuver. When a bass hits, the angler reacts reflexively, bringing his rod back and up sharply while holding the reel handle and reeling the instant he feels the fish. The position of the rod is important. The butt is jammed into the stomach or mid-chest area, and the full arc and power of the rod is brought into play.

Throughout the fight, keep the rod tip up and maintain pressure on the fish. The position of the rod butt remains unchanged. Reel the line in while lowering the rod, then pressure the fish as you bring the rod back up. This technique is used for all but the smallest fish; often referred to as "pumping," it is most effective when fighting a large bass or when using light line.

Often, when a fish is fairly close to you, it is still energetic. Continue to keep the rod high. This is a time to be directing the fish. If you are in a boat and the fish streaks toward it (perhaps to swim under it) you could be put at a disadvantage, particularly when using light tackle. You must reel as fast as possible to keep slack out. If the fish gets under the boat, stick the rod tip well into the water to keep the line away from objects and possibly from being cut.

You should anticipate that a bass will rush the boat, so be prepared to head it around the stern or bow. In some cases, a companion can manipulate the boat (especially with an electric motor) to help swing the stern or bow away from a fish, a smart maneuver that can aid the playing of a very large and energetic bass. If possible, go toward the bow or stern to better follow or control the fish. Don't hang back in a tug-of-war with a large, strong fish; use finesse rather than muscle.

When a fish swims around your boat, keep the rod up (sometimes out, too) and apply pressure to force its head up and to steer it clear of the outboard or electric motor and their propellers.

Eventually the fish is next to you and may be ready for landing. If it still has a last burst of energy, however, this will be a crucial moment. Because of the short distance between you and the fish, a lot of stress will be placed on your tackle. You must act swiftly when the fish makes its last bolt for freedom.

As it surges away, don't pressure it. Let it go. Point the rod at

You have to keep your rod tip up and maintain pressure on the fish at all times.

the fish at the critical moment so there is no rod pressure. A large bass will peel line off the drag, which, if set properly (and does not stick), will keep tension on the fish within the tolerance of the line's strength and provide the least amount of pressure possible. As the surge tapers, lift the rod up and work the fish.

If you are alone and without a net, you must be careful when landing the fish. Keep a taut line, extend the rod well back behind and over your head, and reach for the fish with your other hand. In this position, you are able to maintain some control over the fish, even if it is still active, and avoid creating a momentary slack line situation that may give the bass its freedom.

Remember that fish-playing activities take place in a short period of time. When playing a large, hard-fighting fish the action is often fast. Your reactions must be swift and instinctive, and your tackle, particularly line and reel drag, should be in top condition.

LANDING BASS

All the angling savvy in the world won't help if you are a stumblebum in bringing your catch into the boat. Neophyte anglers panic when they get their catch close to the net, and many otherwise respectable fishermen lose their fish right at the boat due to their own ineptitude in handling. There are some definite do's and don't's for proper fish handling.

Probably the greatest sin of new anglers in this regard is reeling the fish right up to the tip of the rod when the catch is at boatside, as if they were going to spear it. Applying too much pressure on a green fish near the boat is also another sin. Finesse, not muscle, is the secret. The key to properly landing bass is to employ common sense, anticipation, and finesse.

One easy way to boat small bass that are well hooked is by simply lifting them aboard with the rod. This is only practical for small- to medium-size fish caught on tackle that is sturdy enough to permit it.

Landing fish by hand is a tricky maneuver for some species, but a practical and desirable method for bass in many instances. Fish that are small and that are to be released immediately are best handled at a minimum, by leaving them in the water while unhooking them.

Bass can be landed by grasping the lower lip, provided the fish is well tired before the attempt is made. Simply insert your thumb over the lower lip, with remaining fingers outside and underneath. This immobilizes the fish and is good for unhooking as well as landing. Caution: Be sure not to plant your thumb on the hooks of the lure.

Large bass and very active fish can be netted, too, particularly if you intend to keep them. Proper netting technique is as much a matter of attitude as it is ability. My intention is to net a fish at the first good opportunity—there may not be another. The line could break, the reel could freeze up, the fish could get under the boat or scrape the line against the propeller, the hooks could pull out, and so forth. Netting is the culmination of the act of fighting and playing fish.

Many fishermen try to net a green (still vigorous) fish and lose it. Their problem is mostly a matter of poor technique or timing. Many fishermen are poor netters because they have little experience at it and seldom catch fish large enough to require netting. Many avid and successful bass fishermen rarely have a net in their boat and are unaccustomed to using one when the need arises.

Bass are relatively easily landed by hand if you grasp their lower lip. Holding them in this manner immobilizes them for unhooking as well. To net a bass, put the net slightly in the water and lead the fish to it, so the bass can be scooped up head-first.

Proper netting technique is as much a matter of knowing what *not* to do as it is knowing what *to* do. Under most circumstances, you shouldn't put the net in the water and wait for the fish to come close. Nor should you wave the net overhead where a fish might see it. It's best to keep the net solidly in hand at the ready, either motionless or out of sight, until a fish is almost within reach.

You shouldn't go for a fish unless it is within reach and not if it is going away from you or appears to be able to go away from you. The fish should ideally be headed for you so that it must continue forward, or that if it turns, you may still be able to move the net in front of it. As a general rule, I don't try to net fish unless their heads are on the surface or are just breaking to the surface. A fish that is up on the surface has little mobility and cannot do as much as one with its entire body in the water, particularly if the fish is not played out.

You should not try to net a fish from behind. If a fish is completely exhausted you may be able to net it from the side, but the most desirable position is from the front. You also don't want to touch the bass with the rim of the net until it is well into the net. Touching fish, particularly if they are still lively, often initiates wild behavior.

If the fish acts wild, it could roll on your line and break it or simply snap it from the force of its getaway rush. Therefore, you should resist taking a stab at a fish that may be technically within reach of your extended net, but not in the best position for capture.

A major problem that occurs when anglers try to net a fish that is in a poor position to be netted or when they don't get a fish coming squarely into the net is the snagging of a multihooked lure on the mesh or webbing of the net bag. This is one of the surest ways to lose a fish, particularly those that are heavy and cannot be readily hoisted into the boat or scooped up in the now-tangled net. That's one reason to be sure to have the appropriate-size net along.

RELEASING BASS

Because bass are so popular, fishing pressure in many areas has become intense. The "good old days" of ready limits and big fish catches are largely behind us. Size and creel limits have become more restrictive and are helping to provide better bass fishing in many lakes. Limited forms of catch and release fishing, via slot limits, are with us. For these reasons and more, it is important—indeed, it is a tenet of good sportsmanship—that anglers be concerned with the treatment of fish they do not or cannot keep. Those bass present more than just the possibility of being future trophies; they are the fish that will help guarantee angling tomorrow's.

At first glance, releasing bass seems simple enough; unhook 'em and toss 'em back. Unfortunately, it's not that easy. Many factors play a role in the survival of a bass, beginning the moment it is hooked and continuing past its release.

The actual catching, landing, and physical handling during release are the most obvious parts of the process. Luckily, bass are a reasonably hardy fish. They are not too disturbed by moderately re-

Releasing fish you don't need, and proper care of fish to be released, mark you as a sportsman. If a bass is severely stressed, hold it upright in the water and lead it around by the lip to force oxygen through the gills and into the respiratory system.

spectful handling. They can be grasped without harm to fish or fisherman, but always avoid excessive handling.

Potential problems occur the moment you touch a bass. Infection, bodily damage, and suffocation are the principal dangers. All fish have a slimy, mucus-like coating over their bodies, which protects them from bacterial infections. If a portion of this coating is removed, the fish's resistance to disease is lowered, a condition that may be fatal.

Hand-to-body contact with a fish should be minimized for reasons other than possible infection. Fishermen often grasp small bass tightly around their midsections to prevent movement during the unhooking process, and this can cause internal damage to the fish. Such handling, of course, is entirely acceptable for a fish that will be kept.

Another procedure that can be harmful to a bass is netting. The use of a net can remove some of the mucus coating and scales from a fish. Often a plug-caught fish gets enmeshed in a net because some of the loose hooks catch in the webbing during the netting process. As the bass thrashes around he is pulling against the stuck plug, an action which can bend the hooks or tear the mouth of the fish. I net very few of my bass, reserving the net for really big bass or for a companion's fish that I want to be sure is landed. When a bass is netted, I never drop it into the boat; I hold the netted fish aloft and reach in to grab it by the mouth, so the hooks can be freed of fish and net without undue damage.

If you intend to release the fish, don't let it flop around on the

If bass are allowed to flop around in the boat and remain out of water for too long, they will damage themselves in several ways, none of which is conducive to later release and survival.

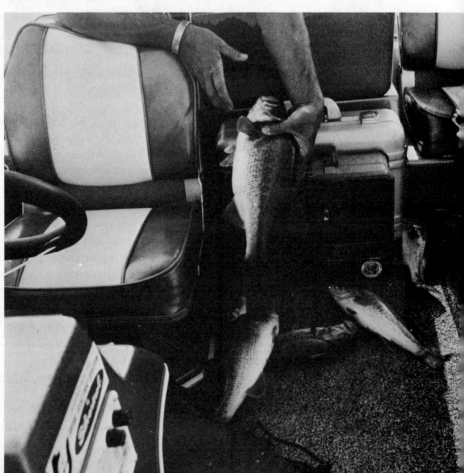

floor of your boat. This, too, results in mucus coating and scale removal, as well as contact with probably harmful elements.

The best technique for landing bass that are to be released is the lip hold, already described. This hold provides the least possible physical contact and does the least damage. There are few other species of fish that can be grasped so handily, either because they have sharp teeth along their lower lip (which a bass does not) or because their mouths are too small for easy thumb insertion. This landing technique requires caution, since a bass is usually hooked in some corner of the mouth, and the hooks are often exposed. If the lure has many hooks, the bass should be well subdued before a lip-landing attempt is made.

Your hand should be wet before you touch the fish, which aids in preventing scale or mucus coating loss. It is also desirable that you do not take the fish out of the water. Almost any fish can be released without being touched at all if you hold your rod high enough to keep the fish's head up and use a pair of needle-nose pliers to unhook the fish. This is a technique I often employ for slimy, toothy fish such as pickerel and northern pike. For general practice, however, I don't recommend it.

An advantage to leaving a bass in the water, besides decreasing harmful physical contact, is that the fish is not exposed to the trauma of harmful out-of-the-water breathing. The longer a fish is held out of its environment for unhooking, photographing, etc., the less will be its chances of surviving.

The best way to release a bass is technically not to catch it. This sounds like facetious advice, but it refers to a hooked fish that can be shaken off at boatside. Sometimes you can bring a bass to the boat and use your rod and line to jiggle the lure free of the fish, especially if the fish is hooked lightly on a single hook or if your lure has barbless hooks (which it won't unless you've crimped the barbs down or filed them off). You have to be careful that you don't break light line or tear the mouth of the fish when heavy line is used, but sometimes, gentle jiggling of the lure while the fish is lying passively near you will permit the hook to slip out. This can be accomplished without touching the fish and is fine for anglers who know they won't keep a bass, yet want the satisfaction of hooking and playing it.

The manner in which bait or plastic worm fishermen set the hook in a bass is another factor in that fish's survival later on. The longer you wait for a bass to swallow your offering, the greater the probability that the fish will be gut- or gill-hooked, and the less its chance of survival. There is no question that fish caught on artificial lures are less severely hooked than those caught on bait. Treble-hooked lures, furthermore, are every bit as practical as single-hook lures, not only for hooking fish, but for ensuring their harmless release.

Deeply hooked fish pose problems because the hook can penetrate vital organs, either when swallowed or through the angler's effort to extricate it. Bass are seldom hooked deeply on lures, but commonly so on bait and occasionally on plastic worms. This makes it vitally important for bait anglers to understand what to do with a sublegal-size bass.

A small fish that is deeply hooked has a much greater chance of surviving if the hook is left in the stomach, and the line is clipped off. Some studies show that line clipping can give a deeply hooked fish a 300 percent greater chance of survival over one with the hook removed. Strong stomach acids will dissolve a hook in time. Stainless steel and cadmium-tin hooks do not break down in saltwater, so you should not use these in bass fishing.

If a bass is bleeding, its chances of survival decrease drastically. Most fish that are gill-hooked will bleed. The gill, a very delicate organ in all fish, should not be touched. If you have a bleeding bass that is of legal size, keep it and eat it. Release another, healthier fish that you may have already caught, or may catch later, in its stead.

The survival of released bass depends on other factors in addition to handling, the two most important being water temperature and how the fish is played. A tired fish is much more susceptible to harm than a fairly vigorous one. Though bass are reasonably able fighters, they do not have to be played for extended periods, unless you are fishing with light tackle and the fish is exceptionally large. Bass have a better survival rate if they are played forcefully (not manhandled, but not coddled either), brought to the boat, and released as quickly as possible. If they do seem severely stressed, as they might be if you had a difficult time removing the hooks, hold them gently in the water and lead them around by the lip to force water and oxygen through the gills and into the respiratory system. Do not move them back and forth, just forward.

Late spring, summer, and early fall are the least advantageous times for released fish to survive. This is because the water temperature is warm and the fish are more stressed by the whole experience or are less metabolically suited to recovery. When the water is cool in spring and fall, bass do much better.

Don't get the impression that bass are fragile fish. They are no more fragile than others and are hardier than most (largemouths even more so than smallmouths). Good handling, adequate water temperature, and ample oxygen are keys to their survival.

As you probably understand, seeing a fish swim off is no guarantee of its survival. That is short-term survival only. What the long-term survival may be is speculative. This depends on the treatment of the bass, considering the circumstances and all the other related factors at that moment. Proper care of the fish you want to or must release will go a long way toward helping perpetuate the sport, as well as marking you as an angler of high caliber.

KEEPING BASS ALIVE

The only reasons to keep captured bass live for any period of time are that you want them to stay fresh till you get them home to be cleaned or that you are participating in a tournament where it is important to be able to release the fish at the end of the day. The only good way to keep bass alive and reasonably fit is with some type of aerated livewell. Bass kept on stringers and dragged around for a long time are seldom suitable for release, even though they may still be alive. It is because of tournaments and their bonus weight allowances for live fish that livewells became a standard feature in conventional bass boats.

Bass boat livewells are good for keeping a few bass alive, but most are not designed to hold many fish or to hold really big bass. There is some serious doubt about the effect of day-long holding in this environment. After all, bass kept in a livewell not only have been hooked, played, landed, and handled, but they have also suffered long- or short-term captivity in a restricted place, been bounced around during travel, been confined with other fish, and then have been released at a later time in a foreign place. Some bass will make it, but many won't. This treatment is not doing the bass any good other than keeping it alive. To retain fish in a livewell that you want to keep for consumption is fine; to retain them to show off at the end of the day and then make a heroic release is false sport and is quite likely to be detrimental to the fish.

There are two types of aerated livewells: plastic, metal, or fiberglass versions built into bass boats, and coolers set up with some type of aeration system. Some boats have two small livewells, others have a single large one with a divider. I prefer the large ones and either take out or don't utilize the divider so that the fish have more room.

Most bass boat livewells have cutoff valves that prevent water from entering or exiting. I leave this valve shut most of the time to keep water out of the livewells because when they are full there is a

In cool to moderate water temperatures, properly aerated livewells are excellent for keeping a reasonable number of fish alive.

lot more weight in the boat (water weighs roughly 8 pounds to the gallon). When I catch a bass to be kept, I then open the valve to allow water into the livewells. When you do have a bass in the livewell, you should shut the valves (or plug the drain), since the livewell water will drain out and the fish will be dry if you have to travel any distance. If you have to fill a bass boat livewell quickly, open the valve or plug, put the engine in reverse, and drive backwards. This forces water to come in, filling the livewells.

Make sure that your aerator system lines are clean and free of debris for best aeration performance. Be careful about using livewells for storage of small baitfish. I've found this to be more trouble than it's worth, with fish getting into drain lines and clogging up the aerator. It's a good idea to clean your livewells once in awhile, as a coat of dirt and scum gathers if you use it enough. You can wash out the drain lines with pressured water from a garden hose.

You can fashion a livewell out of a food and beverage cooler, if you have a bilge pump to use for aeration and a battery to power it. I've used the Bayou Ed Bait Rig, formerly distributed by Attwood, for years, and it works well. This features a bilge pump connected to overhead piping that has holes in it. The cooler is filled two-thirds with water, and the rig nestles snugly into the cooler and pumps water down through the pipe and aerates the livewell. The models I've seen are suitable for use with the medium size (48 quart) Igloo and Coleman coolers, but I've successfully adapted them to larger coolers. These devices are also excellent for keeping bait alive.

Two keys to keeping bass alive are the amount of aeration they receive and the condition of the water. Bass need to be in reasonably well-oxygenated water. They survive best in cold water. If I expect to keep bass alive in warm weather, I sometimes put one or two small blocks of ice in my cooler or livewell. This keeps the water temperature suitable for a short while.

A major help in maintaining well-conditioned bass in a livewell is Catch & Release (from Jungle Laboratories), a chemical formula available in many tackle shops and from mail order suppliers. This product contains a mild tranquilizing agent that helps sedate fish and keeps them from banging around in the livewell; an anti-fungus agent that prevents bacterial infection; and other active ingredients meant to keep bass from requiring more oxygen than normal and suitable for maintaining their well-being. I've used Catch & Release often and

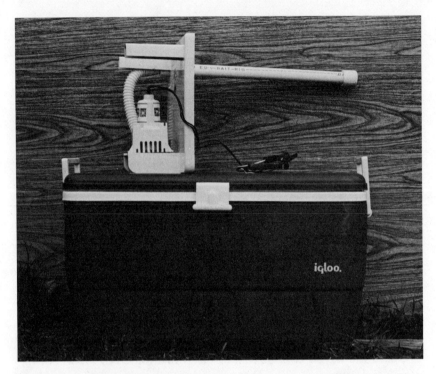

Several aeration devices featuring pumps and plastic pipes are available for use in coolers, making them into functional livewells for up to six medium-size bass.

think very highly of it. When using it, you must keep your livewell plugged so that water will not escape, or you'll find that you have to add this product to it regularly, as treated water will disperse through the overflow line or out the drain when you move quickly.

USING A STRINGER

Although a stringer is perhaps the most utilized device for retaining fish, it is not a good one if your intention is to release the fish later. Stringing a bass is traumatic for the fish, seldom leaving it in good enough condition to be released at the end of the day. Of course, if your intention is to keep and eat all the fish, putting them on a stringer is fine. Once you put them on a stringer, however, they should stay on it—meaning that if you already have a few on the stringer and catch a bass bigger than the rest, don't decide to release one of the previously strung fish and substitute the new one to comply with your state bag limit.

Stringers are made of metal, nylon, and rope, and may have metal or plastic hook snaps on them. Those with hook snaps are preferable to those without because each bass can be well secured, and the hooks are spaced well enough apart to let the fish be relatively unrestricted as it is retained in the water. The best way to fasten a bass to a stringer is to run the hook snap through both lips. To accomplish this, bring the point of the open hook snap up from underneath the lower jaw, through the soft tissue, then up from underneath the upper jaw and through it before closing the snap.

If you have a stringer with snaps, make sure that the snaps are well secured and won't pop open after you've hooked a bass on them. Check the strength of the "O" rings or connectors that affix the snap to the stringer; some won't handle much weight and may need to be replaced.

Many stringers are lost with fish on them because the stringer was not properly fastened to the boat, so be sure that your stringer won't come loose. Also be sure to take the stringer out of the water when the boat is under even the slowest motor speed. If you leave it in the water, the stringer may break or the fish may pull off; it may kick water up in the boat; or it may get caught in the engine propeller if it is long enough. If the latter happens, you'll have minced bass— the swiftest gutting and filleting job you've ever unfortunately seen.

CLEANING AND FILLETING

If you plan on baking your bass or if you want the skin to be cooked with the fish, you'll need to remove the scales. Scaling is best accomplished when the fish is whole and by working from tail to head. I use my fillet knife blade to scale fish, though a spoon, a tooth-edged scaler, or some equivalent implement will suffice. If you're at an outdoor cleaning station, which can be found at some piers, landings, marinas, and fish camps, you might be able to run water on the fish to facilitate scale removal and keep them from flying all over, which they tend to do otherwise. In any event it's best to scale fish outdoors in a suitable locale because of this.

If you aren't going to fillet a bass, you need to gut it by removing the entrails from its body cavity after it has been scaled. Insert the point of a sharp knife blade in the anal area and move it forward until it is near the base of the pelvic fin. Clean out the contents of the body cavity, being especially careful to remove completely the blood-line (kidney) recessed in the cavity.

Cut the head and tail off if they aren't needed. For small fish that will be pan-fried, you should remove the dorsal and anal fins; slice along each side of the base of these fins, then pull free. Flush the cavity with clean cool water. At this point, a bass that has been gutted and scaled is ready for eating or freezing.

The quickest method of cleaning bass is to fillet them, which removes the rib cage bones that anguish many reluctant fish-eaters. Properly done filleting loses little meat and is accomplished easily. One of the keys to good filleting is having the proper instrument. A sharp, moderately flexible blade, 7 to 8 inches long, with an upwardly turned point, is best.

The first filleting step is to make an angled cut behind the pectoral fin down to the backbone. Reverse the direction of the blade so that it is facing the tail and lying flat on the backbone, and slice back toward the tail along the backbone. A smooth cut, rather than a stop-and-go sawing motion, is best. If the fish has been scaled, cut through the skin at the tail.

If the skin is to be removed in the filleting process, do not cut through the tail, but slice to the end without severing, and flop the meat backward. Angle your knife through the meat to the skin, then slice along the skin, separating the meat while exerting pressure on the skin with your free hand. If you accidentally cut through the tail, freeing the fillet from the carcass, you will find it a little more difficult to remove the skin. In this case, press the thumbnail of your free hand on the tail of the fillet (or use a fork), then skin it.

Now, with either scaled or skinned fillet, cut behind the rib cage, slicing the whole section away. Use the same procedure for the other side of the fish. Rinse fillets and prepare for the freezer or for eating.

If you do this correctly, you'll have a clean fillet, and you'll have sacrificed hardly any meat. The two most crucial steps here are the actual cutting of meat along the backbone, and the separation of meat

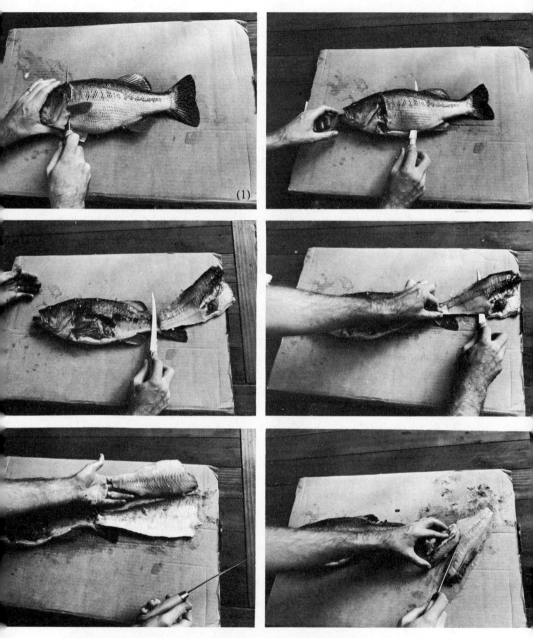

To fillet a bass: Make an angled cut behind the pectoral fin to the backbone (1). Reverse the direction of the blade and slice back toward the tail along the backbone (2). Slice to the end without severing, and flop the meat backward (3). Angle the knife through the meat to the skin, and slice along the skin (4), severing the entire section from the skin (5). Slice the rib cage away (6), and repeat this procedure for the other side of the fish.

and skin. The former requires a smooth slicing motion and attention to detail. Be sure that the blade is as close to the backbone as you can get without slicing off bone chips. Hold the fish firmly. Be careful not to angle your knife downward or you'll cut through the backbone of small fish and have a difficult time trying to undo your error. The latter requires keeping the knife flat, which a slightly flexible blade allows you to do. If you cut through the skin, you'll probably hack some flesh apart and lose a little meat.

Many people use another method of filleting, which produces the same end result. In this method, you make a lateral cut behind the pectoral fin, then run the knife along the side of the dorsal fin and carefully slice the flesh away from the rib cage and remaining carcass. This takes a little longer to accomplish than the method I've detailed, but possibly saves a tad more meat.

CARE AND COOKERY

If you bring home fresh bass that will be eaten in a day or two, you can wrap them tightly in freezer paper and foil or in a sealable plastic bag, and place them in the refrigerator. Let them stay like this no more than two days, and then only if they were refrigerated the same day they were caught.

For longer storage, bass must be frozen. Remember that fish are very perishable, so they must be wrapped properly and won't stay fresh when frozen for extremely long periods of time. It's wise to eat fish as soon as possible. By labeling and dating packages, you can consume stored fish on a rotational calendar basis, using the oldest fish first.

I've stored a lot of fish in one tight wrapping of aluminum foil, which doesn't seem harmful for a short period. But if they're in the freezer like this very long, they'll develop the white-tipped symptoms of freezer burn; plus, it's easy to puncture or scrape corners of foil packages and expose the contents. If you're willing to make the extra effort and expense, the best method is to double-wrap or even triple-wrap fish using wrapping paper, foil, and/or freezer paper. The delicatessen wrap, in which the ends of the paper are brought over the fish to meet one another and then are folded together several times, ensures a good seal.

Be sure to pack fish so there is enough for yourself or your family for a single meal, and, if possible, put wrapping paper in between fish or fillets to make them easier to separate and thaw. Also, label each package by writing on the outside with an indelible marker (or put a piece of masking tape on the package and label that). I note the date, species, quantity of fish, method of cleaning, and origin on packages.

Another method of storing bass is to freeze fillets in blocks of water in plastic containers, empty milk cartons, etc. If you don't have much food in your freezer or only put a few fish in it occasionally, you might try this.

Fish-cookery methods can be as simple or as elaborate as you want them to be. To my knowledge, no one has ever written a book strictly about the care and treatment of fish to be cooked, but there have been plenty of books about fish cookery.

Simplicity and ease of preparation mark the basis of my bass-cooking efforts, which are primarily directed at frying. There's nothing difficult about frying. Where oil is used, it's important that the oil be extremely hot before any fish are deposited in it. Use plenty of oil, enough to cover the fish, for deep frying. If you don't have enough oil to cover the fish, you can still cook them well if you turn the fish over so that both sides have an equal time in the oil. Fish fried in butter must also be turned.

Cut fillets in small fingers or chunks for frying, as small pieces fry best, and use tongs to turn or remove them from the oil. For pan-frying, dip the bass in milk or egg (I prefer egg), then roll well in bread crumbs or batter. My family is partial to Italian-seasoned bread crumbs for this. Lately we've been using Old Guide's Secret prepared batter as well. Fish are fried for a few minutes on each side, then drained on paper towels before serving. Batters that produce a thick coating are best for deep-frying. Take care not to put too many chunks of fish in a deep-fryer at one time; remove after a few minutes when the fish are golden brown.

Many people have a tendency to overcook fish (making them mealy and dry), so it's important to recognize the point at which the fish is done. You have to watch fish while they're cooking and test their doneness by inserting a fork into the flesh and twisting it. If it flakes readily, it's done and should be removed from the heat. The larger the fish and the thicker the fillet, the harder it is to judge doneness and achieve the right moist and flaky texture, but you must keep checking it to achieve the optimum result.

14

NIGHT FISHING

I can assure you that bass fishing at night is hardly ever dull, which is what endears me to the sport. Nighttime bass fishing excitement is largely restricted to the fishing itself, but the general environment also contributes to the entertainment. A pond or lake after dark is markedly different from the daytime environment. Frogs croak. Bats, bugs, and mosquitoes fly freely. Fish splash loudly in the shallows. The air is cool, sometimes chilling. Familiar places and objects seem foreign. Shore lights and moonlight occasionally play tricks on your mind. Every sound, every action is accentuated.

You've probably heard that fishing for bass at night in the summer is a good way to beat the so-called "dog-days" blahs. It's no secret that summer bass aren't eager to further the sporting ambitions of fishermen. Or that success during the day on large lakes is usually achieved by fishing deep. In many places, night fishing for bass in midsummer is consistently more effective than daytime fishing.

Midsummer is the prime time. That is when the amount of daylight is long, and air and water temperatures are regularly high. Daytime human activity on the water—swimming, skiing, boating, fishing—peaks then, too. Most of the time, the lake is all yours after dark, and fishing success can be high.

In my experience the lakes that suffer the heaviest traffic during the day are often the best night producers. I concentrate most of my night fishing on small lakes and ponds, many of which are ringed entirely or partially by residential communities, youth camps, or bungalow colonies, and which host a lot of daytime activity. These places are generally shallow and often blessed with an abundance of cover. The beach area, boathouses, coves, docks, weedy or rocky points, and

Big bass are often caught in the evening or at night in the summer. This large-mouth took a surface plug fished along a stump just before dark.

shallow lily pad and weed areas are prime nighttime bass haunts. Ponds and small lakes also benefit more from cool summer evenings, too, because their temperature drops, often stimulating fish activity. You needn't fish very deep either.

Though there are exceptions, most night bass fishing is done in the shallows, basically in depths of 6 feet or less. This is ideal for surface and shallow-water lures and tactics. Deeper fishing can also be successful at times, particularly in large lakes and reservoirs. Some big lakes, however, are big busts for night anglers. This is often determined by the extent of forage and amount of undisturbed daytime movement.

Surface fishing is the most stimulating form of night bass angling. Because you can't see your lure working and can't see a fish strike, you work primarily by hearing and feeling. It's a special thrill to hear the telltale slurp of a bass inhaling your lure, then feel it on the end of the line. Actually, listening to some surface lures, like a popper or a wobbling surface plug, and anticipating a strike has its own entertainment value. Surface lures are likely to catch some of the biggest bass, too.

Surface lures that are successful at night need to be able to create a commotion. Noise is often a paramount factor for good night bass fishing. Wobbling surface plugs are tops. Crazy Crawlers (Heddon) and Jitterbugs (Arbogast) are equally successful, particularly in large sizes. Maintaining a steady, slow retrieval cadence is the key to effectiveness. At night, bass respond best to and are more likely to be caught on a steady retrieve. The almost monotonous *plop-plop* of these plugs is a come-hither call to nearby bass.

In night fishing, you often miss hits, and fish strike and miss the bait. On dark nights a surface lure offers little, if any, silhouette effect to guide a fish visually. Therefore, the bass responds primarily to sounds. A regular retrieval rate can give a bass a more accurate fix on the precise location and directional movement of a lure. Thus, when it strikes, it has a better chance of connecting. Sometimes it is worthwhile to stagger the retrieval cadence or to use a popping plug retrieved with intermittent jerks, but this is not nearly as reliable as continuous wobbling and is more prone to draw errant strikes.

Missed strikes are one of the chief peculiarities of night bass angling. They have two common causes. One, because bass are primarily guided by sound, a lot of fish miss the intended target, whether it is moving continuously or irregularly. Occasionally, a fish will hit a missed bait a second time, but you'll have a better chance to score if you have a different lure on another rod to toss at it. Shallow-running crankbaits or spinnerbaits could be good lures then because of their detectable vibrations.

The other factor is related to the fisherman. He, too, is usually working on sound. Very often you'll hear a strike before seeing or feeling it. Many times the fisherman is overeager, and he actually sets the hook too soon. It's a very hard technique to master, but a momentary delay in hook setting is advantageous at night. When you actually feel the fish with the lure, set the hook.

If a bass misses the bait and you haven't yanked it out of the water, but kept it coming, he may zero in on it again. Bass are aggressive at night and when they strike, it is with gusto. They don't daintily suck in a bait—they smash it. When they are right on target, you'll know it and you'll have a hookup. Perhaps some anglers will find themselves (as I often do) turning an ear in the direction of the lure to hear better and leaning forward to be ready. It's not necessary. Anticipation is the downfall of many an angler at night.

Perhaps equally effective on the surface as wobbling plugs are buzz baits. They are best in $3/8$-ounce-and-larger sizes for night use. Another surface lure with after-dark value is a propellered stick bait. Instead of retrieving this in the normal pull-pause tantalizing action, speed up the retrieve to a quicker, more direct pace. This lure, in particular, gives the impression of slashing, feeding fish and, used in combination with your partner's lure, can prove to be interesting.

Surface lures don't work all the time, of course, so don't stick with them if results aren't encouraging. Shallow-running crankbaits, spinnerbaits, jigs, and worms all have merit for night bass fishing. I'm most partial to spinnerbaits for fishing in and around grass and pad coverings, along shore, and in shallow water. The spinner blades make vibrations in the water, enhancing the lure's detectability. Worms, though not good for covering a lot of territory in the dark, are great for fishing specific locations, and since they are rigged to be fished weedless, don't invite many hang-ups. (Getting snagged, either on an object in the water or a bush or tree limb on the bank, is the bane of all night bass anglers.)

In small ponds, crankbaits prove more of a burden than a blessing because of the abundance of cover and opportunities to get snagged. The shallowest running crankbaits, including floating-diving minnow imitators, have some merit over submerged weedbeds and along the edges of vegetation and other shallow cover, and hold a lot of promise around rocky environs in locales where crayfish (which are nocturnal) are found.

I like sturdy tackle for night fishing, since you never know what you may encounter. I use only bait-casting gear for lure fishing at night, generally with 12-pound-test line, and heavier line in large bass and snag-infested waters. Usually, you don't know what obstacles are between you and a hooked fish; with stout tackle you can apply a lot of pressure on fish and get them to the boat fast. You can also pull your unseen lure free of most weed and pad tangles. Heavy spinning gear will do, of course, and some may find it preferable because a severe over-run on a bait-casting reel is big trouble in the dark, especially if it occurs during prime-action time.

And when is prime time? Some folks say after midnight. Some say not till two hours after sunset. Some say just before and after a full moon. My experiences have been best on dark moonless or cloudy nights. I have also had exceptionally good success just before and after a sunset. Approximately a two- to three-hour period from 7:30 to 10 o'clock (in midsummer) has been consistently good, with action often nonexistent thereafter. Many other anglers, however, don't have good success until after midnight, fishing from then till daylight. You should try to establish a night-activity pattern by being on the water as often as possible after dark. The more you fish each particular water, the more attuned you'll become to fish activity.

There are a few other points about night fishing for bass that you should consider. One of the most important is to be quiet. Noise from the banging of oars, shifting of tackle boxes, dropping of rods, coughing, loud talking, etc., is magnified at night. Bass are sensitive to this. They like noisy plugs, not noisy fishermen.

It's also a good idea to wear a hat. A hat at night, for me at least, is like a security blanket. Everywhere I've ever fished at night, bats were abundant. I've hit them with the top of my rod, had them bump my line, and had them dart after a cast lure. They sometimes come a lot closer than you'd like, and a hat may make you feel a little more comfortable.

You should also use an electric motor if you have one, keeping it on low power. Keep the shaft down far enough into the water so that you don't churn up the surface with your start-up, and use a weedguard or weedless propeller to make navigation through unseen vegetation less difficult.

Keep light use at night to a minimum. Don't flash your light around looking for the shore or for your lost lure, etc. In a dark atmosphere, such action is usually enough to alert the fish. If you need a light to find a lure or help to see while you tie a knot, discreetly use it low in the boat, preferably masking most of the beam. Although flashing a conventional light in the water or about your boat does not encourage success and serves to impede your own night vision (you'll be surprised how well your eyes adapt to the dark and how much

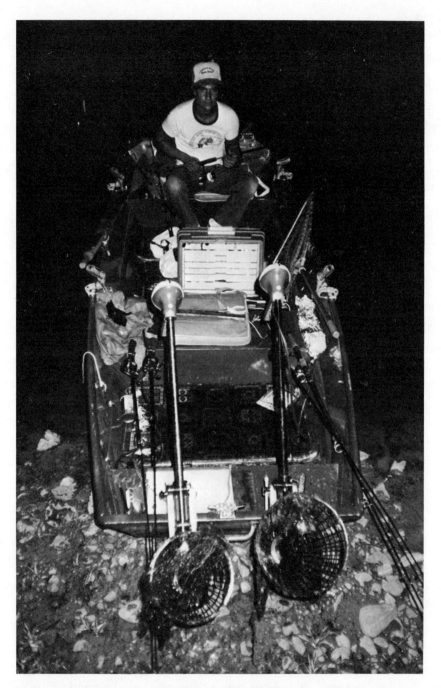

Electric motors are especially valuable at night and allow you to maneuver quietly. Silent stalking, no bright lights, and sturdy tackle are some of the requisites for night success.

you can see without a light), you might look for bright lights on docks, piers, or boat houses. These may attract bugs. If a lot of bugs fall into the water, that will attract small fish, and in turn larger ones. Bright light may also attract small baitfish, bringing bass in with them.

One of the hardships of night bass fishing is tying knots. Holding a lure up to the moon or the feeble light of the stars to help guide the line through an eyelet is exasperating. Tying a knot in the dark by feel can be done if you're adept, but some folks need light for that, too. Using a snap will aid lure changing, but some lures don't work well with snaps. (I prefer not to use them at all.)

I've licked the knot-tying problem by keeping a Zorro black light with me. I have two, a small one that works off flashlight batteries and a larger one that runs off a 12-volt battery and which I keep in my bass boat. If you're so inclined, you can mount these up on the gunwale and use them to watch some of your line, especially the rod tip, while retreving. I keep mine in the floor of the boat and use it when tying on a lure. A black light only works on fluorescent line, making it seem to glow.

Be prepared with your tackle when night fishing. An extra rod or two, prerigged with a lure and ready to use at a moment's notice, is valuable when the action is fast and you get snagged or some other problem arises.

Using boats at night has disadvantages, one being the difficulty of launching in ponds or small lakes, most of which have no, or poor, access locations. With my four-wheel-drive I can put a bass boat, johnboat, or canoe into almost any locale. I may stumble around a bit in the dark pushing boats off trailers or winching them on, but it's usually worth the effort. You may want to install a pair of rear spotlights on the back of your vehicle to illuminate the launch or trailer area and help you see what you're doing.

Watch how you handle fish at night. I once caught what I thought was a bass on a surface plug, brought it to the boat, reached over to lipland it, and found my fingers about to grasp a well-barbed bullhead. Use of a net, on the other hand, can be problematic at night when multi-hooked lures get tangled in the mesh. With sturdy tackle you can swing a medium-size fish onboard and grasp it. Make sure that your bass are well played-out before landing them by hand. Think about what you're doing, and be careful in the dark.

15

SPRING FISHING

Anyone who has to spend free spring time tending to a garden, painting the house, or performing maintenance chores has my sympathy, but not my help. Spring is a time of the year that was especially created for bass fishing. Bass are as accessible and agreeable at this time as they are likely to be all year. The promise and freshness of this season makes anglers enthusiastic, and opportunity matched with optimism is always a potent mixture.

Though you shouldn't expect to have miraculous one-fish-every-other-cast angling, you can experience regular action and catch trophy-size bass, if you are well-versed in the vagaries of springtime angling. Fishing techniques and bass behavior during this season are heavily influenced by natural factors. Understanding nature's calendar will help you focus on the where, when, and how aspects of catching bass.

The most obvious influence on bass behavior in the spring is a gradual warming of the water. In southerly areas this may be very gradual and extend for a considerable period of time, while in northern locales it may be of much shorter duration. If you were a vagabond angler wishing to sample the best spring fishing available, you might start your journey in early- to mid-March in southern Florida or Texas and work north to end up in New England or the Minnesota/Ontario boundary in mid- to late-June. I have experienced fishing in Florida in late March that was quite similar to fishing in Missouri in late April, to Pennsylvania in late May, and to New Hampshire in late June.

Weather in the winter and spring further influences the timetable. A severe winter puts spring conditions two to three weeks behind normal patterns. An unusually warm spring hastens them up. Severe spring weather fluctuations disturb fish behavioral patterns and can lead to poor fishing. Peculiar weather seems to be the norm these days. Instead of planning on routinely expected developments in seasons and fish behavior, it's best to realize this and simply be prepared to capitalize on or adapt to changing conditions.

Comfortable water conditions, preferably in a locale that offers security and feeding opportunities, are important for bass at any season, but especially in the spring. Bass are largely inactive in the winter, since cold water slows their metabolism down, requiring little food and movement. As the days become longer and the sun's influence greater, the water warms; then temperature holds a key to bass activity.

All bodies of water behave similarly in the spring. The surface layer and shallows warm first. Bass begin to move out of deep sanctuaries, becoming more active as the temperature rises. Though bass can be caught in water colder than 50 degrees, it is my experience that when temperatures reach this plateau, bass are most likely to have shaken their winter behavior. When the water warms up enough, in the 60- to 65-degree range for largemouths and 58 to 62 for smallmouths, they spawn. This may occur from late March to late June, depending on locale, species of fish (largemouth or smallmouth), and type of water conditions. Eventually, the water will become too warm in the shallow and upper layers, driving fish deeper or further into thick cover, where their comfort, food, and security requirements can be met.

Paying attention to water temperature is one of the best things that a spring bass angler can do. I installed a surface temperature gauge on my bass boat and refer to it constantly. In other boats I use a pool thermometer hung over the side. Checking water temperature can help you find places that are especially productive for largemouth bass.

There are some interesting spring phenomena at work in each body of water. Small lakes and ponds that are generally shallow throughout are the first to warm up and are often best for early spring fishing. A shallow pond will warm up weeks ahead of a deep lake even if they are side-by-side. In the beginning of the spring, given the option to fish two such lakes, I would focus on the small one first.

Small lakes may warm up entirely by several degrees per day during a warm spring spell. A sustained period of warm weather will activate the fish in this environment. A cool spell, however, will drop the temperature and confuse the fish. Cool nights and mornings have a negative effect on spring fishing, which is countered only by sunlight and mild evening weather.

The surface temperature of large lakes, reservoirs, and small deep lakes doesn't rise as dramatically in a given day, but temperature can vary at different areas of the lake. Shallow flats, coves, feeder creeks, and tributaries are generally much warmer than the main body of the lake, and are prime locales when the rest of the lake is still too cold to induce significant fish activity. Northern and northwestern sectors of a lake, particularly the coves and bays, warm up slightly ahead of other areas, as they are exposed more to the sun.

Regardless of lake type, afternoon fishing is often best in early spring. Water temperature in shallow lakes and in shallow areas of larger lakes can rise several degrees during a sunny day. Fish that have

Tributaries, including creeks and small rivers, warm up before the main body of the lake and may be several degrees warmer in early spring, particularly after a heavy, warm rainfall. Bass are often more active in these areas than elsewhere in the lake prior to spawning.

been subdued by cool nights and cool shallow-water temperatures respond to the afternoon warmth, becoming more acclimated to the conditions and thus more aggressive in chasing bait.

A heavy warm rain is especially desirable in the spring, and bass fishing will pick up shortly thereafter. Large rivers and navigable tributaries that enter a big lake will have significantly higher temperatures than the main portion of the lake. The area of the lake nearest the tributary will benefit from a warm rain, too. Tributaries that drain a large watershed area may not warm up for two or three days after the rain. In small lakes with small inlet creeks, the water temperature difference may be observed the day after it rains. In large lakes you may notice a difference in water temperature from one area to the other if there has been a strong wind that could push warm surface water to one side of the lake. This may spur bass feeding activities for a while until temperatures level out.

You can't rely exclusively on water temperature to guide you to good spring bass fishing, however. If you aren't catching fish in the shallows at a time when water conditions suggest bass should be there, it could be an indication that the fish are still holding in deeper water. If a harsh winter or cold early spring delayed bass activity, yet was followed by a sudden warm spell that brought water temperatures up, bass will probably remain less active than usual for the time of the year because previous environmental conditions had been the dominating influence.

In addition to water temperature, another important factor in the spring behavior of bass is their own biological makeup, condition, and requirements. If your area were to receive a sudden early warm spell this spring, sending surface and shallow-water temperatures up into a range where they are suitable for bass, that doesn't necessarily mean that the bass will rush into the shallows. Some bass may take advantage of this situation to feed, but if they are not ready to spawn, meaning that their biological clocks don't put them in a spawning disposition and their eggs aren't ripe, they will not prepare to do so regardless of the temperature.

Notice that I said "prepare to do so." Bass go through several spawning-related stages of behavior in the spring. In their pre-spawning period, the fish are not biologically ready to spawn, or the water temperature in the shallows is not yet stabilized and conducive to this activity. Nonetheless, bass may be holding near the expected spawning areas, but in deep water.

Not all bass in a lake will be in the same stage at any given time. Some bass may still be relatively immobile in cold deep water while others have reacted to the early signs of impending warmth and have moved toward shallower water. Thus, when some are in a spawning mode, others will be in a pre-spawn mode. Bass in a pre-spawn stage will feed and may be caught more readily than those in the process of spawning. They may feed in deep water on the fringes of the shallows or come into the shallows for a short while and return to deeper water.

When bass are ready to spawn, the male, which is usually the smaller of the two fish, prepares a site and guards it after the eggs have been laid and fertilized. The females are only on the nest for a short time. They are not particularly interested in feeding just prior to spawning, are attracted onto a bed by a male, and leave after all their eggs have been deposited.

Largemouth bass make their beds in fairly shallow water, often 2 or 3 feet deep, on a fairly hard, though not rocky, bottom, and usually near some object, such as a log or stump. Smallmouths make their beds on a hard gravel bottom and don't seem to have the object fetish that largemouths do. Both species may make their beds in deeper water, such as 10 or 12 feet in some places, but they prefer 2- to 6-foot depths.

The worst thing that could happen to spawning bass is for the water level to drop quickly. This will push bass off their beds, expose nests, and possibly cause the fish to make spawning attempts in unsuitable locales or to abandon spawning efforts and absorb the eggs. It is not uncommon to catch a bass in the summer with a small egg mass in its body cavity. Those eggs were never laid, often due to falling water (or a severe cold spell) in the spring when the fish were spawning. If you fish a lake that is missing bass in a particular size range (perhaps the lake has plenty of 9- to 10-inch fish, and some 14- to 16-inches, but few of those in between), this could be the reason.

Immediately after spawning, bass seem somewhat spent and unenergetic for a short while. This is a relatively unproductive angling time. Many bass that are caught now have reddish and split tails, with bruises and sores on their body. This results from the hardships of building nests and mating. Once bass recover from this stressful period

A shallow flat or cove is prime territory for spawning bass.

they are hungry. They will be very aggressive in shallow-water areas that are not only warming, but which provide a host of feeding opportunities as well.

By now the fry of many fish species, including bass, pickerel, pike, perch, and walleye, have hatched. Small bass and intermediate-size fish will prey on this fry, and bass in turn will prey on all small and intermediate-size forage. Their metabolism is in gear and they are starting to exhibit standard patterns of behavior, locating near cover, bottom, and objects, and utilizing these as ambush points to prey on other fish or crayfish. Their willingness to strike a lure now is motivated as much by hunger as instinctive aggressiveness.

Nearly all lures have merit at some time during the spring season, yet crankbaits and spinnerbaits are the most functional throughout this period and throughout the different stages of lake development and bass behavior.

Crankbaits are terrific for scouring the bottom in relatively shallow water. (Shallow water can be considered as 8 feet or less in the spring, 12 feet or more thereafter.) Speed of retrieval is particularly important, and it varies through the spring. Generally, the colder the water the slower the speed of retrieval. That doesn't mean that in warm weather you should blaze the lure along, but for very cold early-spring conditions, you often can't reel a crankbait slow enough. In the first part of the season, bass won't expend much energy to chase a fast-moving crankbait. They usually ignore it. An action that is slow enough to still get the built-in wiggling motion out of a lure is just right in cold water.

It pays to watch your lure as it comes back to the boat at this time. Often, bass swirl after a lure near the boat or take a half-serious swipe at it. This can indicate that you are retrieving your lure too fast, that the bass are only vaguely interested in feeding, or that they are trying to stun their prey before consuming it. Perhaps all of these factors are at work. If bass are poorly hooked or impaled by one barb of the rear treble of a crankbait, it is a similar indication. A slow steady retrieve or a slow stop-and-go retrieve may be the answer.

The type of crankbait to use—shallow-, intermediate-, or deep-diving—depends upon various factors. If the water is very cold, you'll probably have to use a lure that gets down 5 to 10 feet and is worked on points, steeply sloping banks, and shores with a breakline (distinct drop-off to deeper water) at the 5- to 10-foot level. In shallow lakes that have a lot of stumps, flats with cover (though cover is barely starting to emerge when the water is still cold), and the like, a shallow- or intermediate-running crankbait is likely to be best. As the water warms and the cover, which may be grass, milfoil, or cabbage weeds, begins to grow up, the same crankbaits can be used to skim the edges and tops, and only speed of retrieval may vary.

In shallow lakes that have a lot of grass and pad cover, crankbaits will eventually become impossible to use because they hang up on the

A crankbait caught this early-spring bass, which was waiting by a near-shore structure to snatch an unsuspecting meal.

vegetation too much. This will happen by late spring. Shallow-running crankbaits can still be effective at this time, however, if they are worked in a stop-and-go manner over the top of this cover. Minnow-imitation plugs can be worked very effectively in a straight or erratic retrieve over this cover as well.

Crankbaits are particularly productive in large lakes with a lot of deep water. There is usually no vegetative cover in these environments. Largemouth and smallmouth bass begin their spring movement along rocky bluffs and rip rap or craggy shorelines that slope steeply into deep water. Here, crankbaits worked parallel to the shore can be the ticket for early fishing success. Crankbaits can also be hot in lakes with stump fields, timber flats, timbered coves, etc. Bass get into these areas in the spring before and after spawning. Where the outside bends of submerged creek or river channels meet the shore (often by a bluff) can be a choice crankbait locale, too.

Don't overlook the importance of rocks to early season bass. In addition to being an ambush point and feeding locale, rocks in shallow water retain heat. Bass may utilize rocks to help stimulate the development of their eggs and milt. Or the rocks may provide security. Smallmouths, of course, are known as fish that congregate around rocky shores, gravelly areas, rocky shoals, and the like, but largemouths may inhabit such areas as well.

Crayfish dwell in rocky areas; this explains why bass are there. Crayfish are a staple of smallmouth bass through all seasons and are one of many food items for largemouths, depending on their availability. In the spring, when other forage is not yet abundant near shore, crayfish become especially important in a bass' diet.

To some extent, crankbaits imitate crayfish as well as small baitfish, particularly when they are rooting along the bottom and scouring through the sand, rocks, and gravel. Colors or patterns that imitate crayfish are prime bass-catchers in extremely rocky areas (when fishing for smallmouth) and in areas known to have a good population of crayfish.

In places that have large shad or alewife populations, where crayfish are not part of the diet, or where small minnows make up the bulk of early-season bass food, silver- and white-colored crankbaits are especially effective. Most of the time these colors are referred to by manufacturers and anglers alike as "shad."

Other colors that may have merit, especially where largemouth bass are concerned, are bone, chartreuse, gold, and chrome. Color choice in lures has a lot to do with the color of the water being fished. For instance, a lightly colored crayfish-patterned crankbait may work better than a dark one in muddy or tea-colored water (which occurs a lot in rivers and in large reservoirs fed by rivers, due to runoff). Light colored crankbaits that have flash are good in the same waters. Chartreuse is a good color in blue-green water. Gold and chrome are good in dark, tannen-stained lakes.

Natural-finish-style plugs don't necessarily have more fish appeal than lures with standard finishes and colors, since action, vibration, and diving ability are primary attributes. There are times, however, when lures that resemble certain bass forage in nearly every detail are especially successful fish-catchers. In northern lakes where perch and walleye are abundant and where small members of these species are available and eager to prey on bass fry in early- to mid-spring, shallow-running crankbaits with perch or walleye finishes are good largemouth baits. The same can be true with bluegill and catfish imitators.

Though spinnerbaits don't represent an identifiable food source, they certainly appeal to the instinctive nature of bass and are highly effective spring lures. Spinnerbaits are a tempting substantive morsel, offering visual elements of good action and motion (the swimming skirt and spinning blades) plus vibration. They are primarily used on largemouth bass, but can be effective for smallmouths as well. (They are also devastating on pickerel in the spring and on northern pike, and the smallest models are suitable for various panfish species.)

Spinnerbaits can be fished deep, but they are most effectively employed in the shallows, preferably within sight. Spinnerbaits don't become principal spring bass lures until the water warms enough to stabilize fish behavior and keep bass in the shallows. These lures have little effect in very cold water; crankbaits are best then.

Though retrieval speed is not as critical with spinnerbaits as with crankbaits, these lures can be worked too fast. When bass are striking short and nipping rather than nailing lures, it is time to slow down your retrieve.

Watch a spinnerbait closely when you fish it shallow. In the spring, bass commonly take a stab at this lure, yet miss it. Sometimes these fish can be caught by casting the spinnerbait out again, though bass usually spurn it the second time around. Tossing a different lure (such as a floating surface plug, crankbait, or plastic worm) in the appropriate spot is a better strategy.

Whether you catch the fish or not, you have an indication of not only bass' presence, but also disposition. I've experienced frustrating spring trips when only a few bass were caught, but many swiped at a spinnerbait, swirled on it, or chased it momentarily near the boat.

A trailer hook is an indispensable spinnerbait addition in the spring, as long as it can be used without causing the lure to foul up when worked through various cover. A lot of short strikers can be caught on trailer hooks, and if you are catching many fish this way, it may be a good idea to slow retrieval speed. I've tried putting a trailer hook on top of a trailer hook, when fish were missing spinnerbaits, but it never seemed to help. One trailer, the same size as the main hook, and with a wide gap, is best.

I'm partial to tandem-bladed spinnerbaits in the spring because they can be worked very slowly and near the surface, and produce a lot of flash. If you have an assortment of silver- and nickel-bladed spinnerbaits, with chartreuse, white, and chartreuse-and-black (or blue) bodies, you are well-equipped for spring bass fishing. White is good in dark, tannen-colored water and in muddy or milky runoff conditions. Chartreuse is better in blue-green environments and in some clear lakes.

One of the most prominent attributes of spinnerbaits is that they are relatively snag- and weed-free and can be fished in nearly all types of cover. In the spring, vegetation, such as moss, pads, weeds, grass, and the like, ranges from almost nonexistent early in the season to thick by the end of the season. Spinnerbaits are effective here until such cover becomes impenetrable.

Other forms of largemouth cover, particularly stumps, timbered flats or fields, fallen trees, and brush, are ideal places to work a spinnerbait. The trick is to cast beyond the target and bring the lure past it, sometimes nicking or bumping the object. An especially productive tactic is to retrieve the lure up to a stump or log from behind, then let it fall over the object and flutter down in front of it before continuing the retrieve. This technique, called slow-rolling, works best with a large single-bladed spinnerbait.

Smallmouths don't inhabit vegetation or much of the non-rocky cover that largemouths prefer. They may be taken with spinnerbaits when they are in shallow rocky environments close to shore, when they are on shoals to feed, and when they are on beds in sparsely covered terrain. Although I have caught some big-lake smallmouths on spinnerbaits fished along rock- and boulder-studded shores, I have also found them slow to hit these lures under similar conditions on other lakes. I know one excellent spring lake where small in-line spinners will take bronzebacks that refuse spinnerbaits, and another where shallow bass occasionally strike a plug and quickly take a jig, but repeatedly pass up a spinnerbait. So it pays to be adaptable.

Spinnerbaits and crankbaits, of course, aren't the only lures that catch springtime bass. Shallow-running floating-diving minnow imitations in single and jointed models are very effective for both largemouths and smallmouths.

This shallow, timbered shoreline could offer good spinnerbait fishing in the spring.

These lures can be worked as swimming plugs or crankbaits in shallow water on a steady retrieve or in a stop-and-go manner. They are very productive surface lures, worked in a pull-pause twitching action and are the primary spring surface bass bait. The colder the water, the less likely bass are to strike any surface lure. In early- to mid-spring a slowly worked, fairly noiseless plug such as this is more likely to garner results than other surface plugs.

As the water warms, some other surface lures become effective. Among these are minnow plugs with fore-and-aft (or just aft) propellers, stick baits, and wobblers. Buzz baits are ineffective until the water temperature hits the low 60's, though shallow lakes that warm quickly may produce buzz bait action earlier in the season than you might anticipate. Spinnerbaits can be run just under the surface to create a wake, and work as well as a buzz bait, although they are quieter.

Spring bass often won't rise for surface lures. If they also won't move for a crankbait or spinnerbait, you may need to go to jigs or worms.

Though the tendency is to think of jigs as lures for mid- to deep-water fishing, they can be effective spring bass lures, especially for smallmouths. One-eighth- to $1/4$-ounce jigs with bucktail, grub, or curl-tailed soft-plastic bodies work when the fish are in mid-depth, near-shore water prior to spawning; when they are on shoals or reefs to feed; and when they are on the beds. Smallmouth guarding the nest after spawning are also susceptible to jigs. The male guardians may swim away from crankbaits or spinnerbaits, but evidently can't resist a slowly worked jig that bounces through the bedding area.

Brown and black colors work well for hair-bodied jigs, while purple, gray, and green are good in soft-plastic bodies. Though my experience with white and yellow jigs for smallmouths has not been overwhelming, some folks swear by these colors.

Plastic worms are essentially for largemouth bass, though a small worm, fished on a jig head, may be suitable smallmouth fare. Worms don't have much appeal to bass in cold water. I've had little success with this bait in the spring when the water was below 55, and seldom fish a worm until the water gets in the mid-60-degree range. A worm is especially good in the spring as a secondary lure, to throw back at a fish that has struck but missed a crankbait, spinnerbait, or surface plug; for catching bedded bass; and when flipped into heavy cover.

A lot of spring fishing is done with live bait, including worms, crayfish, hellgrammites, shiners, and assorted minnows and small bait-fish. At times, live bait undoubtedly catches fish better than artificials in cold, early-spring conditions. As with artificials, the key to live bait success is putting the offering in the most likely areas and at the proper depths.

Though a still-fishing live bait angler should have success, an experienced lure fisherman who covers a lot of ground in the spring has the upper hand. If bass behavior has stabilized, a lure angler can put his wares before a lot of fish, many of which are likely to be aggressive. Moreover, it is easier for the lure angler to release small or unwanted fish without harm. When bass are spawning, however, live bait may amount to an offer that cannot be refused.

When spawning bass strike a lure or bait, they don't do so to consume it. They merely want to get it away from the nest. They'll grab it sideways and swim off with it a few feet, then release it. It's difficult to hook bass that do this. I've had spawning smallmouths hit a surface lure four or five times until they finally got hooked. They are usually hooked lightly, however, on the corner of the mouth or in the jaw on the outside of the mouth.

A plastic worm is often carted off by the tail. A double-hook rig, with the second hook buried close to the tail and connected to the first with strong line, helps hook spawners. You can also use a standard single hook and thread the shank through the worm so the point can be imbedded far back.

Spawning bass are often able to avoid being hooked by jigs, too. If you don't have a good feel for detecting strikes, a smallmouth may pick up, move with, and drop a jig before you react. Many a smallmouth is missed this way or is so lightly hooked that the jig is thrown the minute the bass takes to the air.

You'll lose a lot of fish in the spring, but you'll also catch a lot. With plenty of action, no hot weather, no water skiers, few boaters, and nature coming alive, it's a great time to be bass fishing.

Spinnerbaits are a prime spring lure, especially when bass are active and aggressive.

16

WORKING THE VEGETATION

As I have stressed before, bass are object- and cover-oriented fish, meaning that they inhabit areas that provide cover security, while at the same time offering a vantage point from which to snap up prospective prey. Bass are particularly attracted to aquatic vegetation because it offers them security, opportunities for food, and suitable water temperature, oxygen, and light conditions. Remember that baitfish require food as well as protection from predators, and they, too, find this in the vegetation, so it is natural for bass to frequent such areas.

Deep in the recesses of lily pads, hyacinths, and other masses of aquatic salad, the environs are protected and cooled to a tolerable level for largemouths. They live there, they feed there, and they can be caught there. Vegetation, particularly when it is found in a moderate depth of water (from 3 to 10 feet), is a very reliable place to locate bass in the summer and fall and should be considered by all largemouth bass fishermen, especially those with limited deep-water angling acumen and limited time.

Most forms of vegetation are quite obvious, but others are not—a fact that may come as a surprise to anglers from some parts of the country. Submerged grass and weed beds are common in many places. Pinpointing the location of weedlines is often a crucial element in determining boat position, lure presentation, and fishing technique. A depthfinder can be a big asset in this situation. The point is to be aware that there is both submerged and emergent vegetation.

There are also varying concentrations to contend with—thin, thick, thicker, and unbearable. All of this can be fished, though you can't get your boat through the worst of it except by poling. Some

Promising vegetation to fish for largemouth bass includes matted weeds and hydrilla (top left), thinner grass (bottom left), lily pads (above), and milfoil (right— in the upper left, you'll see a thick cluster of dense milfoil that appears like a slick on the surface of the water and from which the bass in the photo was caught).

types of vegetation, such as grass, can be found extending through and covering the surface, as well as being submerged several feet, or it can be shallow or deep. You have to adjust to the peculiarities of each situation, but there are some patterns that hold true for all conditions.

I believe that in any given lake from spring through fall, there are usually some bass in the grass all the time. Once you have accepted the fact that bass will reside in even the thickest clumps of vegetation, you must understand how to catch them in such areas. This is easier to say than it is to do. There is no sure-shot one-sentence solution to this problem. After all, there are different types and concentrations of vegetation as well as varying environmental conditions with which to contend. This is true no matter where you go. Nonetheless, some general features related to all vegetation fishing are identifiable, and specific patterns and lure types become prominent.

The most obvious, most often used, and most easily managed way to locate bass in vegetation is to work the edges. In large, fairly thick concentrations of grass, for example, bass stick close to the outside line, most likely because they can see and ambush prey there. This is especially true if the grass is so congested that you can't work any type of lure across the surface without it being fouled up.

Milfoil beds are a prime example of this type of cover. Here, you may have to work the edges with a plastic worm, dropping the worm on top of the milfoil just inside the edge, then slithering it off and letting it drop vertically along the edge. Most strikes will occur within a foot or two of the edge. Any irregularity in the weedline, such as a protrusion, pocket, etc., may be an especially significant place to fish.

Frequently the key to unlocking the bass-catching secret in sparse grass is to fish isolated clumps, patches that are small but thick and that stand off from the main mass of vegetation (they may be inside the main body as well as outside). If you find this to be the case, take care to identify and fish every likely looking isolated patch. Usually there is a lot of ground to cover in weed bed fishing, and if you find a spot that is more worthwhile than others, zero in on it and work it thoroughly.

When the vegetation is thin and sparsely submerged, you won't be able to identify isolated patches such as those I've described. However, if you are using a depthfinder, you may be able to identify the thin and thick sections, as well as dropoffs or holes, by traveling across the area first.

If the vegetation—either emergent or submerged—is thick and has visible pockets or holes in it, start casting. Clearings in the grass are prime fishing locations, and they are easier to fish than the thick spots.

In the case of emergent grass, a worm can be worked in the same manner as in fishing the edges, but in submerged vegetation the chore becomes a little tougher. If the vegetation is too deep to see, you'll only locate pockets by feel; an experienced worm chunker can tell when he eases his worm through the grass into a small clearing and then back into the grass again.

Submerged grass that is at the delicate see/no-see level is also a problem, particularly for the sight angler who's better off if he can watch what he's casting to and fishing. I've fished in areas where the only openings in submerged vegetation were afforded by large flat rocks, and you could only find these by hunting and pecking, watching

FISHING LILY PADS

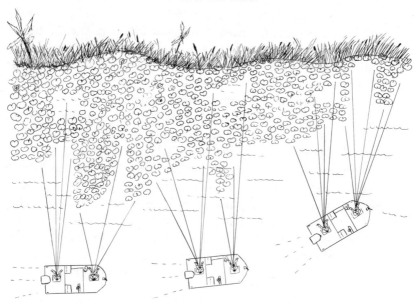

As illustrated here, isolated patches, deep holes, points, and irregular features are the types of location to fish when working thick vegetation.

the depthfinder, and dropping marker buoys, then fishing a plastic worm on the edges of the openings.

A curious fact is that many anglers pass up the best summer fishing locales in the lake—thick pad or grass areas—in favor of shoreline plunking or deep prospecting. I suspect this is because they have not developed adequate continuous weed-fishing techniques. The key to the success and enjoyment of vegetation fishing is a weed-free, or so-called weedless, presentation and, naturally, your lure plays the lead role.

Undoubtedly, you have seen claims regarding the completely weedless or snag-free capabilities of various lures. It's been my experience that the claims are not entirely true. I have found that if a lure has a hook, if it has some weight, and if it is fished in thick cover, it cannot be 100 percent tangle-free. There are relative degrees of weedlessness, just as there are relative degrees of manipulative retrieving skills, but there is no out-of-the-box, guaranteed-never-to-get-stuck bass fishing lure.

The plastic worm can be one of the most tangle-free lures and is the most acclaimed and successful vegetation-fishing lure. But plastic worms will get snagged occasionally in thick cover. If the hook actually gets stuck, it is because the hook point pulled through the soft plastic neck of the worm, or because the point was imbedded too far; perhaps the body has been re-used too often and is incapable of holding another hook. More often the sinker is the culprit, snagged on or wedged into some impenetrable aquatic forest instead of riding over it.

Some folks like to fish a plastic worm without a slip sinker in shallow vegetation, but I almost always use a bullet-shaped sinker. I'm not the patient type who can wait all day for the bait to get down to working level. The key to using a slip sinker is to use the lightest one you can possibly toss and that will still get the worm down adequately, and to peg it with a toothpick. In grass or pad stems or other types of vegetation, a free-sliding slip sinker often pulls off the object, leaving the worm behind. You need to have the two working close together to effect a proper, natural presentation. A slip sinker that has been pegged with a toothpick (see the section on plastic worms)

When fishing submerged weeds, you can try to entice bass out by working a lure above it, or drop the lure into a pocket, or work the weedline and dropoff to deeper water. (*Illustration courtesy of Mercury Outboards*)

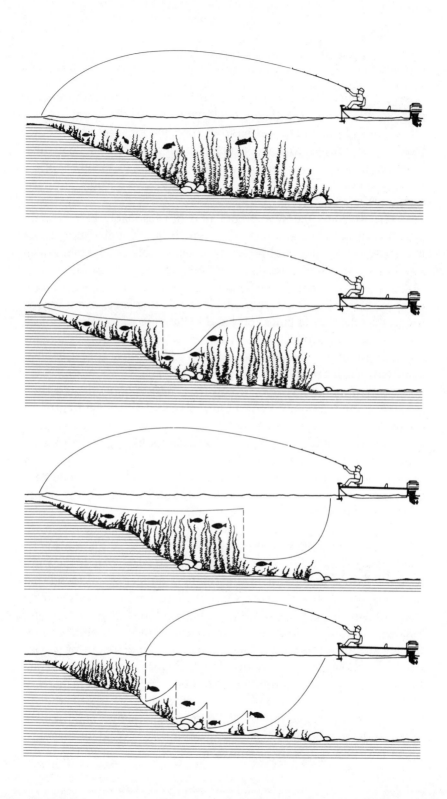

to keep it from sliding does the job. An alternative is to use a weedless jig head or a plain jig with the hook imbedded in the worm.

Although the plastic worm is the prime lure for vegetation fishing, bass do not always go for a worm. Often you need to give them something moving more enticingly, with a flash of metal, to get a strike. Combinations of spoon and pork chunk, or spoon and plastic skirt work then.

The weedless spoon and pork rind has justifiably been a long-time favorite of grass and pad fishermen. In moderately heavy cover it is fairly tangle-free, and its action is reasonably good when drawn into open pockets from the clustered vegetation. The Johnson Silver Minnow and the Strike King Timber King spoons are the most prominent of these baits. Both are available in different sizes, and it is good to have a selection of colors on hand. There are times when a black spoon is far more productive than a silver or gold one. Putting a light-colored strip of pork behind these spoons adds to their appeal, as does a single or twin-tailed curly soft plastic trailer.

Sometimes, though, you'll find that these spoons, despite their good swimming action, do not muster enough flash appeal to interest a bass that passes up or strikes short on a spoon-and-pork combo or a worm. Thus, another popular combination for fishing the green stuff incorporates an in-line spinner, a spoon, and a skirt. This is rather like the old and still popular Snagless Sally (Hildebrandt). The flash of the spinner on this bait is like the whipped cream on top of the parfait—it can make a difference at times.

An offshoot of this arrangement is to take the blade off an in-line buzz bait and place it ahead of a spoon-and-skirt rig. This gives you a noisy surface bait that is essentially snagless, but it does not have the flash appeal of the in-line spinner arrangement. I found that by taking the blade off a Floyd's Buzzer (Blue Fox) and putting it on the split ring of a spoon-and-skirt combo, I had a good topwater weedless buzz bait. There are some relatively weedless buzz baits on the market, and these incorporate a buzzer with a spoon, or spoon-like body, though I can't say that I've had great success with them.

For good measure, you can also add a trailer hook to both of these arrangements. The trailer will mean more hooked fish, though it also means more snagging on pad stems, grass clumps, and the like. You have to be willing to make a tradeoff in fish hooked for snag-ups. If you put on a trailer, be attentive to which hook actually gets the

Plastic worms, weedless spoons, and frogs are effective in the vegetation, as are buzz baits and weedless plugs (not shown).

bass you catch. If it is the main hook, the fish are hitting the lure well and you probably don't need the trailer. But if most of the fish come on the trailer, the fish are swiping at it or hitting short, and you'll have to put up with more snags in order to catch more bass.

In addition to these lures, spinnerbaits can be highly effective when used near vegetation. When pads and grass are not too thick, as is usual in the spring or early summer, a spinnerbait is the best lure to use. For thicker grass and pads, a spinnerbait can be productive when worked on the edges, either fishing parallel along them or by fluttering it down vertically along the breakline. It is when you need to fish deep in thick vegetation that a spinnerbait must yield to other lures.

Keep in mind that bass are sometimes very deep in matted grass or pads or hyacinths and hydrilla beds, if the water is reasonably deep. In Florida, where hyacinths may be so thick that you can't possibly get a lure through them, and where there is ample water extending far back under the matted surface debris, anglers live-line big shiners so that they will run back under this vegetation. This is one reason why live shiner fishing is so popular and successful there.

When you're faced with the problem of fishing vegetation so thick it looks as though you could walk across it and the edges don't produce, you've encountered the most demanding vegetation-fishing situation of all. Fishing effectively is only half the problem. Getting your boat in there and maneuvering it adequately is the rest of the problem. You can hardly row through it and you can't work an electric motor. Poling is about all that works and you spend more time maneuvering than fishing. Using an outboard motor is usually impossible (and harmful to the engine; if the water intake becomes clogged, the engine overheats).

Sometimes there are small holes in this mass that can be readily fished, but more often than not you wind up making your own hole and dunking your bait in it. There's no casting involved here. It's a matter of reaching over a hole, dunking your offering up and down, and then reaching for the next spot. You may even have to use your rod or an oar to poke the hole. Flipping, dabbling, yo-yoing, and doodlesocking are all terms used to describe the technique involved. Usually a weedless jig, jig-and-eel combo, jig and pork chunk combo, or spoon-and-pork-chunk combo is employed, and through the use of a long (7-foot-plus) rod, the angler reaches over a hole, drops the bait, and slowly works it up and down. When bass are concentrated in or under thickly matted vegetation, and you work stealthily and patiently, this technique works admirably well.

A few other types of lures are also suitable for vegetation fishing, particularly over grass that is sparse or submerged. Spinnerbaits and buzz baits can be very effective here, as can shallow-running minnow imitations. The latter can be worked on the surface or beneath it, though retrieved slowly. This type of plug is excellent for determining if fish are present in such vegetation and for locating pockets in which concentraions of fish may be found. When coated, such underwater pockets can be probed more thoroughly and slowly with a plastic worm.

Surface lures are everybody's favorite, and they'll catch their share of bass in areas where they can be properly worked and when the fish are not totally turned off. If bass are actively feeding in submerged grass, surface plugs can be dynamite. Fore-and-aft-propellered stick baits, plus stick baits without propellers, such as the Zara Spook, and wobbling surface plugs will catch bass here.

"Weedless" soft plastic lures also have their place. Some of the best are frog imitations, including the Snag-Proof Frog, and Harrison-Hoge Superfrog. These come as close to true weed-free fishing as possible. They look realistic, have good maneuverability through the salad, and catch fish.

Another product along similar lines is the weedless series of Burke Flex Plugs. Having used these for the past few seasons, I am continually impressed with their ability to work interestingly in snag-infested waters. The popping model is my favorite, and I also like the stick bait version. Although these work well and draw strikes from bass and other fish, for some reason I've found them often fish-less, meaning that I've encountered difficulty in sticking fish with them. That's a problem experienced with some weedless lures and though they are exciting to fish, they are at times frustrating when they don't result in hook-ups. That's a challenge I'm still working on with this kind of lure.

Vegetation fishing generally requires stout tackle. Depending upon the conditions and the maximum size of bass that might be caught, you'll have to be the judge of what is adequate. Where big bass and thick vegetation are common, most old hands will use no less than 17- or 20-pound line, and some will use heavier. Practically, you should leave the real light line and limber tackle for other, more appropriate situations. Even with heavy tackle, there are times when a good-sized bass throws itself behind a thick mass of cover and you have to hurriedly bring the boat over to it, keep rod pressure constantly on, and hope that you can reach down with your hand and scoop it out (you often lose it).

After you've tackled vegetation fishing for a while, you'll find that it seems to be more productive in low-light situations than in bright daylight. Bright days drive bass deeper and further into the vegetation, where they are harder to reach effectively. Dawn, dusk, and overcast days offer the best vegetation fishing conditions. Night is a good time as well.

Keep in mind the types of things to look for in trying to establish a bass-catching pattern in the vegetation. Edges, pockets, irregular breaks, isolated patches, and such, all have potential. If there is current in the lake, seek out those areas that are most affected by it. And if the going is tough and the bass have to be pursued in the thickest vegetation, so be it. Get in there after them.

17

CATCHING BIG
BASS

Experience has convinced me that trophy bass are the most-sought, most revered prize in freshwater. There are more trophies in a given body of water than we suspect. Many die of natural causes, but anglers take their share, too, and not always by mere coincidence.

What constitutes a "big" bass in California may not be the same in Texas or Pennsylvania. Generally, though, any fish that's well above the normal size wherever you're fishing is big. A 4-pound smallmouth is a good fish everywhere, while one 5 pounds or more is a trophy. A 5-pound largemouth is a respectable fish everywhere, but though it's a trophy to some in northern states, it's merely a good one in southern locales. Any bass over 7 pounds, however, is special in almost any body of water.

Size is relative to fish population, fishing pressure, and especially to geography and length of growing season. For instance, on the average, a 7- to 8-year-old bass in New York would weigh 5 pounds, whereas in South Carolina that fish would be about 2 pounds heavier.

The number of big bass in any water is generally small in comparison to the size of the entire bass population. This automatically decreases the odds on catching a trophy. Yet, because relatively few big bass are taken from most lakes, anglers have a tendency to underestimate the actual numbers. This seems contradictory, but many so-called "fished-out" lakes can, and do, produce a good number of cagey old giants.

The prime season for catching big bass, as they say, is anytime, provided it's spring. I've caught large bass in summer and fall, but overall, spring offers the best opportunity for landing a big one. (This is particularly so for smallmouths, which prefer a deeper and more lightly covered habitat than largemouths throughout the season.) For most of the spring, bass are in the shallows and fairly accessible to anglers. During part of the spring they are spawning or about to spawn, and big female bass laden with eggs will weigh considerably more than they will after spawning.

In contrast to my experiences, some good anglers I know, particularly several in Florida's lunker country, prefer summer for catching big bass and land more then than at any other season. This may be peculiar to Florida, because it has predominantly shallower water than lakes in other areas of the country, and perhaps their fish are more vulnerable than deeper and warier fish in other climes. In the big bass spots in the San Diego region, the largest lunkers generally come in late winter and early spring, and often are taken deep.

Regardless of season, you stand a better chance of duping big bass if you use large lures. I've caught big bass, especially smallmouths, on very diminutive lures, but in general, if you want a trophy, feed it a mouthful. There are six different types of lures that I consider big bass baits. When fished in the appropriate places, they can tempt bass of large-than-average size (which means slightly bigger than the standard keeper), as well as appeal to a really big fish.

A big plastic worm is the most effective lunker largemouth catcher throughout the seasons. I thought I knew something about using big worms until I fished a few lakes in Cuba several years ago. In these waters, 12- to 18-inch eels were a major bass forage and the principal bait of local fishermen. Also, 12- to 14-inch worms were the ticket for big and little bass alike, and though smaller worms did catch some fish, they were not as effective. (Mister Twister, incidentally, makes worms this size.)

On our side of the Caribbean, largemouths don't often see such giant forage, so 7- to 9-inch plastic imitations are ample throughout the U.S., though larger ones are occasionally fished in Florida and in other places where water snakes are prevalent. Worms are most effective for big bass from mid- to late-spring through mid-fall.

The same period is also prime time for stick baits. These are my favorite surface bass lures and the most dynamic and predictable of all big bass catchers in the hands of artistic retrievers. The $4^1/_2$-inch to 6-inch-long stick baits exemplified by the Zara Spook and Walker models appeal to the street-fighter side of a bass's nature. No other lures can match stick baits for sheer trickery or ability to bring on

Big lures catch big bass has become something of an axiom, but it can certainly be true and applies particularly to fishing with plastic worms.

angry, electrifying strikes. A lake with a lot of stumps, brush, and vegetation in shallow water is a top candidate for stick bait fishing on non-windy days.

A buzz bait is another excellent big bass surface lure. Primarily effective in warm water, on cloudy days, and when the surface is calm or only lightly rippled, a buzz bait appeals to the instinctive, reflexive nature of a bass. For big bass, a large buzz bait with a trailer hook equal in size to the main hook is the best bet. I use a trailer hook most of the time, but the largest bass usually hammer the bait and get impaled on the main hook anyway. The most effective buzz baits are those that can be worked the instant they hit the water and slowly fished below the surface. They also make a distinctively loud clicking sound as the buzzing blade rotates.

Perhaps most realistic of the big-bass lures are the floating/diving minnow-family plugs. These are 5- to 7-inch lures typified by the Rebel minnow, Rapala Floater in No. 11 or 13 sizes, Bagley's Bang-O-Lure, and the Smithwick Rogue. I favor the wooden plugs here for their added buoyancy, but one big, old tarnished Rebel that I found, repainted, and put new hooks on, has proven to be a treasured bass getter. Another lure of this type that I've used with particular success in the spring in extremely shallow water is a plug I modified and jokingly call the Bag-Head. It was a 6-inch perch-colored stick bait for striper fishing manufactured by Bagley. I replaced the treble hooks and added a small metal lip from a defunct Heddon River Runt, resulting in a plug with a wide sweeping action that won't go more than 6 inches beneath the surface under any condition.

These big minnow baits work best in spring and fall. They can be fished on a slow, steady retrieve, an erratic stop-and-go subsurface retrieve, or strictly as a surface plug in the manner of a stick bait. My better fish have fallen to the latter two techniques.

Perhaps the most versatile big bass lures are spinnerbaits and jig-and-pork combos. There are all kinds of spinnerbaits available, but the larger ones, such as Nos. 5 to 7 single-blade or tandem models, with a rubber skirt and a trailer, are most effective for big bass. A curled twin-tailed white or chartreuse plastic trailer is a lethal spinnerbait addition that adds enticing action and substance to the lure.

Although spinnerbaits can produce big bass through standard retrieves in assorted types of cover, slow-rolling is the next best thing to using an electric shocker. Slow-rolling is a technique of bringing a spinnerbait up to a stump, log, fallen tree, or bush, easing it over the object, then fluttering it down in front of an unsuspecting bass.

Like spinnerbaits, jig-and-pork combinations, in the form of a jig and eel, jig and worm, jig and pork chunk, or jig and frog, have application throughout the fishing season. They, too, will catch bass of all sizes, but have a better-than-average track record on bigger bass. They are effective when flipped into close cover, jigged in deep water, or worked slowly in the edges or pockets of vegetation.

All of these lures have their moments for big bass. Most are at their best when fished in and around very thick cover, and they appeal to the feeding, reflexive, or pugnacious instincts of large fish. Remember that trophy bass are generally not as aggressive as the smaller, more eager members of their species. This is not to say they are docile; when they want something, they'll go for it. But big bass are not accustomed to expending a lot of energy to get their food. You have to show them something worth taking, something that's irresistible, something that's easily had.

Most fishermen who catch a big bass have a tendency to move off from the place they've caught it. Or they eliminate the possibility of catching more bass from that same spot by drifting over it or making a big commotion. Some people get so excited when they hook a big bass that they don't think of anything except that fish and that fight. The angler who keeps a cool head is able to work the fish properly while also noting exactly where it came from, and adjusting the position of the boat with the electric motor to stay away from the spot, keeping down boat noises, and otherwise minimizing disturbance, in case the area turns out to be a haven for big fish or a cafeteria for bass on a feeding frenzy. Some of the best short-haul catches I've made have come from a single locale late on a spring day, when bass had turned on in the warm shallow waters.

A lot of fishermen forget where they've caught, lost, or seen big bass. They forget the exact location, i.e., the specific stump along a row, the particular bush on a brushy bank, etc. It's important to know, to the most precise detail, where you encountered a good fish so you can return to that spot. It's not a bad idea to mark these places, if they are near shore, in some way.

I fish a lot of unfamiliar water each year and spot all kinds of markers in the form of cans, ribbons, glow-in-the-dark cloth, etc. Some of these mark trotlines, nets, or brushpiles, but I suspect some

Many big largemouths, including this Florida-caught 11-pounder, come from thick cover, and an angler has to be able to wrestle a tough old fish out of such conditions. A lot of big bass are lost because anglers are unable to do this.

also mark a particularly desirable fishing spot. Stakes, poles, and other objects driven into the bottom also serve as markers. In the Arctic, the Eskimos traditionally place rock piles along the shore of lakes to mark places where the fishing is good. (A tip on marking big-bass locales: don't mark the exact spot. Place a marker a certain distance to the side of the exact spot, so it's more difficult for others to decipher.) Such marking is particularly advantageous in lakes that experience water-level fluctuations.

The first time I fished a local reservoir, I caught a $6\frac{1}{2}$-pound largemouth at the base of a bush. The bush was out of water a few weeks later, but nearby was a row of tree stumps barely visible under the water. One of the stumps yielded a $7\frac{1}{4}$-pound largemouth. When the water is low the bushes are out of water and when it's extremely low so are the stumps. When it's high you can find the bush, but you can't see the stumps and have to hunt for them. Here's an instance where a shore-based marker would help locate the stump(s) for precise high-water fishing.

Don't get the impression that big bass are found only near the shore. In deep lakes with a lack of thick shoreline cover, in heavily pressured lakes, and in shallow lakes with good cover throughout, you're just as apt to find the monsters in deep or open water, so check the terrain on all sides of the boat.

You also shouldn't be timid about trying something out of the ordinary when seeking big bass. I once had a letter from a *Field & Stream* reader who caught a $7\frac{1}{2}$-pound smallmouth on half a cricket he'd been using for crappies, which shows that anything is possible at times (and that luck or circumstance often plays as big a role in catching big bass as does skill and technique). A few years ago I was fishing a Cuban lake for big bass, and it occurred to me that if giant bass will take 12-inch shiners in Florida, why wouldn't these bass hit a properly presented big crankbait? Fishing with a 5-inch deep-diving muskie plug seemed weird to my companions, and I'll admit I felt a bit awkward doing it, but I landed an 8-pounder and lost a bigger fish when it leaped and broke off. Yes, those fish may have been a bit naive, not having had much hardware tossed their way, but who's to say this sort of experimentation is unwarranted elsewhere?

On another occasion in a Florida phosphate pit I was fishing a small pit from shore near a sluice pipe that was pouring water out from another pit, creating a lot of current in the immediate locale. I

Occasionally it takes something different, like the big crankbait hooked to the mouth of this bass, to catch a large fish. Don't be afraid to experiment with something a bit out of the ordinary when prospecting for lunkers.

tried fishing with a Bagley DB3 crankbait, but thought I needed to get deeper and replaced that with a 5-inch deep-diving Bagley Bang-O-Lure (a muskie and saltwater bait). On my first cast I landed a 4-pound largemouth. A few casts later, in the same spot, I took a 6-pounder. I know that few people would think of using such a big crankbait for bass, yet I've seen big bass (including smallmouths) hit a big bait meant for stripers or muskies or pike, and while I admit it doesn't happen often, occasionally going outside the norm and trying a different kind and size of lure might hook that big bass.

Note that I said "hook," not "catch." There may be twice as many big fish hooked each year as landed. Everyone loses big bass, though some seem to do so with more frequency than others. It's the fishermen who see only one or two big bass a year who get my condolences when they lose a good one. Most big bass are lost because the line was too light for the conditions; the hook was not set properly; the drag was too loose or too tight; the tackle was inadequate (usually too limber); the fisherman didn't know how to net a fish; or he didn't play it properly. Many fish are lost when they jump, although some would-be jumpers can be duped into not jumping if you thrust your rod tip into the water and change the angle of pull.

I don't subscribe to the theory that a big bass should be thoroughly played out before you land it. Play the fish as hard as your tackle and the conditions will allow, and land it as soon as you are able. This increases your chances of catching it and enhances the fish's well-being if it is to be released. The longer a big fish is in the water and the less pressure you apply, under routine circumstances, the more there is to go wrong, and the greater the likelihood of losing it. If you do lose a fish, it will rarely hit again without being rested. However, it is possible that you can return to the same spot and catch the same fish, if not later the same day, then the following day or a few days later.

It is also important to pay attention to those places where you have seen big bass strike and miss or boil after a lure but never feel a hook. Sometimes these fish can be caught immediately on a subsequent cast with a different lure. A plastic worm is the best secondary lure in this situation, but a spinnerbait or minnow plug is also very effective.

Confidence, patience, and determination go a long way toward helping the trophy bass seeker. There are some anglers who can spend many hours casting one type of bait or lure in selected places, and though they don't fill the boat with fish, they do manage to catch big bass with enviable regularity. I'm not patient, but at times on lakes with which I'm intimately familiar, I can psyche myself into capturing a big bass. I may deliberately pretend that a real trophy lies in every spot. When a big one does hit, I'm so ready that it hardly stands a chance.

Fishing for big bass is a worthwhile challenge, provided you don't do it strictly for show and do release the majority of your fish unharmed. It is a pursuit that sets you apart from the average bass angler. Trophy bass don't come easy, but, as someone once cryptically observed, "Anybody can catch small bass."

18

IMPROVING BASS FISHING'S FUTURE

Every now and then I become reflective about fishing experiences and daydream about good times, good catches, and other memorable angling moments. I've been lucky to have had a wide variety of experiences, with bass as well as with other species of fish. I'm especially fond of bass, naturally, so with all the experiences I have to remember, nothing is more pleasant than recalling the capture and unharmed release of those big, memorable bass.

There is a satisfying feeling associated with the release of a prized fish, both at the moment it occurs and in recollection of it later. Some writers describe the release of a memorable fish, usually trout, as a reward and an expression of gratitude toward a remarkable fighting performance and fishing experience. This is an emotion I do not feel. There is a sense of power involved in the ability to control the immediate life-or-death destiny of the captured, a power usually reserved for a higher authority. There is the pleasing element of being able to succeed in the quest without having to kill that which is sought. But, mostly, there is personal satisfaction with one's own expression of the ultimate in good sportsmanhip.

Oddly enough, I don't hear much about releasing big bass. I don't hear too much about releasing bass, period, except from the self-serving tournament promoters. Most of the talk and the writing centers on catching more and bigger bass. At times it seems as though bass fishing has become more of a business than a sport. Where bass once meant cane poles and bobbers, it now means highly sophisticated equipment. Where it once meant leisurely rowing and casting, it now means selective bait presentation, problem analysis, structural-fishing adaptations, and efficient use of time. Where it once meant the enjoyment of a total outdoor experience, it now means the production of fish to warrant the effort and investment.

Not that there's anything wrong with the use of highly sophisticated equipment; it's only natural that fishing techniques should become more complex as different forms develop. But what is alarming is the fact that bass anglers on the whole have become a highly aggressive, intense bunch, with the emphasis almost entirely on the catch, not the sport. Too many anglers are interested only in big bass, and the comment, "Did you get any good (meaning lunker-sized) ones?" is heard all too often.

The emphasis, then, is not only on production—having fish to show for your time and involvement—but on the capture of lunker bass as a measure of quality fishing and self-proficiency. That is human nature at work; a preoccupation with size and stature is part of the American way—bigger is better and biggest is best—and there is no form of fishing in which you will not find importance attached to the catching of large fish.

Although it would be nice if people recognized that being able to entice any fish, regardless of size, is the basis of the angling sport, it is hard to find fault with attention to size. Bass anglers, perhaps even more so than other fishermen, are devoted to the pursuit of lunkers. So be it. Sadly, it has been my observation that most of the big bass they catch, they keep. And with this we can quarrel.

Remember the photos you have undoubtedly seen of men fishing in the "good old days" when legal limits were nonexistent and the bounty of the earth was thought to be endless? Doesn't happen any more, you think?

Symptoms of gluttony occur on many bass lakes, with some anglers intent on keeping the biggest fish they catch all the time, feeling compelled to stringer a slew of fish for the folks at the ramp or marina to see. There are plenty of travel organizers, tourist promoters, tackle dealers, and overeager bass fishermen who wantonly exhibit the spoils of their success to attract attention, and by so doing encourage the same behavior in other fishermen.

Most bass anglers don't realize that their numbers are greater now than ever. It doesn't occur to them that the amount of water available is not increasing and that the water quality is worse in many instances

---

than before, or at least no better. Nor do they stop to think that bass populations are stabilized or generally decreasing. Or that the big bass they do catch have overcome substantial odds to get that way.

A bass is very lucky to grow large. When initially spawned, it was just one of between 5,000 and 45,000 eggs in the nest. Twenty percent of those eggs never even hatched. The majority of the fry failed to survive their first few months of existence, and a comparatively small percent achieved adult size (10 to 12 inches). Hardly any make it to the trophy size.

The lifespan of the lucky bass varies from 8 to 15 years. Bass that have reached lunker size generally have been the faster growing individuals of their species. Studies have indicated that female bass, which grow largest, seem to outlive males, and this is significant since it is the females that lay eggs for spawning; one would think that fish that grow large may possibly pass along this trait to their progeny.

When you put all the factors together you can make the following profile of a big bass: a relatively rare fish; a fish that has been one of

Reason, need, and good sportsmanship dictate moderation in the taking of big bass. The small fish you release today will be the big fish of tomorrow, and the big fish you release will help propagate more big fish.

the "fittest" of its species; and, likely, a female with high reproductive value.

Numerous factors contribute to the size and composition of a bass population in any given water. Fishing pressure is one of the foremost of these, and it is known what the effects of this pressure will be on the percent of distribution among the bass population.

In a moderately fished lake, approximately 35 percent of the bass population will consist of fish 10 inches long or more. The remainder are young-of-the-year fish and bass in the intermediate sizes. In a heavily fished lake, however, only 10 percent of the population will be 10 inches or better, with 10 percent being young-of-the-year and 80 percent being bass in the intermediate range. This is relatively meaningless unless you know the size of the total population (which even biologists seldom do). If the total population in a heavily fished lake is very high, than 10 percent would still be a lot of fish, but regardless, in all but near-virgin lakes, the amount of chest-thumping bass in the population is small.

The fate of the popular and intensely sought lunker bass is a dubious one when you consider the circumstances of its existence: there are more bass anglers now than ever before; the anglers are more skillful, more knowledgeable, and better equipped than ever; the lakes get older and the bass populations stabilize; and big bass are selectively picked off.

Not all anglers are tearing up the bass populations and reaping continual harvests of big fish. The vast majority of fishermen meet with only fair success over the course of an angling season, and the capture and keeping of one or two lunkers is reasonable and completely justifiable. Keeping fish is an important element of catching fish for many anglers. It is within the bounds of reason, need, and good sportsmanship that the suggestion to be moderate in the taking of bass is made.

Tom Bankhead, formerly executive director of the Bass Research Foundation, once commented to me that fishermen ought to release big bass because "they won't get any bigger if you don't." That's a simple, truthful declaration. But more than that, a big bass is a very special creature.

Smaller bass usually taste better than the old ones, anyway, so if dinner is what you're after, let the lunkers go and keep the small bass. If a wall mount is what you want, fine. But if you already have a mounted bass, is another really necessary? You might consider spending the money on an art print or replica carving instead.

In many cases, it is neither food nor mount that motivates a fisherman to keep a bass. Often pride or a chance of winning the local fishing contest is the reason. But remember, a picture is lasting and is said to be worth a thousand words. A good, portable scale will verify your weight guesstimate, and a pocket camera will produce the proof of the report. Maybe that won't win any contest, but it will become part of a treasured memory.

Some well-meaning fishermen, seeking the best of all worlds, stringer a bass for a while or keep it in a livewell to show the folks before releasing it. Forget this. Big bass happen to be rather delicate fish and highly susceptible to handling-related mortality. The further north you go, the more this is so. Big bass, especially smallmouths, seldom last very long cooped up in a livewell or clipped on a stringer unless the water temperature is cool.

If you're going to take a few snapshots of your bass before releasing it, do so quickly. The longer the fish is held out of water, the less is its chance of recovering from the experience. Take a half-dozen photos from different angles and with the fish held in a few positions, handling it as little as possible.

It is best if you can tire a big bass enough to lip-land it, but with big strong fish and multi-hooked plugs, this often is impossible or dangerous. But a lower-lip-held bass is fairly well immobilized and free from possible harmful handling. Remember that netting can take some of the scales and mucus coating off, but this is generally the safest and surest way of landing a big bass. Remove the fish quickly and hold it by the lower lip. Do your best to prevent the fish from squirming free and flopping around in the net or on the floor of the boat.

When you release it, do so gently. Lay the bass in the water by the boat, and if it does not make an effort to swim off, carefully guide the fish forward through the water to bring water and oxygen into its system until it revives.

Watch that fish as it swims away. You have just made a personal contribution for improving bass fishing's future, a guarantee for tomorrow. You'll almost surely never see that bass again. But someone else may. And you may see its progeny in time. You will see that bass in the eye of your mind and feel it in your heart. And that is especially satisfying.

The future of bass fishing is up to you.

APPENDIX I
==
STATE AND PROVINCIAL FISH AND GAME AGENCIES

If you are interested in discovering bass fishing opportunities in other areas beside your own state, usually the best source of information is the fish and game agency responsible for management of the bass fishery in that area. They may not only be able to give you information about good fishing opportunities and fishing regulations, but can be of assistance to you in non-technical information ways. Many such agencies have a wealth of booklets, brochures, maps, and other published literature available at nomimal cost. When writing to them, it might help expedite matters if you included a self-addressed, stamped envelope for reply. Also, address your correspondence to the Information and Education Section.

ALABAMA
Dept. of Conservation and
Natural Resources
64 N. Union St.
Montgomery, AL 36130

ARIZONA
Game and Fish Dept.
2222 W. Greenway Rd.
Phoenix, AZ 85023

ARKANSAS
Game and Fish Comm.
#2 Natural Resources Dr.
Little Rock, AR 72205

CALIFORNIA
Dept. of Fish and Game
1416 Ninth St.
Sacramento, CA 95814

COLORADO
Div. of Wildlife
6060 Broadway
Denver, CO 80216

CONNECTICUT
Dept. of Environmental
Protection
165 Capitol Ave.
Hartford, CT 06115

DELAWARE
Div. of Fish and Wildlife
P.O. Box 1401
Dover, DE 19901

FLORIDA
Game and Fresh Water Fish
Comm.
620 S. Meridian St.
Tallahassee, FL 32301

GEORGIA
Game and Fish Div.
270 Washington St., SW
Atlanta, GA 30334

HAWAII
Div. of Aquatic Resources
1151 Punchbowl St.
Honolulu, HI 96813

IDAHO
Fish and Game Dept.
600 S. Walnut, Box 25
Boise, ID 83707

ILLINOIS
Dept. of Conservation
524 So. Second St.
Springfield, IL 62706

INDIANA
Dept. of Natural Resources
608 State Office Bldg.
Indianapolis, IN 46204

IOWA
State Conservation Comm.
Wallace State Office Bldg.
Des Moines, IA 50319

KANSAS
Fish and Game Comm.
Box 54A, RR 2
Pratt, KS 67124

KENTUCKY
Dept. of Fish and Wildlife
#1 Game Farm Rd.
Frankfort, KY 40601

LOUISIANA
Dept. of Wildlife and Fisheries
P.O. Box 15570
Baton Rouge, LA 70895

MAINE
Dept. of Inland Fisheries and
Wildlife
284 State St.
Augusta, ME 04333

MARYLAND
Dept. of Natural Resources
Tawes State Office Bldg.
Annapolis, MD 21401

MASSACHUSETTS
Dept. of Fisheries and Wildlife
100 Cambridge St.
Boston, MA 02202

MICHIGAN
Dept. of Natural Resources
Box 30028
Lansing, MI 48909

MINNESOTA
Dept. of Natural Resources
658 Cedar St.
St. Paul, MN 55155

MISSISSIPPI
Dept. of Wildlife Conservation
P.O. Box 451
Jackson, MS 39205

MISSOURI
Dept. of Conservation
P.O. Box 180
Jefferson City, MO 65102

MONTANA
Dept. of Fish and Wildlife
1420 E. Sixth St.
Helena, MT 59601

NEBRASKA
Game and Parks Comm.
P.O. Box 30370
Lincoln, NE 68503

NEVADA
Dept. of Wildlife
P.O. Box 10678
Reno, NV 89520

NEW HAMPSHIRE
Fish and Game Dept.
34 Bridge St.
Concord, NH 03301

NEW JERSEY
Div. of Fish and Game
CN 400
Trenton, NJ 08625

NEW MEXICO
Game and Fish Dept.
Villagra Bldg.
Santa Fe, NM 87503

NEW YORK
Dept. of Environmental
Conservation
50 Wolf Rd.
Albany, NY 12233

NORTH CAROLINA
Wildlife Resources Comm.
512 N. Salisbury St.
Raleigh, NC 27611

NORTH DAKOTA
Game and Fish Dept.
2121 Lovett Ave.
Bismarck, ND 58505

OHIO
Dept. of Natural Resources,
Div. of Wildlife
Fountain Square, Bldg. C-4
Columbus, OH 43224

OKLAHOMA
Dept. of Wildlife Conservation
P.O. Box 53465
Oklahoma City, OK 73152

OREGON
Dept. of Fish and Wildlife
P.O. Box 3503
Portland, OR 97208

PENNSYLVANIA
Fish Commission
P.O. Box 1673
Harrisburg, PA 17120

RHODE ISLAND
Dept. of Environmental
Management
83 Park St.
Providence, RI 02903

SOUTH CAROLINA
Wildlife and Marine Resources
Dept.
P.O. Box 167
Columbia, SC 29202

SOUTH DAKOTA
Game, Fish and Parks Dept.
445 East Capitol
Pierre, SD 57501

TENNESSEE
Wildlife Resources Agency
P.O. Box 40747
Nashville, TN 37204

TEXAS
Parks and Wildlife Dept.
4200 Smith School Rd.
Austin, TX 78744

UTAH
Div. of Wildlife Resources
1596 W. N. Temple
Salt Lake City, UT 84116

VERMONT
Fish and Game Dept.
Montpelier, VT 05602

VIRGINIA
Comm. of Game and Inland
Fisheries
P.O. Box 11104
Richmond, VA 23230

WASHINGTON
Dept. of Fisheries
115 General Administration
Bldg.
Olympia, WA 98504

WEST VIRGINIA
Dept. of Natural Resources
1800 Washington St., East
Charleston, WV 25305

WISCONSIN
Dept. of Natural Resources
Box 7921
Madison, WI 53707

WYOMING
Game & Fish Dept.
Cheyenne, WY 82002

CANADA

ALBERTA
Dept. of Energy and Natural
Resources
Petroleum Plaza Bldg.
Edmonton, Alberta T5H 2C9

BRITISH COLUMBIA
Ministry of Environment
Parliament Bldgs.
Victoria, B.C. V8V 1X5

MANITOBA
Dept. of Natural Resources
Legislative Bldg.
Winnipeg, Manitoba R3C 0V8

NEW BRUNSWICK
Dept. of Natural Resources
Centennial Bldg.
Fredericton, N.B. E3B 5H1

ONTARIO
Ministry of Natural Resources
99 Wellesley St.
Toronto, Ontario M7A 1W3

QUEBEC
Dept. of Recreation, Fish and
Game
Place de la Capitale 150 East
Quebec City, Quebec G1R 2B2

SASKATCHEWAN
Dept. of Parks and Renewable
Resources
3211 Albert St.
Regina, Saskatchewan S4S 5W6

Appendix II

ADDRESSES OF MANUFACTURERS

A lot of products mentioned in this book and applicable to bass fishing are not available in all sections of the country. Because of this and because I regularly receive many inquiries through *Field & Stream* regarding specific fishing tackle products, I thought it would be a service to readers of this book to know how to contact specific manufacturers directly in order to obtain information about their products, to find out where they may be purchased locally, or, in a few cases, to order directly from the manufacturer or a mail-order supplier. This listing is fairly comprehensive in regard to bass fishing equipment and covers more than just the many products mentioned in this book.

ABU-Garcia, Inc.
21 Law Drive
Fairfield, NJ 07006

Jim Bagley Bait Co.
Drawer 110
Winter Haven, FL 33880

Arbogast
313 W. North St.
Akron, OH 44303

Bass Pro Shops
P.O. Box 4046
Springfield, MO 65808

Arkie Lures, Inc.
P.O. Box 1460
Springdale, AR 72764

Bead Chain Tackle Co.
110 Mountain Grove St.
Bridgeport, CT 06605

Attwood
1016 N. Monroe St.
Lowell, MI 49331

Beckman Net Co.
1810 Cameron Dr.
Madison, WI 53711

Berkley & Company, Inc.
Trilene Dr.
Spirit Lake, IA 51360

Blakemore Sales Corp.
P.O. Box 505
Branson, MO 65616

Blue Fox Tackle Co.
645 N. Emerson
Cambridge, MN 55008

Bomber Bait Co.
Box 1058
Gainesville, TX 76240

Brawley Lures
1450 Carpenter Ln.
Modesto, CA 95351

Browning
Route 1
Morgan, UT 84050

Bumble Bee Bait Co.
Hwy. 5 No., Box 1169
Mountain Home, AR 72653

Burke Lures
Box 72
Traverse City, MI 49684

Cabela's
812 13th Ave.,
Sidney, NE 69160

Lew Childre & Sons
110 Azalea
Foley, AL 36535

Cordell Tackle
3601 Jenny Lind
Ft. Smith, AR 72902

Crankbait Products
9300 Midwest Ave.
Garfield Heights, OH 44125

Creme Lure Company
Box 87
Tyler, TX 75710

Crispin Lures
Box 9622
Kansas City, MO 64134

Daiwa Corporation
7421 Chapman Ave.
Garden Grove, CA 90249

Ditto Mfg., Inc.
Box 222
San Mateo, FL 32088

Down-East Sportscraft
198 Main St.
Yarmouth, ME 04096

Du Pont Co.
1007 Market St.
Wilmington, DE 19898

Dura Pak Corporation
Box 1173
Sioux City, IA 51102

Eagle Electronics
Box 669
Catoosa, OK 74015

Earie Dearie Lure Co.
2252 Greenville Rd.
Cortland, OH 44410

Eppinger Manufacturing
6340 Schaefer
Dearborn, MI 48126

Fenwick
14799 Chestnut St.
Westminster, CA 92683

The Fishin' Worm Co.
5512 So. Florida Ave.
Lakeland, FL 33803

Gapen's World of Fishin'
Hwy. 10
Big Lake, MN 55309

Gould Batteries
Box 43140
St. Paul, MN 55164

Harrison-Hoge Industries
104 Arlington Ave.
St. James, NY 11780

James Heddon's Sons
414 West St.
Dowagiac, MI 49047

John J. Hildebrandt Corp.
Box 50
Logansport, IN 46947

Hopkins Fishing Lures
1130 Boissevain Ave.
Norfolk, VA 23507

Luhr Jensen & Sons, Inc.
Box 297
Hood River, OR 97031

Johnson Fishing, Inc.
1531 Madison Ave.
Mankato, MN 56001

Jungle Laboratories
P.O. Box 630
Cibolo, TX 78108

Knight Manufacturing
Box 6162
Tyler, TX 75711

Kunnan Tackle
9707B Candida St.
San Diego, CA 92126

L&S Bait Co.
1500 East Bay Dr.
Largo, FL 33541

Lake Systems Division
Rt. 3, Box 233-M
Mt. Vernon, MO 65712

Bill Lewis Lures
Box 4062
Alexandria, LA 71301

Lindy-Little Joe, Inc.
1110 Wright St.
Brainerd, MN 56401

Lowrance Electronics
12000 East Skelly Dr.
Tulsa, OK 74128

Mann's Bait Co.
1 Humminbird Lane
Eufaula, AL 36027

Maxima Fishing Line
18239 S. Figuero St.
Gardena, CA 90248

Mr. Twister, Inc.
Drawer 996
Minden, LA 71058

Motor Guide
P.O. Box 825
Starkville, MS 39759

Nautical Interiors Corp.
5009 Rondo Dr.
Ft. Worth, TX 76106

Norman Mfg. Co., Inc.
P.O. Box 580
Greenwood, AR 72936

Normark Corporation
1710 E. 78th St.
Minneapolis, MN 55423

Okie-Bug
3639 S. Sheridan Rd.
Tulsa, OK 74145

OMC Parts and Accessories
100 Sea-Horse Dr.
Waukegan, IL 60085

The Orvis Company
Manchester, VT 05254

Penn Fishing Tackle
3028 W. Hunting Park
Philadelphia, PA 19132

Plano Molding Co.
P.O. Box 189
Plano, IL 60545

Producto Lure Co.
590 Rinehart Rd.
Lake Mary, FL 32746

Ranger Boats
P.O. Box 262
Flippin, AR 72634

Johnny Ray Sports
P.O. Box 1608
Gadsden, AL 35902

R&W Lures, Inc.
P.O. Box 423
Lamar, MO 64759

Rebel Lures
3601 Jenny Lind
Ft. Smith, AK 72902

Ryobi America Corporation
1158 Tower Lane
Bensenville, IL 60106

Scientific Anglers/3M
3M Center, 223-3S
St. Paul, MN 55144

Sears Roebuck & Co.
Sears Tower
Chicago, IL 60684

Shakespeare
P.O. Drawer S
Columbia, SC 29260

Sheldon's, Inc.
Box 508
Antigo, WS 54409

Shimano American Corporation
205 Jefferson Rd.
Parsippany, NJ 07054

Silstar Corp.
2122 Platt Springs Rd.
West Columbia, SC 29169

Lee Sisson Lures
Box 666, 305 McKean St.
Auburndale, FL 33823

Si-Tex Marine Electronics
Box 6700
Clearwater, FL 33518

Smithwick Lures
P.O. Box 1205
Shreveport, LA 71163

Snag-Proof Lures
4153 E. Galbraith
Cincinnati, OH 45236

Storm Mfg. Co.
P.O. Box 265
Norman, OK 72070

Strike King Lures
2906 Sanderwood
Memphis, TN 38118

Techsonic Industries, Inc.
1 Humminbird Lane
Eufaula, AL 36027

Tru-Turn
Drawer 767
Wetumpka, AL 36092

Uncle Josh Bait Co.
P.O. Box 130
Fort Atkinson, WI 53538

Weed Master, Inc.
249 N.E. 32nd St.
Ft. Lauderdale, FL 33334

Whopper Stopper
Box 1111
Sherman, TX 75090

Woodstream Corporation
Front and Locust
Lititz, PA 17543

The Worth Company
Box 88
Stevens Point, WI 54481

Wright & McGill Company
Box 16011
Denver, CO 80216

Zebco
Box 270
Tulsa, OK 74101

Zorro Baits
509 Edison Circle
Smyrna, TN 37167

INDEX